LESSONS OF THE LOCKER ROOM

LESSONS OF THE LOCKER ROOM

The Myth of School Sports

Andrew W. Miracle, Jr., and C. Roger Rees

Prometheus Books

59 John Glenn Drive
Amherst, NewYork 14228-2197

Published 1994 by Prometheus Books

Lessons of the Locker Room: The Myth of School Sports. Copyright ©
1994 by Andrew W. Miracle, Jr., and C. Roger Rees. All rights reserved.
No part of this publication may be reproduced, stored in a retrieval system,
or transmitted in any form or by any means, electronic, mechanical,
photocopying, recording, or otherwise, without prior written permission of
the publisher, except in the case of brief quotations embodied in critical
articles and reviews. Inquiries should be addressed to Prometheus Books,
59 John Glenn Drive, Buffalo, New York 14228-2197, 716-691-0133. FAX:
716-691-0137.

98 97 96 95 94   5 4 3 2 1

Library of Congress Cataloging-in-Publication Data

Miracle, Andrew W., Jr.
    Lessons of the locker room : the myth of school sports / by Andrew
W. Miracle, Jr., and C. Roger Rees.
        p.   cm.
    Includes bibliographical references and index.
    ISBN 0-87975-879-1 (acid-free paper)
    1. School sports—United States—Moral and ethical aspects. 2. School
sports—Social aspects—United States. I. Rees C. Roger. II. Title.
GV346.M57   1994
796'.0973—dc20   93-48666
                                                                      CIP

Printed in the United States of America on acid-free paper.

Contents

Preface

Does sport in our schools promote education by keeping students in school longer? Does sport help keep youth off drugs and out of trouble? In short, does sport build character? Or, as Heywood Hale Broun has suggested, does sport just build characters?

This book is an examination of the beliefs that commonly surround the question of sport in American schools. The answers may not please the critics of sport or its promoters, but they are based on the best available data. We have assembled findings published in social science journals and combined them with data from our own research to provide a scientific basis for evaluating these issues.

When and where did the notion that sport builds character originate? Why have so few Americans questioned it until recently? Why is it being challenged now?

Within the past few years some districts have eliminated sport programs and some states have passed controversial no pass/no play legislation. School athletics are being challenged and appear vulnerable. As public debate is waged, we ask, what is responsible for the change in the perceived role of sport in American schools?

We find the answer through the use of the anthropological concept of myth—a story we tell about ourselves that needs no proof. We use this understanding of myth to analyze school sport in America. We trace the history of the idea that sport builds character and we examine the impact of sport on schools, communities, and youth.

We compare the myths of school sport to the existing "scientific" or empirical evidence, mindful of the fact that it is but one version of the truth. In doing so, we find little empirical evidence that sport builds character or has any positive effects on youth, even though the idea that it does has been around more than a century. So, we ask, why?

What caused the widespread acceptance of this myth, this belief which needed no proof? The search for answers leads us to examine the relationship between school sports and the communities in which they are played, as well as the corporate needs of nineteenth-century industrializing and late twentieth-century postindustrial America.

What we discover is that the early captains of industry perceived that sport would help American industry by supplying healthy workers who valued teamwork and respected authority, not ones who were well-schooled. However, the contemporary CEO is more likely to believe that America's economic future looks bleak unless schools begin to produce highly skilled, informed, even creative workers. Forced to choose between sport or academics, industrialists today invariably argue for more homework.

The ultimate question is, what next? What will happen to high school sport as we enter the twenty-first century? We examine the alternatives and predict that most American communities will de-emphasize sports in schools. At the same time, these communities will create other institutions to house sport and thus continue to provide local communities with the positive benefits that can result from sport.

School sport interests us for a number of reasons, both personal and professional. We are fascinated by the power of sport as an institution in American life. We find it ironic that, while much has been written about professional and college sports by academicians and journalists, there have been few attempts to describe how sport functions at the high school level, where most people experience it live. That these experiences are meaningful to people can be judged by the extent to which sport-related memories are so much a part of the recalled high school experience.

Our goal in writing this book has been to increase the understanding of school sport. We have tried to explain the social functions of this institution at several levels, to analyze its impact on education, and to show how and why it is viewed in such a positive light by most Americans.

There were several motives behind our endeavor. On a personal note, we both played high school sports, one in America and the other in England. We both were college athletes. One studied to become a physical education teacher, the other had a father who was a high school coach and school superintendent. We both had teachers for parents.

As social scientists we are professionally interested in sport, both as a subject in its own right and for what it tells us about society. To paraphrase anthropologist Clifford Geertz, sport is part of a story we tell about ourselves. In it are found the rituals and myths that are keys to our culture. One such key is the myth that sport builds character, which has provided the theme for this book.

In writing this book about school sport we have attempted to decode the rituals and to examine the myths made real by them for the athletes, the student body, the institution of the school, the local community, and, ultimately, the culture that is America. We also have addressed the importance of school athletics for educational policy and practice. What role should athletics play in the education of the youth of our nation in light of the cultural myths that we identify? Teachers, coaches, administrators, parents—and, indeed, all taxpayers—have a stake in this discussion.

1

The Myth
An Introduction

In order to form a just estimation of the character of any particular people, it is absolutely necessary to investigate the Sports and Pastimes most generally prevalent among them.

—Joseph Strutt (1838)[1]

It's a Friday evening in early November in a small town in mid-America. The center of town is deserted, but bright lights and music are emanating from an area on the outskirts of town. Here a majority of the town's inhabitants are huddled around a flat, open, grassy area on which white lines of lime mark off a grid. People of all ages are sitting in bleachers surrounding the field. The entire assemblage seems to be color-coded. Most individuals in the concrete bleachers on the east side of the field are wearing green and gold clothes, many are waving green and gold pennants, and there are green and gold signs seemingly hung so as to be read by those sitting across the field. There is a slightly smaller crowd, proudly sporting blue and white, seated in the wooden bleachers on the west side of the field.

11

Many individuals on both sides seem agitated, and there is a general sense of excitement and anticipation.

The undefeated season of the local high school football team is on the line tonight in the game against their archrivals from the next county. The winner goes into the record book as the first undefeated state champion since 1929. The loser goes home.

Team members have not been doing much studying recently. It's hard to concentrate on school work when something else is so important. Actually, the players have been preparing for this game since the first victory in September when the coach told them they had a shot at going undefeated. He had used the idea of this game to get them motivated for the lesser teams they had beaten during the regular season. With all but one game of a perfect season behind them, tonight they are fired up and ready to kick ass. This is the big one and they are going to win!

The school really has come together in anticipation of the game. The principal has a bet with his counterpart at the rival school. The pom-pom squad and marching band have practiced every evening. The nerds[2] in the math club have written a program for the school computer lab that simulates the game. The program has been running continuously all week with minor variations in weather conditions, injuries, and coaching decisions, and the home team has not lost yet.

The usual disagreements and animosities have been forgotten in a frenzy of football fever. The teachers have not been sarcastic to the dumb jocks who have been polite to the band fags, and everyone has been nice to the cheerleaders. Even the burnouts, who usually reject everything to do with school, sang the school fight song along with everyone else at the pep rally. The whole school is psyched for the game. All week "We're number one" has reverberated through the halls, which are covered with posters supporting the home team and maligning the opponents.

There is a lot riding on tonight's outcome. Several players are hoping for college scholarships to Division I universities. How they perform under the pressure of a big game will be of particular interest to the college coaches in the audience. A "free ride" to play college ball could mean the big time, maybe a shot at the pros. At least they could use football to get an education and make something of themselves.

For other players, particularly seniors who are not good enough for college football, this will be the most important day of their lives. This is it; there is no tomorrow. How they do tonight will be remembered in the diners, bars, and barber shops of the town for generations. Through victory they can achieve hero status bordering on immortality. Defeat, however, would dog them for the rest of their days. Win or lose, this game is destined to become part of the local folk history, part of the story its residents will tell about themselves for years to come.

Will the home team "win the big one"? Will they grab the cup of destiny with both hands in a character-building come-from-behind victory, or will it be dashed from their grasp by a costly fumble in the waning minutes of the game? Will the faithful gather at Al's Bar down the road to celebrate the victory or to drown their sorrows? You will have to write your own script for this game. The usual questions about winning and losing are less important to us than decoding the meaning of the event and understanding the social functions of school sport.

The Nature of Myth and the Locker Room

Community members all over America gather to watch high school football games, basketball games, hockey matches, and other sport events. In so doing they establish a sense of collective identity that unifies the school and the community, and binds them with certain cultural traditions. For much of the country, high school sport in general, and high school football in particular, is a series of ritual events that makes real a set of shared beliefs about particular ways of thinking and feeling. These myths, as we call them, are cultural blueprints for understanding our society.

The social values epitomized by sport are the ones that "make

America great." You can find them, along with slogans reflecting the American ethic, on the locker room walls of any local high school.[3] Here is the emphasis on success: "Winning isn't everything, it is the only thing." Here is the dedication to hard work of the Protestant work ethic: "No one ever drowned in sweat." Here is the need to keep trying in the face of adversity and never give up: "Winners never quit." Here is the importance of self-sacrifice for the good of the group: "There is no 'I' in team"; and the need to keep competing despite seemingly insurmountable odds: "It's not the size of the dog in the fight, it's the size of the fight in the dog." Above all is the overriding need to "be a winner."

Winning in sport, like winning in life for Americans, is outcome-oriented, not process-oriented. The usual question asked after a game is not how well you played or how enjoyable it was, but "What was the score?" or, more to the point, "Did you win?" According to George Allen, former coach of the Washington Redskins, losing is worse than death because you have to live with losing! The bottom line is victory.

It is because winning is so highly valued that it is made difficult. Our sports are usually examples of negative-sum games, there being more losers than winners. This is invariably done by placing teams in leagues and emphasizing winning the league as the ultimate achievement. Only one team can win the league, or in individual sports, only one player can be number one. To be number one is the ultimate goal; Americans are not interested in being second best.

For example, when professional soccer was introduced into the United States, the promoters of the North American Soccer League were concerned that the public would be dissatisfied with the tied games so common in Europe and South America. Therefore, they introduced the shoot-out, in which members of each team took turns taking penalty shots on goal after the end of regulation time, until one player missed. This rule has since been adopted by Fédération Internationale de Football Associations (FIFA), the international governing body of soccer, and was used in the World Cup games for the first time in 1990. Clearly the most important characteristic of our sport is that it produces a winner—and being labeled or thinking of oneself as a winner is an important measure of status in American society.

Everywhere sports and games are presumed to reflect the values of the cultures in which they are played. For example, the young men of the Tangu culture of New Guinea play a game called *taketac,* which cannot end unless the score is tied. This is necessary because the culture is based on the sharing of food (and most everything else) among the members of the society. If some Tangu defeated other Tangu, it might tear the basic social fabric of their society. No Tangu wants to "win" at such a price.

Or, consider British cricket. In Britain one game of cricket may last as long as five days, if it is not stopped by rain, and at the end still might not produce a winner. The game allows players to show sportsmanship and to behave like gentlemen, so the score is not too important. On the other hand, in American sport everyone knows that "A tie is like kissing your sister."[4]

The British anthropologist Mary Douglas has stated that the term "myth" is used to denote an axiom we reiterate about ourselves or our institutions that needs no proof.[5] Myths are made legitimate by references to nature and tradition.[6] For a century we have believed strongly in the myth that participating in, or, more specifically, winning in, sport builds character. Americans are convinced that competition brings out the best in us, and when we win, we prove our moral worth. People at high school football games know this to be true. It is only natural, a matter of common sense, they assume. Certainly no scientific data is needed by most fans to support this contention.

Studying the Myth of School Sport

Like all myths, the notion that sport builds character is strengthened by examples that seem to provide support for a popular, firmly held belief. Any evidence to the contrary tends to be ignored, and cases or examples not conforming to the belief (e.g., Bob Hayes,

Mercury Morris, Len Bias, Babe Ruth, or Pete Rose*) are dismissed as aberrant or "exceptions which prove the rule."

A majority of the respondents in a comprehensive study of American attitudes toward sport[7] felt that sport competition is good for children because it teaches them to strive to do their best, it reduces delinquency, and it is likely to bring the family together. Three out of every five Americans surveyed agreed that athletes are often the best role models a child can have.

We propose to examine this sport myth as social scientists might study any other myth. Thus we ask, "What's the story?" Can the myth be substantiated scientifically? What are the consequences of challenging this myth? In writing this book we explore these issues as they pertain to school athletics.

Why focus on school sport? First, if sport does build character, the effect must occur at a young age in order to impact an individual's basic character through socialization. Our schools seem the ideal places to investigate the proposition since the student athletes have the benefit of several years of sport participation. Moreover, high school sports, unlike professional sports, are not just for elite athletes; they often are more inclusive. Thus, they comprise a broader, more representative spectrum of Americans.

In addition, our schools and their sports are worthy of investigation because of the attention now being focused on education. As the possible relationship between schooling and the decreased international role of the United States is examined, politicians, industrialists, professional educators—indeed, all citizens—have a stake in what happens in our schools. During most of the twentieth century, much of what happened outside the classroom was sports related.

Strangers to America would not have to look far to see the importance of sport in American schools. All that is necessary is to go through the main school entrance and see the spoils of scholastic warfare prominently displayed in glass cases near the principal's office.

---

*Hayes and Morris were football superstars and Bias a famous basketball player all of whom achieved notoriety due to involvement with illegal drugs. As baseball players, Ruth was known for his drinking and Rose for his gambling.

The big trophy in the middle was awarded to the boys basketball team for winning the championship. The little cup in the corner was won by the school debate team. Sport in our schools, particularly in the form of interscholastic athletics, is extremely important.

According to the myth, school sport is supposed to pay off in a number of ways. First and foremost, it has socialization value. Through sports, according to the myth, adolescents are supposed to learn the pro-social values necessary to be successful in business and in life. They learn the importance of success and the need to dedicate themselves to attain success. They learn respect for authority, self-sacrifice, sportsmanship, and fair play. They learn to get their kicks on the playing fields and in the gymnasium rather than through deviant experiments with drugs and alcohol. In short, they learn to be winners. It is expected that this lesson should be applied to whatever they do after they have finished school. Thus interscholastic athletics is an integral part of the role of the school in inculcating the values necessary for the perpetuation of American society.

Not only is it assumed that lessons learned in athletics can be transferred to master other challenges in life, but interscholastic athletics also are supposed to provide another path of upward mobility via a college education. The logic of the myth is that participation in interscholastic athletics helps motivate athletes academically, especially the ones on the scholastic borderline, because a specific grade point average is required to maintain eligibility for participation. If the athletes are good enough, they may have a chance to go to college on an athletic scholarship and, while representing their college in sport, attain an education and a degree. This college education can lead to occupational mobility, the attainment of a high-status job, and success in society. It is deeply ingrained in our social mythology (if it is not a historical fact) that thousands of athletes from poor backgrounds have been able to use athletics to achieve an education that they could not have afforded otherwise.[8]

Thus the supposed importance of school athletics is two-fold. First, it socializes students into a belief system that prepares them for a life of competition in the business world. The values of victory and competitiveness learned in athletics will be transferred to the working world. If they are winners in school sport, they will be winners in the game of life.

Second, a student can use sports skills to obtain a college education, which will lead to a better job and upward mobility. The bottom line for high school sport is that it pays off in terms of character development, educational aspiration, educational attainment, and occupational advancement. Thus, school sport delivers the goods for American business and American society.

These two claims have helped to make interscholastic athletics the most popular extracurricular activity in our schools, and the principal method by which students think of themselves as unified members of the institution. It also is the most important, if not the only, form of interaction between the members of the local community and the school. By catching "Friday night fever," students, teachers, parents, and the larger community attain a sense of unity and solidarity. Through this means, traditional values of America are being taught and reinforced. High school sport is part of the American heritage, along with Thanksgiving and the Pledge of Allegiance.[9]

School Sport as Public Ritual

Even though on one level it is "just a game," an athletic contest can have a sacred, quasi-religious quality.[10] This is because high school sport serves an important function as public ritual in America.

Ritual marks the transition of individuals through different roles in life (i.e., as rites of passage) and it marks the passage of time through the cyclic changing of the seasons (i.e., rites of intensification). Ritual is sacred because it denotes a special time in which we do things that confirm the importance of deeply held beliefs. As we shall see, sport in general, and high school sport in particular, has these characteristics, whether boys football in Texas or girls basketball in Iowa.

Groups use ritual to mark changes in the social status and roles of their individual members.[11] Some ritual of this type occurs at relatively fixed points in the life cycle of every individual. Such rituals are usually termed rites of passage or transition rituals. The second type of regularly occurring ritual has been called rites of intensification or calendrical rituals because they occur at regular points in the annual cycle. It has been suggested that these rituals serve to regulate the changes in interaction affecting all members of a group.[12]

Observing that human societies always have endowed time with sacred meaning, the British anthropologist Edmund Leach[13] sought to explain the ritual process whereby this occurred. Changes in the seasons, patterns in animal and plant life, and celestial phenomena tend to coincide with events in our social and religious life. Leach examined the use of festivals or other rites of intensification to mark such points on the calendar. Even our contemporary calendar continues to provide testimony to the connection between rituals and the annual cycle.

Sports in America largely have replaced the seasonal markers of planting and harvesting rites of an earlier agrarian America on the ritual calendar that simultaneously signals the cyclic nature of life and the passage of time. Today basketball is what happens for most of us between football and baseball. Longer periods of time are marked by the number of such intervals. We can refer to last season, or the time of three seasons ago, or even the era of "The Babe." Years on the official Gregorian calendar are less important than the sequence of seasons for a particular sport.

Sports define sacred time for most Americans.[14] Thus high school athletes can be counted among the ritual actors who help the rest of society keep time by ushering in each new season with the first game and celebrating its passage with the championship play-offs.

The cyclic nature of ritual as it occurs in modern institutions has been demonstrated by anthropologist Jacquetta Hill Burnett[15] in her examination of ritual in a midwestern high school. Ritual events were noted in relation to the school calendar. Burnett observed that the rites of intensification were more or less evenly distributed throughout the school year.[16] These included homecoming, the football banquet, the Christmas dance, the New Year's Eve party, the sweetheart dance, the athletes' banquet, and honors day.

In addition, pep rallies were held on a regular basis during the football and basketball seasons.

Rites of passage, which mark the transition of individuals into new status positions and roles, also were evidenced in the school. Freshman initiation occurred early in the fall, but all of the other rites of passage occurred at the end of the school year. These were baccalaureate, graduation, the alumni banquet, and the senior trip.

Not only does ritual make sacred the passage of time, it also symbolizes group solidarity and unity.[17] In sport, individuals are socialized through common participation—whether as players or spectators—to accept certain social norms. The nineteenth-century French sociologist Emile Durkheim, often called the father of modern anthropology and sociology, would have appreciated the sense of collective identity that is fostered through athletics. In modern in- dustrialized societies there may be no other context in which one is as likely to feel union with others to such an extent as that which is possible at an athletic event. During the crucial moments of the game, especially a game that is perceived to be particularly impor- tant and is closely contested, players and spectators are as one; the individual gives way to the collective. Hundreds or thousands of voices become as one. Almost simultaneously, many individuals may ex- perience ecstasy, that is, an altered state of consciousness, a tremen- dous natural high.

It is the force of public ritual that gives sport the kind of cultural power usually attached to religion. As the anthropologist Clifford Geertz[18] notes with regard to religion, it is a system that acts to "establish powerful, persuasive and long-lasting moods and motivations" by "formulating conceptions of a general order of existence and clothing these conceptions with such an aura of factuality that the moods and motivations seem uniquely realistic." Sport has done this for American culture in a way that traditional religion could not.[19]

The Sport Myth and Education

The study of school sport is especially important at this juncture in American history. Criticism of sport in general has increased, e.g., criticism of the crass commercialization of professional sport with its highly paid superstars, the tarnished image of collegiate sport where athletic revenues often seem much more important than educational considerations, and youth sport where disgruntled coaches have attacked umpires with guns. Simultaneously, public education stands accused of failing its mission to keep America competitive. The combined criticisms of sport and education are forcing an examination of high school sport.

As citizens we are continuously making decisions about secondary education. Many of these decisions, directly or indirectly, involve sports. Recently, for example, the Dallas Independent School District (DISD) laid off 245 teachers just two weeks into the 1991–92 school year. Forced to cut expenditures, it fired mostly secondary teachers of core academic subjects, along with some elementary school teachers. Only after one school board member threatened rebellion did the DISD administrators add a small reduction to the district's athletic budget. The effect was a reduction in the number of middle school coaches and equipment. The budget for high school sport was not affected.

When a school board votes to spend funds to build a new stadium, they are electing not to spend those monies to expand library holdings or to raise salaries or to hire new teachers in order to reduce the average class size. Moreover, if the myth is accurate, when a school district or state agency imposes a tough policy on athletes' academic eligibility, e.g., no pass/no play, it may affect dropout rates in its schools.

When school authorities make such decisions, we need to feel confident that these decisions are based on appropriate, fully informed bases, not just emotion or tradition. Not only parents with school-aged children, but all citizens have a need to know the facts, or at least the probabilities, regarding education and athletics.

In addition, sport directly affects the lives of a large percentage of American youth. The results of a 1990 survey released by the National Federation of State High School Associations show a total of 5.2 million youth (just under 3.4 million boys and just over 1.8 million girls) participating in high school athletics. Add the numbers who additionally participate in marching bands, spirit clubs, and as spectators at athletic events and the potential impact of sport swells. It is not an exaggeration to conclude that, directly or indirectly, high school sport affects the lives of virtually all American youth. Therefore, it seems reasonable that we examine the impact sport has on high school athletes, our schools, and American society.

How should this important subject be examined? The typical American's response is, "Look at the facts." This is what we propose: an objective, empirical, scientific examination of the existing data. Still, there may be those who would ask why such an examination is necessary. After all, aren't the benefits of sport obvious? Isn't it just common sense?

There is a common belief in the value of sport, which we have chosen to view as a myth not because it is untrue, but because it is generally accepted without question. If this common understanding, this myth about sport, is valid, it ought to withstand scrutiny. If it is not valid, we tax-paying citizens who make decisions about the future of our educational system need to know.

In school districts across the United States, American taxpayers spend hundreds of millions of dollars annually on high school sports. To us it seems reasonable to determine whether or not sport builds character, and if it does, whether athletes are any different than members of the band or glee club in this regard.

Moreover, we want to explore other aspects of school sport. Does participation in sport actually prevent delinquency, reduce prejudice, promote cooperation, motivate students academically, improve participants' life-long health, or lead to improved economic opportunities?

In this age of science and technology, we need to know, and our knowledge must be based on the best data available. That is something we demand of all businesses and advertisers, not just engineers and physicians. We make scores of daily decisions after evaluating options based on the best information we have or can obtain: where to live, which day care to choose for our children, which food to purchase for our pets. Should decisions about schools and their activities be any less reasoned?

If sport does live up to the myth surrounding it, even if only in part, perhaps we should invest more heavily in sports. For example, we could make room for all students in sport, not just the athletically superior. On the other hand, what if it were demonstrated scientifically that most or all of the myths about school sport have no empirical basis, that there are no data to support them, no evidence of positive effects? As a taxpayer, parent, educator, or concerned citizen, what would your response be? What should it be?

These are the issues we discuss in the chapters that follow. We begin with a review of the myth, i.e., our understanding about sport. We trace the origins of the myth and explain why the myth was embraced initially and why it has continued to survive without need of proof. Then we examine the empirical evidence which might support or refute the myth.

The primary proposition of the myth is "sport builds character." It is generally assumed that character primarily is built through the skills taught and the discipline demanded in sport. The nature of this character development, in turn, affects morals, as evidenced through positive personality traits.

An important component of the myth is that sport decreases delinquency and, recently it has been alleged, drug use, by increasing positive self-concept, enhancing skills, and demonstrating to the individual that success can be obtained by following rules. Furthermore, sport is believed to build character by increasing educational motivation and furthering educational attainment. As a result of increased educational achievement, sport participants may enjoy increased economic rewards during their adult lives.

After examining the data on these points, we turn our attention to the current state of education, and the changing role of sport in modern society. We review the traditional position of school sport in American communities in order to demonstrate its power. Then we explore the changes in American society at the end of the twentieth century that are affecting the traditional relationship between schools and their constituent communities.

We conclude that there is a perception of crisis regarding American education, and that this will continue to affect school sport. In public debates over the future of school athletics, three different models of high school sport might be considered. We explore the ramifications of each of these and evaluate the current force and probable future of the myth that sport builds character.

Summary

The rituals of school sport are as important to our society as bull fighting in Spain or *carnival* in Brazil. Football or basketball provides a quasi-religious celebration of who we are and at the same time a process by which boys may become men.[20] Such sacred rituals are endowed with special meaning, myths that become part of the story we tell about ourselves. These myths do not need proof; they are grounded in nature and tradition.

Since these myths are part of our cultural heritage, they are highly valued and resistant to change. As author Buzz Bissinger discovered in Odessa, Texas, criticizing high school sport is often seen as an un-American activity. Bissinger's book, *Friday Night Lights*,[21] describing a season of high school football, was not well received by the local population. Although no one has claimed that his exposé is untrue, many have been angered by what he said. The fact that Bissinger himself was for a time persona non grata in Odessa is a modern example of the ancient tradition of punishing the bearer of bad news.

Sociologist Christopher J. Hurn[22] has said that schools are invariably the subject of controversy because they are agents of cultural transmission, and in our heterogeneous society there is little agreement over what our culture is or should be. Moreover, since formal education is the major avenue for upward mobility in America, access to it is valued greatly and guarded jealously.

To the extent that involvement in school athletics is part of formal education, then the debate over the value of school athletics has to be controversial. Yet the controversy over school athletics is even greater because of its value as myth.

While we do not expect to settle such a controversy in this book, we do hope that we can raise the level of awareness about what the role of school athletics is now and what it should be in the future. Perhaps athletic directors, physical education teachers, school administrators, and parents can use the information as a starting point to help make school athletics the educational force that its advocates wish it to be.

Notes

1. Joseph Strutt, *Sports and Pastimes of the People of England* (London: Thomas Tegg, 1838), pp. xvii–xviii.

2. While it is not our intention to reinforce stereotypes, terms such as "nerd," "dumb jock," and "band fag" are frequently used by adolescents to describe their school peers. (See chapter 3.)

3. For a more complete review of locker-room slogans, see Eldon E. Snyder, "Athletic Dressing Room Slogans as Folklore: A Means of Socialization," *International Review of the Sociology of Sport* 7 (1972): 89–102.

4. This phrase says as much about traditional male/female relationships as it does about sport. Why shouldn't males kiss their sisters? Perhaps because it is not macho to show your emotions except in sport. For "real men," kissing is only a prelude to sex, which certainly is inappropriate with your sister.

5. Mary Douglas, *Implicit Meanings: Essays in Anthropology* (London: Routledge and Kegan Paul, 1975).

6. Mary Douglas, *How Institutions Think* (Syracuse, N.Y.: Syracuse University Press, 1986).

7. *Miller Lite Report on American Attitudes Toward Sport* (Milwaukee, Wis.: Miller Brewing Co., 1983).

8. James Michener, *Sports in America* (New York: Random House, 1976).

9. All three of these traditions were invented at the end of the nineteenth century, at the time of the industrializing of America. This was an era of rapid technological change and social unrest. The stabilizing effects of traditions, even newly invented ones, was sorely needed in American society. See chapter 2 for an explanation of the notion of "invented traditions."

10. For example, see Shirl J. Hoffman, ed., *Sport and Religion* (Champaign, Ill.: Human Kinetics Publishers, Inc., 1992).

11. Arnold van Gennep, *Rites of Passage* (Chicago: University of Chicago Press, 1960).

12. Elliot Dinsmore Chapple and Carleton Stevens Coon, *Principles of Anthropology* (New York: Henry Holt and Co., 1942).

13. Edmund R. Leach, "Two Essays Concerning the Symbolic Representation of Time," in *Rethinking Anthropology,* ed. Edmund R. Leach (London: The Athlone Press, 1961), pp. 124–36.

14. Emile Durkheim proposed the polarized concepts of sacred and profane. The profane is the sphere of the routine, the mundane, the taken-for-granted, workaday world. The profane is characterized by attitudes of blasé acceptance based on common familiarity. On the other hand, the sacred is the sphere of the unusual, the extraordinary, the not-to-be-taken-casually, that which is out-of-this-world. The sacred is characterized by attitudes of awe, a sense of mystery, and circumspection in dealing with something special. While few contemporary social scientists still use Durkheim's concepts analytically, they are often applied to various cultural phenomena for illustrative purposes.

15. Jacquetta Hill Burnett, "Ceremony, Rites and Economy in the Student System of an American High School," *Human Organization* 28 (1969): 1–10.

16. For the following data, see ibid., p. 5.

17. British sociologist Basil Bernstein has defined ritual as relatively rigid patterns or acts, the meaning of which gets generalized beyond the specific situation. Following this line of thought, sport can be seen as a consensual ritual that gives participants and spectators a sense of purpose and solidarity; see Basil Bernstein, *Ritual in Education: Class Codes and Control,* vol. 3 (London: Routledge and Kegan Paul, 1975). This theme is developed in chapters 3 and 7.

18. Clifford Geertz, *The Interpretation of Cultures* (New York: Basic Books, 1973), p. 90.

19. Religion could not do this for two reasons: (1) The religious diversity of American immigrants has been too great. Religious synthesis would have been a slow and precarious process, and the rapidly emerging corporate economy of the nineteenth century needed an immediate homogenizing mechanism. (2) Traditional religion, especially much of nineteenth-century Christianity, held onto values that were antithetical to the needs of industrialization and the emerging corporate economy. The social gospel movement of the late nineteenth century, which shared common tenets and traditions with the playground movement discussed in chapter 2, is an example of the tensions between traditional, agrarian Christian values and the needs of the corporate economy. The social gospel movement was overwhelmed.

It was the development of sport as a new public ritual that was to provide the corporate economy with the integrating mechanisms it needed. It is because sport has become ubiquitous and because no one in society can comfortably escape nominal participation in sport ritual that it is so sacred.

20. It is clear that school sport can serve as a rite of passage for boys into manhood, but a similar function of sports as a rite of passage for girls into womanhood has not been documented yet. Although girls' athletic participation in school has expanded greatly over the past twenty years, it is rarely seen as having the sacred qualities of boys' sports. However, for an exception to this generalization, see Madelaine H. Blais, "A Season in the Lives of the Amherst Hurricanes," *New York Times Magazine* (April 8, 1993): 25–30.

21. H. G. Bissinger, *Friday Night Lights: A Town, a Team, and a Dream* (Reading, Mass.: Addison-Wesley, 1990).

22. Christopher J. Hurn, *The Limits and Possibilities of Schooling: An Introduction to the Sociology of Education,* 2d ed. (Boston: Allyn and Bacon, 1985), p. 40.

2

The History of the Myth

A lot of character building is achieved when we put children in
swimming pools and on playing fields.
>—Donna E. Shalala, former president of Hunter College
>and Secretary, U.S. Department of
>Health and Human Services (1984)[1]

Broadly speaking, outside of national character and an educated
society, there are few things more important to a country's growth
and well-being than competitive athletics. If it is a cliché to say
that athletics builds character as well as muscle, then I subscribe
to the cliché.
>—President Gerald R. Ford (1974)[2]

It is a vital character builder. It molds the youth of our country
for their roles as custodians of the republic. It teaches them to
be strong enough to know they are weak, and brave enough to
face themselves when they are afraid. It teaches them to be proud
and unbending in honest defeat, but humble and gentle in victory. . . . It gives them a predominance of courage over timidity,
of appetite for adventure over love of ease. Fathers and mothers

29

who would make their sons into men should have them participate in sport.

—General Douglas MacArthur[3]

Only aggressive sports can create the brawn, the spirit, the self-confidence, and quickness of men essential for the existence of a strong nation.

—President Theodore Roosevelt[4]

In reviewing these statements by educators, military leaders, and presidents, one is struck by the power of the belief in the value of athletics. This power is demonstrated first in the range of social values that are believed to be affected by athletic participation, and second by the longevity of these beliefs. These statements span over eighty years of history, and most Americans today still endorse the positive social values of involvement in sport.

As powerful and wide-ranging as these statements are, they all seem to be meant for males. The "boys-into-men" theme is prominent, but nothing is said about "girls-into-women." The origins of the "sport-builds-character" myth reflects the historical reality of a society dominated by males.

The belief that sport builds character is a relatively recent phenomenon. Social historian Donald Mrozek[5] states that "to Americans at the beginning of the nineteenth century, there was no obvious merit in sport . . . certainly no clear social value to it and no sense that it contributed to the improvement of the individual's character or the society's moral or even physical health." By the second decade of the twentieth century these sentiments had been reversed.

In this chapter we shall trace the development of the "sport-builds-character" idea with particular reference to how it affected and was affected by the process of education. We shall trace its origins in the athleticism movement of the British public schools in the mid-nineteenth century and show how it was imported to the exclusive boarding schools of the eastern United States in the 1870s and 1880s. These schools trained the men who became the leaders of America in the early twentieth century, and an important part of that training included athletics.

We also shall investigate the playground movement that developed in the large Eastern cities at the turn of the century. Although independent of the athleticism movement of the rich, it similarly stressed the importance of team sports. Some of the leaders of the playground movement went on to establish athletics as part of the education of the masses in the public schools. This early form of athletics was much more inclusive than the high school sports of today.

Play Up and Play the Game: Athleticism and the British Public School

"Everybody knows that there are certain actions which an honorable English gentleman will not commit. He will hate whatever is mean, fraudulent, or disingenuous. According to a well-known phrase, which in itself may be taken as symbolical of English life, he will always and everywhere 'play the game.' "[6]

While the concepts of physical activity and moral development are linked in the philosophy of Jean Jacques Rousseau and the gymnastics of the German educators Jahn and Guts Muths,[7] it is in the games of the British public schools that they first received widespread exposure and legitimation. The "sport-builds-character" myth made its entrance to American education via the phenomenon known as British athleticism.[8] So great was the effect of this movement, both on the British system of education and on educational systems all over the world, that a summary of it is justified.

English public schools are the opposite of what the name implies. It has been cynically suggested that they are called English because they teach Latin and Greek, public because they are private, and schools because they are devoted to athletics.[9] At no time in their history have they ever been public as we know the term in America. In the 1830s and 1840s, before the development of athleticism, they were the places where the landed gentry and aristocracy sent their sons, and by all accounts you probably would not want your child to go there.[10] The curriculum consisted almost entirely of Latin and Greek and the students found it boring and irrelevant. Compensation for this boredom was sought in their leisure time with traditional and often brutal field sports such as poaching, shooting, and hare-and-hounds.

These schools were not nice places. Discipline was poor; homosexuality, cruelty to animals, bullying, riots, and brutality were common.[11] Formal games and sports were played, but these were mostly mob games organized by the boys and often banned by the school authorities.[12] For example, Samuel Butler, headmaster of Shrewsbury School from 1798 to 1836, felt that the game of football was "more fit for farmboys and laborers than for young gentlemen."[13] No hint could be gained from this picture of the transformation that would occur in these schools during the second half of the nineteenth century, a change so great that it has been called an educational revolution and one in which athletics figured prominently.[14]

This educational revolution was partly a result of the Industrial Revolution during which time the children of the new middle class became the main clientele of the British public schools. The schools began to exert more control over the leisure activities of the boys, and the rough unorganized games that characterized the time became institutionalized. This means that they became organized and regulated. Rules were agreed on and written down, and the headmasters and teachers began to support them.

The movement responsible for the institutionalization of games in the British public schools has been termed *muscular Christianity*.[15] While the origins of this phenomenon are unclear, they are often placed in the romantic novels of Charles Kingsley and Thomas Hughes.[16]

The essence of muscular Christianity was the belief that physical activity, especially team sports like cricket and rugby, made a significant contribution to the development of morality and patriotism, and that these values learned in sport at school would be transferred to other situations later in life.[17] Nowhere was this union of athletics and morality stronger than in Thomas Hughes's instant best seller, *Tom Brown's Schooldays,* published in 1857. Based on the author's own experiences as a pupil at Rugby School, it depicted the importance of sport in the moral development of the boys. For example, the moral value of cricket was described by one of the masters at Rugby as follows: "The discipline and reliance on one another which it teaches is so valuable I think . . . it ought to be such an unselfish game. It merges the individual in the eleven; he doesn't play that he may win, but that his side may."[18]

Thomas Arnold, who became the headmaster of Rugby School in 1828, is usually credited as the founder of school athleticism, although it was former pupils of his such as C. J. Vaughan, and assistant masters at Rugby such as G. E. C. Cotton and John Percival, who really developed athletics when they became headmasters in their own right at Harrow, Marlborough, and Clifton College, respectively. These and others were important agents for change. By 1880 the public schools were committed to athleticism[19]—so much so that Mangan reports that by the 1880s compulsory games, sometimes every day (at Harrow), or three times a week (at Lancing), were the norm.

It is one of our basic assumptions that educational reform does not take place in a vacuum. Events do not just happen. There were reasons why the philosophy of muscular Christianity and the curriculum of compulsory games that demonstrated this philosophy were so acceptable to the public school system and Victorian society at that particular time. Certainly in the social context of public schools, athletics provided some useful social control mechanisms.[20] Sociologist Christopher J. Hurn[21] has pointed out that schools, like most organizations, have to solve problems of order, control, and motivation. In the British public schools, almost all of which were boarding schools, authority was shared by the teachers and the older boys called "prefects." The prefects were responsible for exerting authority over the younger boys in after-school hours. The mechanism to sustain this relationship was the "fagging" system by which the younger boys were forced to act as "fags" or servants for the older boys. The tasks could include anything from cleaning rooms and polishing shoes to preparing food and, in one case, even warming the toilet seat. This particular act is described by British author Roald Dahl when he was a pupil at Repton Public School in the late 1920s.[22]

By all accounts, the "fagging" system was repressive and brutal beatings were common. By encouraging games-playing, the headmaster could create a "moral elite" among the prefects, who became his lieutenants in the aim of turning the boys into Christian gentlemen, which was more in keeping with the philosophy of the school.[23] Historian James Mangan notes that "a boy who had won his flannels [i.e., was a member of the cricket or football eleven] at Harrow probably never possessed such power again."[24] The era of the athletic hero had arrived.

There is evidence that in some cases compulsory games as a medium of moral education were rather stretched. In many schools compulsory cross country running in all weather became an integral part of compulsory games. This was used as a device for occupying the poorer games-players when no games were available, or as a means of occupying all boys in impossible playing conditions.[25] At Uppingham, for example, boys participating in such runs would be accompanied by prefects on bicycles with whips "lashing out at any fellow with a stitch or a cramp."[26] It is difficult to see how the values of fair play and self-sacrifice, so admired by the muscular Christians, were developed under such conditions. Here sport was used as an instrument to discipline and control the boys. Whether or not these activities taught them any values, they must certainly have toughened up the boys and tired them out.

The rigors of mandatory running and games, indeed the generally harsh discipline of public school life, helped to develop "manliness," an integral part of muscular Christianity. The link between manliness, character development, and the public school education was described in a contemporary article as follows.

> Boys like nations can only attain to the genuine stout self-reliance which is true manliness by battling for themselves against their difficulties, and forming their own characters by the light of their own blunders and their own troubles. It is the great benefit of our public schools that they help character to grow . . . a benefit that

would be wholly lost if their system were not based on salutary neglect. The object of the public school is to introduce a boy early to the world, that he may be trained in due time for the struggle that lies before him.[27]

The struggle that is referenced here is the struggle for the British Empire, and Mangan has noted the paradoxical link in muscular Christianity between Christian gentility and social Darwinism.[28] Under the guidance of athletics, the public schools provided the training necessary for the British gentleman to go out and fulfill his God-given right to govern the inferior races in the far-flung corners of the British Empire. According to Bertrand Russell, public school education in general, and athletics in particular, stressed toughness rather than kindness, firmness rather than imagination, certainty rather than intellect, and harshness rather than sympathy. According to one commentator, this was "Darwinism misrepresented as survival of the most belligerent rather than the most adaptable."[29]

Athletics in the British public schools of the mid- to late nineteenth century taught the future rulers of the empire to "play up and play the game." In the ideology of muscular Christianity we see the fusion of idealism and practicality typical of the Victorian age. Through sports, the boys would develop character, which would later be used in imperialist domination. As sport historian Ralph Wilcox[30] has suggested, the poem "Vitai Lampada," published by Sir Henry Newbold in 1897, remains the greatest testimony to this cause. In it we see the British version of manliness and character development linked to military service in a classic example of the socialization power of the school.

> There's a breathless hush in the Close to-night—
> Ten to make and the match to win—
> A bumping pitch and a blinding light,
> An hour to play and the last man in.
> And it's not for the sake of a ribboned coat,
> Or the selfish hope of a season's fame,

But his Captain's hand on his shoulder smote—
Play up! play up! and play the game!

The sand of the desert is sodden red,—
Red with the wreck of the square that broke;—
The Gatling's jammed and the Colonel dead,
And the regiment blind with dust and smoke.
The river of death has brimmed his banks,
And England's far and Honour a name,
But the voice of a schoolboy rallies the ranks:
Play up! play up! and play the game!

This is the word that year by year,
While in her place the school is set,
Everyone of her sons must hear,
And none that hears it dare forget.
This they all with a joyful mind,
Bear through life like a torch in flame
And falling, fling to the host behind—
Play up! play up! and play the game!

Historian Eric Hobsbawm[31] has pointed out that the growth of sport in Britain in the latter part of the nineteenth century was part of a process of "inventing traditions" that gave stability to society and helped make the existing power relations legitimate in a time of unprecedented political and social change. Private education, expanding to meet the needs of a growing middle class, became the means by which this group could establish identity and claim leadership positions in business and commerce.

Before 1868 about twenty-four schools could seriously claim the status of "public" schools, but by 1902 this number had grown to between 64 and 104 depending on the criteria used for inclusion, or, more specifically, exclusion.[32] The best criterion for acceptance into this community of elite schools was athletic competition. That schools would play games against each other was symbolic of a shared identity.

To some extent, *Tom Brown's Schooldays* helped to invent the tradition that sport builds character. Although the sentiments of muscular Christianity previously had been expressed in children's literature,[33] and the memories of Hughes's school life may have been embellished by more up-to-date experiences,[34] this book certainly captured the spirit of the times. It sold eleven thousand copies in six editions in the first year of publication and was reprinted fifty times by 1890.[35]

It was stated at the outset that this chapter would have little to say about girls' sports, and as yet they have not been mentioned. Victorian educational and political leaders would not have taken to the idea of middle-class girls learning "manliness" by playing sports, and drawing upon these experiences to defend queen and country in far-flung corners of the British Empire. By emphasizing boys' sports as essential to the development of manliness, prevailing myths of male superiority were reinforced.[36]

Historians of sport only recently have begun to investigate the topic of girls' sport in Victorian times. However, a small but growing body of historical evidence suggests that the muscular Christianity movement did have its female equivalent, and that sports did figure prominently in the girls' private schools of the time.[37]

Specifically, historian Kathleen McCrone[38] notes the commonly accepted belief was that women's bodies and minds were incapable of hard labor. Medical theories in vogue at the time held that females had a limited amount of energy, which, during puberty, went into the development of the reproductive organs. Subjecting adolescent girls to the rigors of intellectual and physical pursuits during this developmental period would compromise their ability to produce children as adults. In the male-dominated world of the Victorians, what better calling could there be for a woman than to bear children?[39]

By the middle of the nineteenth century, some educators (usually female) believed that moderate exercise for girls would not compromise their femininity or gentility, and that playing games would provide for girls the same moral qualities as their male counterparts, without the Darwinian emphasis.[40] Moderate exercise would help girls to become "fit" mothers and to produce physically healthy and morally sound children.[41] In general, the emphasis on sport in the Victorian private schools for girls seems to have paralleled that of boys, but at a slightly later date. In reality, much less is known about girls' sports because they remained cloistered in schools, and their games did not get the widespread exposure afforded male play.

For boys, however, muscular Christianity was an idea whose time had come. In it was found the first real articulation of the "sport-builds-character" myth. In games of the British public schools are to be seen rituals that establish solidarity for one's house, one's school, and one's country. In these rituals were forged the myths of fairness, pluck, and courage that made middle-class English boys into men.

Sport historian James Mangan[42] has described how the rituals of intra- and interschool sports sustained and encouraged loyalty to house, school, and, later, country through the belief that team sports were at once the training ground for the typically British values of fairness and leadership, and at the same time the vehicle through which these values could be demonstrated. Through cricket and rugby the fittest would survive, and in surviving would "play up and play the game."

Such a belief served the vested interests of the leaders of the public schools who were attempting to control the lives of the boys and bring them more in line with the philosophy of the schools. This socialization was reinforced by the needs of the country to govern the large and expanding British empire. Although the quote by the Duke of Wellington that the battle of Waterloo was won on the playing fields of Eton has doubtful authenticity,[43] there is little doubt that to most Victorians these playing fields and others like them made a significant contribution to the empire. They also contributed greatly to the American view of athletics as educational. A century and a half after Wellington, another famous general, Douglas MacArthur, is supposed to have expressed similar sentiments about football.

> Upon the fields of friendly strife
> Are sown the seeds
> That, upon other fields, on other days,
> Will bear the fruits of victory.[44]

In fact, the muscular Christianity movement of the British public schools laid the philosophical foundations of worldwide amateur sport. Moreover, amateur sport was one of Britain's major exports to the colonies and to America. The diffusion of this concept to American education is the subject of the next section.

Muscular Christianity and American Sport: Diffusion

Muscular Christianity was imported to North America at almost the same time that it was being developed in Britain. During the mid- to late nineteenth century, the exclusive private schools of New England were modeled after their British counterparts. Team sports at Groton, St. Paul's, and Worcester Academy performed the same functions as they did at Eton and Harrow.[45] In fact, several of the headmasters of the American boarding schools had firsthand knowledge of the British system. Endicott Peabody, headmaster and founder of Groton in 1885, was a former pupil of Cheltenham College in 1867, where he would have been exposed to the current ideas of the importance of sport in character development.[46] Peabody loved athletics and made it of central importance at Groton. Other headmasters such as Poland at Worcester Academy and Coit at St. Paul's had similar philosophies.[47]

The novel *Tom Brown's Schooldays,* so influential in Britain in popularizing muscular Christianity, had a similar effect in America. Its author, Thomas Hughes, came to America in 1870 and visited St. Mark's School, which was described as "a sort of American Rugby."[48] In the late nineteenth century America developed its own Tom Brown in the person of Frank Merriwell. According to Gilbert Patton, his creator, Frank Merriwell stood for "truth, faith, the triumph of right, mother, home, friendship, loyalty, patriotism, the love of *alma mater,* duty, sacrifice, retribution, and strength of soul as well as body."[49] He was truly the archetype "all American boy" and was, of course, good at sports. Patton, writing under the nom de plume of Burt L. Standish, wrote 208 Frank Merriwell books in which the moral value of athletics was consistently demonstrated. Sport historian

Benjamin Rader[50] has noted that there was a flood of boys' books in the late nineteenth and early twentieth centuries in which the "manliness" idea of the British public schools was reinforced.

It appears that sport in the exclusive private schools of America and Britain went through similar stages of development. Just as in the English public schools, the rough and unorganized recreational activities of the students became institutionalized and were used by American school authorities to control the boys. Under the guise of building character, athletics, particularly team games, became compulsory for all students.[51] Sociologist Christopher Armstrong[52] has suggested that team sports fulfilled the same functions on both sides of the Atlantic, specifically, extending institutional control, allowing students contact with games-masters who acted as surrogate parents, teaching "manliness," developing school leaders, and preparing athletes for elite colleges and universities. As with the British system, the social-control value was never far from the surface. Ted Harrison, long-time coach and school master at Andover, called the games-masters "triple-threats" because they were teachers, coaches, and dormitory or house supervisors.[53] They therefore had the boys under surveillance twenty-four hours a day. Legitimating this supervision was the overriding idea that through participation in organized sports the boys would learn to be "gentlemen" by developing the "masculine ideal of self-control and fair play."[54]

In the early days, at least, this "play-up-and-play-the-game" philosophy was maintained. Commenting on this facet of British sport, McIntosh notes that "while games were played to the very limit of human endurance and the element of competition was often overdone, yet 'victory at any price' was not an idea that ever found favor."[55] An article in the Worcester Academy paper in 1879 reiterates this idea: "Half the pleasure and benefit arises from the zest in which we play; so don't stop to consider the probabilities of victory but play for exercise and fun."[56]

Even the early intercollegiate football games were characterized by this gentlemanly, sportsmanlike behavior. After the first college football game between Princeton and Rutgers in 1869, both teams ate supper together and sang songs. Harvard and Yale did likewise after their first game.[57] Indeed, the rules of the game of rugby, developed in Britain in the 1870s, did not even create a referee. It was felt that any differences of opinion could be settled by the two captains in a gentlemanly manner.[58]

Despite this early "play-up-and-play-the-game" mentality, the exclusive private schools in America were beset with problems of overemphasizing victory. By the 1890s, while athletics in American boarding schools was generally still in the early stage of development and under the control of the boys, the morality idea was being undermined. Incidents of boys from outside the school being used in key games (i.e., "as ringers"), of boys being recruited for the sole purpose of playing athletics, and boys being paid to play began to occur. The following comments about interscholastic squabbles between Andover and Exeter will serve as an example.

Disagreement and mutual distrust had resulted in no football games between the two schools in 1889 and in 1895. There had been no baseball games in the four years from 1893 to 1896. One reason why the formula of "fun and games" was not working is illustrated by the following incident, related by a member of the class of 1892. Andover, it seems, had a player named Jim White, who was paid a salary of $200. Two Exeter brothers succeeded in enticing him to transfer to Exeter for a $100 raise. "White pitched for our team in 1889 and won the game 3–2, precipitating a knockdown and drag-out fight between the two schools that took place at the railroad station. Athletic relations were severed for a year."[59]

The use of "ringers" was a problem not limited to the elite private schools. Sport historian Jeffrey Mirel[60] notes that "professionalism" was a criticism of the development of high school sports in Michigan since the 1880s. He suggests that this occurred because the boys were adopting the college model where such behavior was common and cites "an inherent tension between the desire to win and the rules of the game which prescribe what can be done in order to win."[61]

Whatever the reasons for the emphasis on winning in the private schools and high schools, the issue was used to take athletics away from the boys and put it into the hands of adults. The history of adult organization does not show that they were any more successful in controlling abuses than were the boys.

Whether tension between winning and fairness is inherent in sport or not, it is exacerbated by emphasizing the outcome of sport contests via leagues, championships, and large audiences.[62] In these situations the elements of play are replaced with the elements of display.[63] This implies that it is the emphasis socially placed upon sport that may be a problem. Victory in sport and winning in general were part of the social fabric of American society and remains so today.

The leaders of America who received the values of athletics at Groton and other exclusive boarding schools accepted this view. They shared the emphasis on manliness and social Darwinism with their British counterparts. In his address at the Harvard commencement in 1896, Senator Henry Cabot Lodge noted the importance of athletics in his education: "The time given to athletic contest and the injuries incurred on the playing field are part of the price which the English-speaking race has paid for being world conquerors."[64] However, there was a new twist. Mrozek has characterized it as a combination of social efficiency and the spirit of victory.[65] Athletic competition shaped character because it gave the opportunity for action, and as a result of this action, success and victory.

Training and competition in sport were understood to create a pattern of conduct and to shape a habit of success, and the conscious pursuit of sport had the effect of producing an unconscious but deep commitment to victory. The process worked not through a ritualistic appeal to sentiment but by the practical governance of behavior, introducing physical order and discipline into the actual experience of young men fated to serve their country as leaders.[66]

Victory can be attained by social efficiency, which in sport is characterized by team work or what Henry Cabot Lodge called a "capacity for acting together." This was perceived as a typically American characteristic and it was imputed to American sports such as football and baseball.[67] Americans were winners and showed their moral worth through victory. This victory demonstrated social efficiency. As former Green Bay Packer Willie Davis said after a Super Bowl victory, "We went out and played great football and we whipped them good and preserved our manhood."[68] Mrozek points out the circuity of this argument in that moral attitudes were indistinguishable from their expression in action. In other words, how do you question whether or not sports builds character if the "proof" is always provided after the fact, in this case by whether or not the game was won.

If there was one individual who personified the idea that action was the basis of moral character, it was Theodore Roosevelt. He endorsed athletics as a valuable developer of character, maintained involvement in vigorous physical activity, and personally interceded in the college football controversy of 1905.[69] He was a friend of Endicott Peabody, headmaster of Groton, and his first wife was Peabody's cousin. Roosevelt believed that sport could toughen moral fiber and impart character, and he sent his sons to Groton. He became nationally identified with the American version of the "sport-builds-character" myth and acted as a living advertisement for it.

In summary, men like Roosevelt and Lodge epitomized the American version of British muscular Christianity. At the same time, they demonstrated the change from the play-up-and-play-the-game mentality to the victory mentality. Morality was associated with sports, but now "moral power was transmuted into physical power."[70] The implication of this is that, all other things being equal, if you win you are morally better than your opponent.

Perhaps the change in the British and American interpretation of muscular Christianity was symptomatic of the difference in the status of the two societies at the time. America needed to show the importance of winning as the country grew toward the status of a world power. The British "gentleman" had already won, by way of being born, and there was no need to advertise this obvious fact. Much better to play up and play the game and keep a stiff upper lip.

Another reason for the difference between British and American interpretations of muscular Christianity could be the need for American institutions to adapt to the effects of unprecedented immigration. Since so many people came to this country who were not American by birth, the idea of America had to be invented.[71] Sport played an important part in this invention of tradition. For example, team sports such as baseball and football were thought to demonstrate typical "American" characteristics, and winning was one such quality.[72]

On the other hand, as we study the myth that sport builds character, we must be mindful of the possibility of other myths surrounding sport. That the British were more interested in playing fairly than winning could itself be a myth developed by the British to demean their transatlantic rivals when they were bested by them in sport, a common occurrence as the sporting craze took off in America around the turn of the century. Certainly the critics of the compulsory-games movement in British private schools claimed elitism, spectatorism, and a preoccupation with victory as problems.[73]

At any rate, by the turn of the century, the "sport-builds-character" idea, or perhaps more precisely the "winning-at-sports-builds-character" idea, was accepted widely in American society. Sports, particularly football and baseball, were required activities for the future leaders of America.

That these future leaders were male goes without saying. Middle-class concepts of women were similar on both sides of the Atlantic. Historian Roberta Park notes the tendency of American commentators of the late nineteenth century to view American women as in relatively poor health compared to their English counterparts. These negative comparisons might have been part of a general inferiority complex toward England that was not removed until later in the 1880s and 1890s when American sport teams began to beat their British rivals.

Park notes that in the 1850s Americans could read more books about English sport than American sport, and in 1858 only *Little Dorrit* sold more copies than *Tom Brown's Schooldays*. Another reason might have been the specter of immigration, which increased the pressure on middle-class "Anglo-Saxon" females to bear as many healthy children as possible. In so doing they would be defending the "racial health" of the country in the face of an influx of vast hordes of fecund immigrants from lower-class origins. Middle-class wives who did not have children were held responsible for "race suicide."[74]

As in England, then, sport for women was linked to childbirth, and the belief that mild exercise could turn weak girls into "fit" mothers was common by the 1880s.[75] Although the social importance of games for girls did not reach the level of significance attached to boys' games, American commentators did accept their importance in moral and physical development. Basketball, in particular, was supposed to help teach women self-control, physical and moral courage, and teamwork.[76]

By the turn of the century, Americans were asserting that they were the world's foremost nation. That they could achieve victory in sport demonstrated their physical and moral superiority. Winning in sport was symbolic of national dominance. "Young, strong, courageous, competent, the athlete was the idealized hope of the future: imperialistically, economically, socially, *and* biologically."[77]

Football, in particular, "exemplifies all the best in American manhood."[78] If sports were required activities for the future leaders of America, could they be used to "Americanize" the children of immigrants? The impetus to broaden this idea to the view that sport has valuable character development properties for everyone came from a different source, the playground movement.

YMCA, PSAL, and Playgrounds: The Democratization of Muscular Christianity

"[O]rganized play, particularly team sports for adolescents, was seen by reformers as an ideal means of integrating the young into the work rhythms and social demands of a dynamic and complex urban-industrial civilization."[79]

The playground movement[80] sprang from a concern with the problems of urbanization and immigration that were perceived to be threatening American values. Among these problems was the belief that the family's role in socialization was being eroded to the extent that it could no longer teach morality. It was felt that the city environment had a corrupting influence on youth that had to be countered. A group of progressive educational reformers believed that the answer to these social ills could be found in the transformation of unorganized, unstructured play in the city streets into adult-supervised, organized play in city playgrounds and gymnasiums.

This group, often called "play organizers"[81] or "boy-workers,"[82] included Luther Gulick, president of the Playground Association of America; journalist Jacob Ries; Henry Curtis, founder and first secretary of the Playground Association of America; and Jane Addams, social worker and winner of the Nobel Peace Prize. They believed that organized play would help teach cooperation, group loyalty, and subordination of self, and thus act as a brake against unrestricted capitalism, which they thought was a danger to American society. At the same time, it was felt that organized play would help to counter juvenile delinquency, perceived to be common in urban areas, and give a sense of moral purpose to youth.[83] Furthermore, this deemphasizing of individuality would help to integrate the children of different ethnic groups which were flooding into America at a great rate. The play leaders believed that the immigrant families were incapable of doing this, so organized play would enable immigrant children to break away from their ethnic roots and become "Americanized."[84]

The organizations that brought sport to the young masses were the Young Men's Christian Association (YMCA), the city playground movement, and the Public School Athletic League (PSAL). One man, Luther Halsey Gulick, Jr., was involved in all three institutions. He was responsible for changing the curriculum of the YMCAs from gymnastics and calisthenics to team sports. With genetic psychologist G. Stanley Hall, he developed the evolutionary theory of play that gave physical activity a central role in child development, and provided the philosophy behind the playground movement. In this influential theory the history of the human race was supposed to be recapitulated by each individual during play activities. Organized, adult-monitored games constituted the most advanced form of play in which the evolutionary stage of man as the savage hunter submitting to the leadership of a chief was being enacted. Although in retrospect this view of play appears to be rather bizarre, at the time it was widely accepted and influential. Like the muscular Christianity movement, it endowed games with the highest moral principles of teamwork, self-sacrifice, obedience, self-control, and loyalty.

In 1903 Gulick became director of physical training of the public schools of greater New York City and organized the PSAL so that the boys of the city schools could have "the physical benefits and moral and social lessons afforded by properly conducted games and sports."[85] According to sport historian Thomas Jable, the PSAL "was a progenitor of and leader in public school athletics,"[86] and brought programs to hundreds and thousands of children. In doing so it remains true to the principles of the play leaders that participation in sport and play rather than observation of it was the key to moral development.[87] Among the innovative programs of the PSAL was class athletics, in which participation of at least 80 percent of the class was required, and the average of the class, not the best individual performance score, was used as the criterion measure of victory. Class athletics encouraged participation of the mediocre and poor athletes, and, according to Jable, participation was enormous. For example, in 1914, 63,901 boys representing 2,248 classes took part in the broad jump; 34,377 boys from 1,192 classes competed in the dash; and 43,345 boys from 1,609 classes did pull-ups.[88]

Another program, the athletic badge test, was perhaps the first to link athletic and academic performance. Any boy meeting PSAL standards in running, jumping, or chinning could qualify for entry provided he had a "B" average in effort, proficiency, and deportment if he was in elementary school, or had a "satisfactory" grade for classroom work in high school. In 1915, the number of boys qualified for athletic badges reached 24,576. In the first "no pass/no play" policy, scholastic standards also were required for participation in interscholastic competition organized by PSAL. By 1907 this competition included soccer, cross country, swimming, tennis, lacrosse, roller skating, ice skating, and rowing.

PSAL, which laid claim to the title of the largest athletic body in the world,[89] was a monument to the power of the athletic ideology that sport builds character. So strong was this belief that Gulick and the other league founders could find large cash contributions ($40,000 during the first four years) from prominent New York businessmen such as John D. Rockefeller, Andrew Carnegie, J. Pierpont Morgan, and William K. Vanderbilt, as well as volunteer help from thousands of teachers and free newspaper publicity. In 1905, President Theodore Roosevelt served as PSAL's honorary vice president. In his letter of acceptance he said, "You are doing one of the greatest and most patriotic services that can be done and you are entitled to the healthiest backing in every way from all who appreciate the vital need of having the rising generation of Americans sound in body, mind, and soul."[90]

Although it was an organizational tour de force, PSAL did not touch the two-thirds of the "rising generation of Americans" living in New York City who did not attend school. Attempts to enrich their bodies, minds, and souls were made through the development of playgrounds. Between 1906 and 1917 cities with managed playgrounds grew from 41 to 504. In 1906 the number of cities spending $15,000 for playgrounds was 41, but by 1916 the number of cities expending more than $3 million on recreation was 480.[91] As with PSAL, the evolutionary theory of play provided the theoretical underpinnings, and the "class athletics" and badge tests of PSAL were among the common athletic activities.[92] Fueled by a fear of the problems of corruption and delinquency in the cities, the middle-class and higher-income taxpayers footed the bill.[93]

The YMCAs, PSAL, and the playgrounds were the organizations by which the "sport-builds-character" idea was broadened from a necessary component in the training of the future leaders of America to a mechanism through which to Americanize the lower classes. While the democratization of the muscular Christianity ideal seems to have owed more to Stanley Hall than to Thomas Hughes, by the second decade of the twentieth century the "sport-builds-character" idea was firmly fixed in the social fabric of American society. Athletics was not exclusively the right of the rich, but valuable for all boys in America. Child's play and sports were now considered much too important to be left to the children, and adults had taken control in the exclusive private schools, in the YMCAs, and in the streets of the large eastern cities. By 1920 "play organizers had convinced some influential Americans that organized play had moral and political implications. Americans were now persuaded that play was a vital medium of cultural transmission, and that team games were essential for promoting ethnic harmony, physical vigor, moral direction, psychological stability, and specific social skills in urban young people."[94]

Benjamin Rader has characterized the time from about 1920 to the present as the age of the spectator. This characterization is as valid for high school sport as it is for college and professional sport since the high schools followed rather than led sporting trends. The challenge was to adapt the "sport-builds-character" myth to this development. This did not prove difficult in spite of the myth's origins in compulsory participation for all at the British and American boarding schools[95] and the playground movement's fear of the moral hazards of spectatorship.[96]

Summary

Writing in the *New York Times* of Sunday, October 21, 1984, on the responsibility of the coach, Robert Mastruzzi, the superintendent of Manhattan high schools, spoke of the coach's moral and professional obligations. He noted that the qualities that the coach seeks to develop are preparation for competition, winning spirit, pride and tradition, tenacity and perseverance, sound moral fiber, teamwork, and sportsmanship. This chapter has shown that historically Mastruzzi was in good company. What he said was not markedly different from the muscular-Christianity headmasters of the British public schools in the 1860s, or their counterparts in America. His statements would have found approval with the fathers of the playground movement, such as Luther Gulick, and with presidents such as Theodore Roosevelt and Gerald Ford. The uncanny similarity of all these beliefs attests to the power of the myth that athletic involvement is the key to society's success, or, simply put, that sport builds character.

Behind these statements is the philosophy that action speaks louder than words, that sport action shows character, and that on the football field or in life, success demonstrates morality. Winners are morally better than losers, and this can be demonstrated in sport. That sport has been a predominantly male activity reinforces the importance of success as primarily a "male" rather than a "female" outcome of socialization.

On the shoulders of athletics has been placed the reason for the rise (and fall) of the British Empire and the "Great Society." Even today, when drug scandals, cheating, gambling, and recruiting violations are common practices in the world of sport, the "sport-builds-character" myth is dominant, the criticism of a few radicals, feminists, and liberal educationalists not withstanding. The majority of Americans still believe that sport is a valuable socializing experience for youth.[97]

Does sport build character? Certainly the weight of evidence presented in this chapter indicates that people believe that it does. Who are we to question the belief of moral educators on both sides of the Atlantic, leaders of the British Empire, American society, the free world, and the great American public? Historians Cavallo, Mangan, Mrozek, and Rader have described eloquently the power of this belief during the late nineteenth and early twentieth centuries. However, an underlying theme of this chapter has been that all the groups described had their own vested interests in perpetuating the "sport-builds-character" myth.

British and American headmasters in exclusive boarding schools could use it to bring the boys into line and socialize them into muscular Christianity. Military leaders could use it to demonstrate what they considered to be social Darwinism, which legitimized colonial conquest and exploitation. Altruistic social reformers, community leaders, and powerful captains of industry believed that they could use it to "Americanize" the youth from different ethnic backgrounds. Twentieth-century educators could use it to justify quasi-professional interscholastic athletics, which established the high school as an integral part of the community and gave the students something to shout about. The "sport-builds-character" myth has served the interests of all these groups.

This chapter has laid the historical foundations for our exploration of the rituals and myths of modern high school sport. Through sport, players and, by association, the spectators have the opportunity to be winners, and through winning to demonstrate their moral worth.

This sport ritual is something special, something old, and something uniquely American. Few Americans, however, understand the historical roots of these beliefs.

It is probable that the crowd hysteria and emotionalism of present-day school sports would cause a curl in the stiff upper lips of the likes of Thomas Hughes and Charles Kingsley. The leaders of the playground movement also would be shocked by the spectacle of so many thousands of children watching the elite few (usually males) play sport instead of actively participating themselves. However, the power of myth is that it allows us to believe that things always have been this way. The "tradition" of sport, although of relatively recent invention, adds historical legitimacy to the phenomenon. We believe that our traditions have stood the test of time. The next chapter brings the "sport-builds-character" myth up to date and discusses some of its intended and unintended consequences for schools.

Notes

1. Donna E. Shalala, "Sports: Active Ingredient in the Pursuit of Discipline," *New York Times*, November 11, 1984: Section 5, p. 2S.

2. Gerald R. Ford with John Underwood, "In Defense of the Competitive Urge," *Sports Illustrated* 41, no. 2 (1974): 17.

3. Douglas MacArthur, cited in "Education in America," *Saturday Review* (October 16, 1971): 35.

4. Theodore Roosevelt, cited in Benjamin G. Rader, *American Sports: From the Age of Folk Games to the Age of Spectators* (Englewood Cliffs, N.J.: Prentice-Hall, 1983), p. 149.

5. Donald J. Mrozek, *Sport and American Mentality, 1880-1910* (Knoxville, Tenn.: The University of Tennessee Press, 1983): preface.

6. J. E. C. Welldon, *Forty Years On* (London: Nicholson and Watson, 1935), p. 112; cited in Ralph Wilcox, "Muscular Christianity: Synthesis of the Victorian Body and Mind," unpublished paper, Hofstra University (1984).

7. Dominick Cavallo, *Muscles and Morals: Organized Playgrounds and Urban Reform, 1880-1920* (Philadelphia: University of Pennsylvania Press, 1981); Richard D. Mandell, *Sport: A Cultural History* (New York: Columbia University Press, 1984); Wilcox, "Muscular Christianity."

8. James A. Mangan, *Athleticism in the Victorian and Edwardian Public School*

(Cambridge, England: Cambridge University Press, 1981); Peter McIntosh, *Physical Education in England since 1800* (London: G. E. Bell, 1968); Peter McIntosh, *Fair Play: Ethics in Sport and Education* (London: Heinemann, 1979); Wilcox, "Muscular Christianity."

9. Ralph Wilcox, "Sport in Bristol (UK) and Boston (USA), a Cross-National Comparison, 1870-1900" (Ph.D. diss., University of Alberta, 1982).

10. McIntosh, *Physical Education in England since 1800.*

11. Ibid.; Wilcox, "Sport in Bristol (UK) and Boston (USA)."

12. Eric Dunning, "The Development of Modern Football," in *The Sociology of Sport,* ed. Eric Dunning (London: Frank Cass, 1971), pp. 133-51; McIntosh, *Physical Education in England since 1800;* Wilcox, "Muscular Christianity."

13. Cited in McIntosh, *Physical Education in England since 1800,* p. 25.

14. Mangan, *Athleticism in the Victorian and Edwardian Public School.*

15. Wilcox, "Muscular Christianity."

16. Charles Kingsley, *Two Years Ago* (Cambridge, Mass.: Macmillan and Co., 1857); Charles Kingsley, *Alton Locke, Tailor and Poet: An Autobiography* (Cambridge: Macmillan and Co., 1876); Charles Kingsley, *Westward Ho* (Cambridge, Mass.: Macmillan and Co., 1885); Thomas Hughes, *Tom Brown's Schooldays* (London: Macmillan, 1857).

17. Gerald Redmond, "The First Tom Brown's Schooldays: Origins and Evolution of 'Muscular Christianity' in Children's Literature," *Quest* 30 (1978): 4-18; Peter McIntosh, *Sport in Society* (London: C. A. Watts, 1963); McIntosh, *Physical Education in England since 1800.*

18. Hughes, *Tom Brown's Schooldays,* p. 351.

19. Mangan, *Athleticism in the Victorian and Edwardian Public School,* p. 94.

20. Ibid., p. 111.

21. Christopher J. Hurn, *The Limits and Possibilities of Schooling: An Introduction to the Sociology of Education,* 2d ed. (Boston: Allyn and Bacon, 1985).

22. Roald Dahl, *Boy: Tales of Childhood* (London: Johnathon Cape, 1984), pp. 143-45.

23. Dunning, "The Development of Modern Football."

24. Mangan, *Athleticism in the Victorian and Edwardian Public School,* p. 171.

25. Ibid., p. 84.

26. Ibid., p. 85.

27. *Saturday Review* (December 8, 1860): 727; cited in Mangan, *Athleticism in the Victorian and Edwardian Public School,* p. 135.

28. Mangan, *Athleticism in the Victorian and Edwardian Public School,* p. 136.

29. John Bowles, *The Imperial Achievement: The Rise and Transformation of the British Empire* (London: Secker & Warburg, 1974), p. 290.

30. Wilcox, "Muscular Christianity."

31. Eric Hobsbawm, "Introduction: Inventing Traditions," in *The Invention of*

Tradition, eds. Eric Hobsbawm and Terence O. Ranger (Cambridge, England: Cambridge University Press, 1983), pp. 1–14.

32. Eric Hobsbawm, "Mass-Producing Traditions: Europe 1870–1914," in Hobsbawm and Ranger, *The Invention of Tradition,* pp. 263–307.

33. Redmond, "The First Tom Brown's Schooldays."

34. Earle R. Anderson, "The Barby Hill Episode in 'Tom Brown's Schooldays': Sources and Influences," *Arete* 2, no. 2 (1985): 95–110.

35. Wilcox, "Muscular Christianity."

36. Roberta J. Park, "Sport, Gender, and Society in a Transatlantic Victorian Perspective," in *From "Fair Sex" to Feminism: Sport and the Socialization of Women in the Industrial and Post-Industrial Eras,* eds. James A. Mangan and Roberta J. Park (London: Frank Cass, 1987), pp. 58–93.

37. Mangan and Park, *From "Fair Sex" to Feminism.*

38. Kathleen McCrone, "Play Up! Play Up! And Play the Game! Sport at the Late Victorian Girls' Public Schools," in *From "Fair Sex" to Feminism,* eds. Mangan and Park, pp. 97–129.

39. The traces of these medical theories still exist today in the physiological myths suggesting that women's bodies are more fragile than men's and therefore more susceptible to injury. These myths have been used to limit female involvement in competitive sports, particularly contact sports.

40. McCrone, "Play Up! Play Up! And Play the Game!" pp. 97–129.

41. Park, "Sport, Gender, and Society in a Transatlantic Victorian Perspective," p. 65.

42. Mangan, *Athleticism in the Victorian and Edwardian Public School,* chapter 7.

43. McIntosh, *Physical Education In England since 1800,* p. 15.

44. Cited in Paul Hoch, *Rip Off the Big Game* (New York: Anchor/Doubleday, 1972), p. 70.

45. Christopher F. Armstrong, "The Lessons of Sport: Class Socialization in British and American Boarding Schools," *Sociology of Sport Journal* 1 (1984): 314–31; Axel Bundgaard, "Tom Brown Abroad: Athletics in Selected New England Public Schools, 1850–1910," *Research Quarterly for Exercise and Sport,* Centennial Issue, 56 (1985): 28–37.

46. Wilcox, "Sport in Bristol (UK) and Boston (USA)."

47. Bundgaard, "Tom Brown Abroad," pp. 28–37.

48. Ibid.

49. Robert H. Boyle, *Sport: Mirror of American Life* (Boston: Little, Brown, 1963), p. 242.

50. Rader, *American Sports,* p. 150.

51. Bundgaard, "Tom Brown Abroad," p. 29.

52. Armstrong, "The Lessons of Sport," pp. 314–31.

53. Bundgaard, "Tom Brown Abroad," p. 34.

54. Armstrong, "The Lessons of Sport," p. 329.

55. McIntosh, *Physical Education in England since 1800*, p. 73.

56. Bundgaard, "Tom Brown Abroad," pp. 28–37.

57. Parke H. Davis, *Football: The American Intercollegiate Game* (New York: Charles Scribner, 1911), p. 50; Morton H. Prince, "History of Football at Harvard," in *The H Book of Harvard Athletics*, ed. John A. Blanchard (Cambridge, Mass.: The Harvard Varsity Club, 1923), p. 374.

58. C. Roger Rees, "The Relationship between the Development of British and American Football" (Unpublished paper, University of Maryland, 1972).

59. Cited in Bundgaard, "Tom Brown Abroad," p. 32.

60. Jeffrey Mirel, "From Student Control to Institutional Control of High School Athletics: Three Michigan Cities, 1883–1905," *Journal of Social History* 16 (1982): 83–100.

61. Ibid., p. 95.

62. C. Roger Rees and Andrew W. Miracle, "Conflict Resolution in Games and Sports," *International Review of Sport Sociology* 19, no. 2 (1984): 145–56.

63 Gregory P. Stone, *Games, Sport, and Power* (New Brunswick, N.J.: Transaction Books, 1972).

64. Henry Cabot Lodge in *Harvard Graduates' Magazine* (September 1869): 67, cited in Wilcox, "Sport in Bristol (UK) and Boston (USA)."

65. Mrozek, *Sport and American Mentality, 1880–1910*, pp. 33–34.

66. Ibid., pp. 32–33.

67. Wilcox, "Sport in Bristol (UK) and Boston (USA)," p. 594.

68. Jerry Kramer, ed., *Lombardi: Winning is the Only Thing* (New York: Thomas Y. Crowell, 1971), p. 111.

69. Guy Lewis, "Theodore Roosevelt's Role in the 1905 Football Controversy," *Research Quarterly for Exercise and Sport* 40 (1969): 717–24.

70. Mrozek, *Sport and American Mentality, 1880–1910*, p. 169.

71. Hobsbawm, "Mass-Producing Traditions," p. 279.

72. Park, "Sport, Gender, and Society in a Transatlantic Victorian Perspective," p. 71.

73. Gerald Redmond, "Alarm, Amusement, and Contempt: Early English Critics of Muscular Christianity," paper presented at the annual meeting of the North American Society for Sport History, Hamilton, Ontario (1981); Malcolm Tozer, "From 'Muscular Christianity' to 'Esprit de Corps': Games in the Victorian Public Schools of England," *Stadion* 7 (1981): 117–30.

74. Carrol Smith-Rosenberg and Charles Rosenberg, "The Female Animal: Medical and Biological Views of Women and Their Role in Nineteenth-Century America," *Journal of American History* 60 (1973): 332–56.

75. Park, "Sport, Gender, and Society in a Transatlantic Victorian Perspective."

76. Ibid., p. 86.

77. Ibid., p. 74.

78. Ibid., p. 69.
79. Cavallo, *Muscles and Morals*, p. 2.
80. Ibid.
81. Ibid., p. 1.
82. Rader, *American Sports*, p. 148.
83. Cavallo, *Muscles and Morals*, p. 17.
84. Ibid., p. 124.
85. Luther Halsey Gulick, Jr., "Athletics for School Children," *Lippincott's Monthly Magazine* 88 (1911): 201; cited in Thomas J. Jable, "The Public Schools Athletic League of New York City: Organized Athletics for the City School Children, 1903–1914," in *The American Sporting Experience: A Historical Anthology of Sport in America*, ed. Stephen Reiss (West Point, N.Y.: Leisure Press, 1984), pp. 219–38.
86. Jable, "The Public Schools Athletic League of New York City," p. 235.
87. Cavallo, *Muscles and Morals*, p. 22.
88. Jable, "The Public Schools Athletic League of New York City."
89. Mrozek, *Sport and American Mentality, 1800–1910*, p. 61.
90. Jable, "The Public Schools Athletic League of New York City," p. 227.
91. John Rickards Betts, "The Technological Revolution and the Rise of Sport, 1850–1900," *The Mississippi Valley Historical Review* 40 (1951): 231–56.
92. Cavallo, *Muscles and Morals*, p. 43.
93. Rader, *American Sports*, p. 156.
94. Cavallo, *Muscles and Morals*, p. 48.
95. Bundgaard, "Tom Brown Abraod."
96. Cavallo, *Muscles and Morals*, p. 22.
97. Stephen J. Grove and Richard Dodder, "A Study of the Functions of Sport: A Subsequent Test of Spreitzer and Snyder's Research," *Journal of Sport Behavior* 2 (1979): 83–89; Elmer Spreitzer and Eldon E. Snyder, "The Psychological Functions of Sport as Perceived by the General Population," *International Review of Sport Sociology* 10 (1975): 87–93.

3

Sport and School Unity

An air of anticipation hangs over Madson High School. Students leave their classrooms in small groups and walk purposefully toward the gymnasium. Their conversation is animated and their behavior is generally uncharacteristic for a Friday afternoon, as school winds down and students get ready for the weekend. An important event is about to take place. The whole school is involved.

Madson is having a pep rally for tomorrow's football game against cross-town rival Pascelle High. As we enter the gym our senses are assaulted by an excess of color, sound, and movement. The school band is playing; cheerleaders dance, perform acrobatic movements, and lead the student body in ritualized chants and cheers. A few teachers patrol the perimeter of the throng in a mock show of authority, occasionally issuing directives or warnings to students who have too quickly become overly enthusiastic, or who have not waited for the official start of this event to exhibit behaviors that soon will be expected.

Large pictures of red hornets, the school mascot, adorn the walls. An enormous sign, at least ten feet tall, a memorial to the collective calligraphy of one homeroom, says "BEAT PASCELLE." In one corner of the gym there is a picture of a hornet biting a cat (Pascelle's mascot is a wildcat) on the butt.

Other signs are being waved by the students who are assembled on the gymnasium floor. "TAME THE CATS," "GO MADSON," and "PASCELLE ARE PUSSYCATS" reflect the theme, but some signs are in questionable taste. One, held by a small knot of boys who have painted their faces red, proclaims that "MADSON EATS PUSSYCATS FOR LUNCH."

Seated on a raised platform, symbolically above the hubbub, sits authority—vested in the school principal, his lieutenant (the football coach), and the foot soldiers who will do battle for the school's honor tonight. The warriors are clad in red and white jackets adorned with large letters.

The pep rally is an exciting event and one that frequently is considered an essential element of high school athletics. Classes may be excused so all students can attend, indicating that at least on some occasions athletics may be given priority over academics.

The school principal or that person's designate initiates the formal content of the event with a few remarks about the school that are designed to heighten sentiments about the institution. This speech invariably mentions the high quality of the school, its sense of tradition, pride, and spirit—all of which are supposedly better than any other school's. The principal then introduces the coach who remarks about the critical nature of the upcoming game and the worthiness of the opponent. Then the coach introduces the players, or else the team captain who then introduces the other players. The players usually appear nervous as attention is focused on them in this uncharacteristic and socially uncomfortable setting.

As the band plays and the cheerleaders exhort the crowd, many students laugh and yell, cheer and sing, clap and dance, and generally appear to have a good time. Other students seem to be fairly blasé. At the end of the scheduled time period for the pep rally, the principal dismisses the assembled students with an enthusiastic reminder that everyone should attend the game and support the team in its quest for victory.

The pep rally is a symbolic event in the culture of the high school. Like rituals in general, it helps to heighten respect for the status quo and make it acceptable to the participants.[1] Among other functions, such ritual can instill acceptance of the school culture. Even at a pep rally, students are learning to accept the view that success is the goal, that you win by working hard and following orders, that people differ in their ability to be winners, and that whether you win or lose is up to the individual, not the system.

Anthropologist Clifford Geertz notes that the governing elite of any society is distinguished by many symbols, rituals, and ceremonial forms that bestow charisma on those involved.[2] The ritual ceremony of the high school pep rally confirms the sacredness of the central authority of the school. In no other instance are all the elements of the school—the principal, the teachers, and the various cliques which comprise the student body—unified in their pursuit of a common goal. In other domains of high school education, these elements may be at odds, and even within the assemblage of the pep rally they may isolate themselves by claiming distinct territories during the event.

It is clear that the authority structure of the school is vested in the principal, who initiates the pep rally and terminates it. The principal, or principal's designate, is in control throughout the event, setting the tone with a brief speech and then introducing subsequent major participants. Even though students may appear to act with abandon during the height of excitement generated by the pep rally, it also is clear that teachers and staff control student behavior so that in reality students' freedom to act is more apparent than real. Teachers control students and coaches control players. It has not always been this way, however. A review of the historical development of school sports will provide insight into the evolving role of sports in the American school.

We shall begin by tracing the development of adult control in school sports. We shall show how the rituals used so effectively in the private schools of England and America during the nineteenth century have been put to work to build morale and esprit de corps in high schools all across America. Today the ubiquitous myth that sport builds character is still alive. It convinces coaches and educational administrators of the value of athletics in providing a moral elite for the school, individuals whom the rest of the student body can respect.

We also shall demonstrate how sport has become central to the social life of the school, more important to some students than intellectual growth, yet often rejected by other students who are in revolt against school values and education in general. Finally, we shall focus on the macho subculture of the high school jock, a subculture in which the value system is often at odds with the official values of the school. By stressing winning in athletics, the school runs the risk of turning dumb jocks into the real heroes of high school, and in so doing, subverting the very myth that athletics originally was supposed to enshrine—the symbol of moral and intellectual growth of our youth.

From Student to Adult Control of Athletics

In general, athletics in high schools developed in the wake of college athletics in the United States, which had been influenced by the emergence of athletics in universities in England. While the first interscholastic baseball team was organized in 1859 at Worcester High School in Massachusetts, it was not until the 1880s that football was first played on an organized basis in high schools.[3]

A report of the Carnegie Foundation for the Advancement of Teaching described the period from 1886 to 1906 as the crucial stage in the development of modern school athletics.[4] The Carnegie study was conducted in 1926 and included a survey of 148 colleges and secondary schools in the United States and Canada.

Prior to the 1890s, athletic contests were conducted between school clubs controlled entirely by students. Student managers and captain-coaches provided club leadership. Players paid all of their own expenses. However, by 1906 the situation had changed drastically for those schools surveyed by the Carnegie Foundation. Historian

Joel Spring provides a good summary of what had transpired. "Coaching became a technical profession, and paid coaches were hired to manage the teams. Management and control were taken from students and given to faculty, administration and alumni. Fees began to be charged for admission to athletic events, particularly football, and national athletic associations were formed [for colleges]."[5]

The Public Schools Athletic League (PSAL), described in the previous chapter, was formed in New York in 1903, and by 1910 there were school-based leagues in at least seventeen additional cities.[6] By the 1920s, athletics had been institutionalized in virtually every school district in America. Institutionalization meant that it was brought under the control of school authorities with coaches who were full-time faculty members. Control was extended outside the local community through membership in leagues that were deemed necessary to prevent abuses by individual schools and communities. In fact, as early as 1902 faculties in Wisconsin, Illinois, and several eastern boarding schools had taken control of interscholastic sport.[7]

In the first decade of this century, it was not clear that public education would become the ubiquitous institution that it is today. High school attendance was low, and earning a diploma was not a common achievement. Graduation was not necessary for employment, its chief function being to mark social status. At that time education was hardly a profession. For example, there was no graduate school of education in the United States. There was no specialized course work for school administrators.[8]

During the early years after the turn of the century, educators were looking for new activities to add to school programs in an effort to make them more attractive to students and to the community. It was precisely at this time that educators began to encourage school sports. Sports, especially baseball and football, were popular with adults who enjoyed watching boys play. Educators sought to capitalize on this popularity.

Football provides an interesting illustration of education's institutionalization of athletics. Prior to and during the first decade of this century, football was an especially violent sport. Injuries were common and deaths were reported in the press. Teams at some schools and colleges were hiring professional coaches in an effort to be more competitive, a move that was greatly resisted by faculties and administrators alike. Several attempts were made to institute rules to curb some of the abuses noted by educators. These were difficult to enforce since the teams were affiliated with the institutions only in a rather loose fashion.

The institutionalization of athletics effectively solved the problem. Teams were made official entities within the educational institutions. This new status granted the teams certain benefits, such as better training facilities and financial assurances. In exchange, the institution gained control over the previously autonomous teams; now educators could regulate athletics.

By the 1920s schools had usurped the functions of the playground movement, adding to and strengthening its institutional foundation. Consequently, children's play became more institutionalized as athletics, which meant it became elitist (i.e., designed for the athletically superior) and adult-dominated.

The successful incorporation of athletics into school programs, coupled with the passage of compulsory education laws, had a tremendous adverse effect on the organized playground movement. Organizations such as Boys Clubs, the YMCA, and the Boy Scouts are surviving remnants of the turn-of-the-century playground movement, and they have survived by specializing so as to avoid direct competition with schools.

Between the organization of the first interscholastic baseball team in 1859 and the promulgation of the Carnegie study in 1926, high school sports grew, not only in numerical terms, but in relative stature within the institutional structure of the American educational system.

Today students exercise no control over organized school athletics. National, state, regional, and local bureaucratic agencies staffed by professionals determine every aspect of school sports: the rules of the game, who is eligible, who may coach, what may constitute practices, how many games may be played, and when and where those games may occur.

Gaining control over athletics simply completed the autocratic control that adult educators have exercised over every sphere of American schooling since colonial times.

The forces of muscular Christianity and immigration were behind the institutionalization of school athletics. If participating in, or preferably winning at, typically American sports such as football built character, then these sports could be used to socialize the children of immigrants into traditional American values.

Athletics became an important democratizing influence in the growing institution of public education, which experienced a spectacular expansion. By 1913, for example, there were 38.6 students per 10,000 population in America, compared with 9 to 11.5 in Europe, and less than 8 in Britain.[9] That these athletic activities were linked to Anglo-Saxon traditions (e.g., those of British public schools) helped to quell fears that American institutions would be swamped by immigrants from Eastern Europe.

The value of sports in secondary education was recognized as early as 1919 by a report from a special committee of the National Education Association entitled "The Cardinal Principles of Secondary Education."[10] Echoing the thoughts of the leaders of the playground movement, the report noted that urbanization had reduced the power of the family to socialize youth. Schools should pick up the slack by achieving two educational goals: preparing students for vocations and teaching the social values perceived to be essential for coping with modern life. These social values were cooperation, social cohesion, and social solidarity. Athletic games were among the common activities suggested to instill these values.

The Functions of Athletics Within the School System

It may be easier to understand the evolution of high school sports, the rise of sport myths, and the role that mythology has played in school sports after examining the functions of sport in the American high school. When we speak of the functions of sport, we mean those effects that sport has on schools and on the participants.

The functions are of two types. There are those that are openly acknowledged by the school authorities, such as character building. These are known as *manifest functions*. Manifest functions oftentimes are offered as explanations in response to questions about why traditional customs and practices exist. In addition, there are those functions, which generally are not readily apparent to parents, students, and educators, nor admitted to by school authorities. These are called *latent functions*. It is these functions that allow insights into how social institutions work.

For example, adults took control over high school athletics from the boys ostensibly to curb abuses and allow "fair" competition; this was the manifest function of the action. Once in control of athletics, the school authorities could claim that sports helped to socialize students into the "American" way; this rationalization is another manifest function. However, these values were those of the white Anglo-Saxon Protestants who were the leaders of the country. This class of Americans was concerned with preserving its own power in the face of massive immigration by Europe's "huddled masses." Thus, in effect, they could use coaches as "paid agents of the ruling class" to teach obedience to authority and acceptance of the status quo through athletics.[11] This effect can be understood as a latent function of the institution of high school athletics.

Primarily we are concerned with the latent functions of sport, those which may not be easily perceived, those which lie outside the consciousness and concern of most students, parents, and educators. Indeed, such functions are called latent precisely because they generally are hidden from view. When social scientists discuss particular latent functions attributable to a social institution, the likely response of the layperson may range from disbelief to blasé acceptance to gradually increasing insight. It is the last response that we hope to generate here. That is, by openly discussing the latent functions of athletics, we may be able to understand more clearly why sport has become so important in American high schools.

Schools are bureaucracies. They have a hierarchical system of authority stretching from school boards to superintendents to principals to teachers; students are at the bottom of this pyramidal system.

As do all bureaucracies, schools have explicit rules and regulations that define duties and responsibilities. To a large extent, professional educators define policies and establish routine procedures, and enforce the rules and regulations. In fact, today American schools are almost totally controlled by professionals.

As a mass institution charged with the uniform and fair treatment of an endless supply of students, schools are faced with a nearly impossible task. As the educational sociologist Christopher J. Hurn has noted,[12] schools have to coordinate the activities of many individuals, insure some degree of uniformity and predictability of performance, and treat individuals fairly. These are essential to promote the growth of bureaucratic organizations and to insure the maintenance of smooth operations.

Hurn believes that the most distinctive dilemma schools face is the problem of motivating and attempting to teach a captive audience that might prefer to be elsewhere, but has no choice.[13] Schools must socialize students, who are not in school entirely of their own volition, to become passive receptors of education or at least to become sufficiently submissive so as not to disrupt the overall functioning of the institution.

To some extent, schools are custodial institutions. To some "inmates" who are not interested in what the school has to offer, schools may indeed seem like prisons. In order to function efficiently, schools must exercise careful regimentation and control over the behavior of students, even over seemingly inconsequential details (e.g., hair length and clothing styles) in order to minimize individual differences and promote reliance on the authority structure of the school. As will be shown, athletics have served schools well in their needs as custodial institutions.

Educational administrators have learned that the cultural value placed on athletics can be used to bureaucratic advantage. For example, control over sport in the school increases the authority of the principal. The power of the administrator is great indeed when it can prevent a student from playing school sport or attending a sport-related event since these are generally considered to be the most important school functions by students and many community members.

Sport and the Social Organization of the High School

The powerful presence of sport has continued unabated for most of the twentieth century. In the 1920s sociologists Robert and Helen Lynd noted that sports were significant in the social system of the high school. They wrote that "the highest honor a senior boy can have is captaincy of the football or basketball team."[14] Writing about schools in 1932, the educational sociologist Willard Waller concluded that, "Of all activities athletics is the chief. . . . It is the most flourishing and the most revered culture pattern."[15] In the 1940s sociologist August Hollinshead observed that high school football and basketball were a central focus of student and public life.[16]

The serious study of high school sports began in earnest with James S. Coleman's examination of ten high schools in Illinois in the late 1950s.[17] He found that regardless of school size, location, or socioeconomic composition, athletics dominated school life. Stanley Eitzen and George Sage have summarized Coleman's findings on athletics as follows[18]:

(1) Membership in a school's leading crowd was based on different criteria for males and females. While girls' status was determined by ascribed characteristics such as parents' achievement, good looks, and possessions, status for boys was based on achievement, especially in athletics.

(2) The most important attribute for male popularity was "being an athletic star." This was consistently considered more important than (in order of importance) being in the leading crowd, being a leader in activities, making high grades and being on the honor roll, having a nice car, or coming from the right family.

(3) When asked how they would most like to be remembered, in Coleman's 1961 study 44 percent of the boys said as an athletic star, 31 percent said as a brilliant student, and 25 percent replied as the most popular. This contrasted with the parents' response to the same question; three-fourths of them said that they wanted their sons remembered as brilliant students.

Given the way that athletics affect the status system of high school males, Coleman characterizes sport as a democratizing factor.[19] For boys, sports undercut ascribed characteristics such as social background as a basis for status, utilizing achievement through sport as an important status determinant.

More recent research[20] has found that being an athlete is still the foremost criterion for male popularity. It seems that athletic participation is more highly valued by nonwhite males, those who are younger, and those who are sons of less well-educated fathers.[21] Sport also is valued more highly by those more centrally involved in school activities, those given parental encouragement to play sports, and those in noncollege, as opposed to college preparatory, curricular tracks.[22] In addition, sport participation is more highly valued by those who attend smaller schools with a more rigid authority structure in smaller, more rural, and less affluent communities.[23]

For females, being an athlete has been given fairly low social status in the past.[24] It seems that girls in elementary school enjoy playing sports,[25] but many stop participating in games by the age of thirteen or fourteen.[26]

In recent years, the number of girls participating in high school sports has grown dramatically, increasing over 600 percent since 1971. Today, as much as 35 percent of all high school athletes are females.[27] Furthermore, high school girls perceive athletic participation as having a direct effect upon their popularity.[28] However, these findings must be placed within a school culture wherein sport still figures prominently as a "male" activity, an issue which is addressed in the next section.

Sports may function positively for schools as institutions, quite apart from any effects on the individual players. For example, in addition to helping define the status hierarchy of students within the social organization of the school, athletics also may serve to integrate the distinct cliques and social groupings within the school. Sports can serve this function because they are given such importance by school authorities and because so many students have been socialized to believe that sport is important.

For example, a football game brings to one place band members, cheerleaders, and pep squad participants. In addition, groups of friends from the various social strata of the school population may attend the game, as well as pre-game rallies and post-game dances. At least for a short time, the attention of a school's diverse constituencies is focused largely on a unifying theme.

Every institution depends upon the energies of its members; if it cannot obtain these energies through appeals to loyalty or motivational incentives, the institution is in jeopardy. This is an especially difficult challenge for a custodial institution such as a school.

Coleman observes how ineffective grades and academic goals are in this pursuit. "[E]ven for students with the right backgrounds, grades are a poor motivating mechanism, because they are unique to the school and useful only in comparison with grades of fellow students. This generates invidious comparisons, sets each student in competition with his fellows, and is a powerfully divisive force among students."[29] In a sense, grades can be compared with incentive pay, which often encourages informal norms restricting productivity. Coleman believes that a "much more successful mechanism of control in an institution is one which generates strong positive identification with the institution."[30]

Coleman notes that schools are distinct institutions in that, except for sports and other extracurriculars, they have no collective goals, only individual, scholastic ones. "Athletic contests with other schools provide, for these otherwise lifeless institutions, the collective goals that they lack. The common goals shared by all makes the institution part of its members and them part of it, rather than an organization outside them and superimposed upon them."[31] Sport can transform a disorganized, individualistic student body into a close-knit community with strong common goals, thus solving a difficult problem for the institution: "the problem of generating enthusiasm for and identification with the school and drawing the energies of adolescents into the school."[32]

"As with any collective enterprise, there is a mutual reinforcement, because the effort of each benefits all. When the team wins the school wins. When the school wins, all its members feel a little better about the school, and because they are part of the school, about themselves."[33] This is similar to the shared pride that workers feel in their joint accomplishments. However, in schools, except for sports and other extracurriculars, there are no arenas for achieving this feeling of unity. This is unfortunate because "collective enterprises, in which people work together toward a common goal that is not entirely selfish, make people feel good about themselves and about their activity. And wholly individualistic activities, in which a set of individuals work separately toward separate goals, has no such force."[34]

As we have suggested, school sports can serve to integrate various groups and categories of individuals within the school. This is especially important in heterogeneous schools, with student populations drawn from various social strata and ethnic populations. The natural patterning of these diverse elements tends toward voluntary segregation. Organized athletics is one of the few systems that can serve to unite and focus the energies of these disparate elements, and thus contribute toward the maintenance of equilibrium within school and community.[35]

Sport and Student Cliques

The myth that sport builds character has been used by educational administrators to build conformity and solidarity in the student body. The reward systems of schools, reflecting the perspectives of school officials, reward those students who contribute to its prestige and well-being, whether they are National Merit Finalists or trophy-winning athletes. A closer look at the informal culture of adolescents shows that students do not always passively accept the messages of the school and may have a different view of what high school athletics actually represent.

Sport certainly provides the central force in the social life of the typical American high school, and because of this athletes usually are among the most popular members of the student body. However, what comprises status among adolescent cliques is often different from what well-meaning adults would like to believe.

The study of adolescent cliques, small friendship groups which define and reflect what is "in" and "out" in the social lives of students, provides insights into the socialization of youth and the role of athletics in this process. Research on high school cliques[36] confirms the popularity of athletes, but not always for the reasons that educators and coaches might suppose. A typical clique hierarchy consists of numerous sets of cliques, often colorfully labeled by students.

The following is a generalized description of a high school clique structure. Of course, there are many local variations and the student social structure and behavior of clique members can differ greatly from school to school. However, we believe that the description provided here applies to many, if not most, high schools across the country.

The terms[37] by which adolescents categorize themselves and their schoolmates are descriptive and reflect the perspective of the dominant groups within the school. That is, an individual might disagree with the label applied to him or her by members of the dominant groups.

Membership in cliques often is structured around characteristics such as race, gender, and social class, as well as preferences for clothes and cars, and lifestyle or behavior differences, including extracurriculars and leisure pursuits. Moreover, virtually all cliques have single-gender memberships. Mixed-gender cliques are rare, though commonly a male clique and a female clique will be paired for general social activities, including dating.

High status is all about being cool, which defined in adolescent terms means being able to "handle" what are perceived to be adult issues such as sex, drugs, and alcohol. In many schools it also can mean being good at sports, especially with regard to male, aggressive, team sports such as football.

The male jocks are at the top of the status hierarchy in most high schools.[38] Male jocks are cool because they are macho and date the best girls. Other male cliques that are found on the fringes of the athletes' cliques or are associated with the band, use athlete norms as the standard by which to measure social success. Athletes are perceived as macho, and being seen as macho is important. Anyone who is not macho is a fag or a wimp, derogatory terms in male cliques. The following example is taken from anthropologist Douglas E. Foley's description of a high school in southwest Texas.

The main masculinity test for band fags was to punch their biceps as hard as possible. If the victim returned this aggression with a defiant smile or smirk, he was a real man; if he winced and whined, he was a wimp or a fag. The other variation[s] on punching the biceps were pinching the forearm and rapping the knuckles. North Town boys generally punched and pinched each other, but this kind of male play towards those considered fags was a daily ritual degradation. These were moments when physically dominant males picked on allegedly more effeminate males and reaffirmed their place in the male pecking order. Ironically, however, the players themselves rarely picked on those they called band fags. Males who emulated jocks and hoped to hang out with them were usually the hit men. The jocks signaled their real power and prestige by showing restraint towards obviously weaker males.[39]

Another issue in the status hierarchy is intellectual aspirations and ability. Intellect can be a respected secondary trait for individuals within the clique structure, but intelligence alone is insufficient to get one into a high-status clique. For example, jocks who do well in school receive high status. However, since athletic ability counts for more than intellectual ability, dumb jocks also are respected. Nerds or brains are usually among the low-status cliques, just above the burnouts. The nerd label signifies no social poise or success with girls, and a unidimensional interest in studying. The nerd's only chance for increased prestige is to take a test for a jock or to do a jock's homework for him. Some intellectual non-jock males who are rich and popular (e.g., preppies), or who have success with girls, will not receive a negative label for being bright, but intellectual ability by itself has few social rewards.

For female cliques, the effect of athletics tends to be indirect. The high-status clique may be labeled "the rich and populars," although there are many variations on this label. High-status female groups tend to dress well, get good grades, and take part in student government. They also provide support for the male jocks, either as cheerleaders, which remains the highest-status female activity, or as dates. That high-status female groups generally provide support roles for high-status males reflects the traditional power relations between males and females in our society.

Female jocks can provide exceptions to this trend. As a group, they are generally assigned lesser status than male jocks. However, it is important to recognize that playing sports is more likely to be a truly voluntary activity for female athletes than for their male counterparts. Certainly they are generally under much less pressure from parents and peers to participate in athletics.

Although sociologist Joyce Canaan[40] did identify a subgroup she called "cool female jocks" based on their ability to dress well, act with self-confidence, and date cool jock males, many female athletes do not enjoy such high status. If not part of this cool group, female jocks, often labeled jockettes, are usually given middle status alongside the regulars or nobodies, and just above the nerds. To the extent that they reject the norm of dating males, they may be labeled lesbian, a low-status characteristic in most adolescent groups.

Although adolescents often claim that clique membership is "no big deal," or sometimes nonexistent,[41] most can readily describe the clique structure of their school, and the terms "jock," "nerd," and "freak" are part of the lexicon of adolescent culture. These cliques reinforce some social mores, for example, heterosexuality and athletic ability, while rejecting others, for example, intellectual ability. This sometimes puts the male athlete in an ambivalent position. On the one hand lionized by his peers for his cool behavior, and on the other held up by the school authorities as a moral leader, he is trapped by the myth that sport builds character. Perhaps being macho is the modern equivalent of the muscular Christianity idea of "manliness."

When high school football players describe the meaning of football,[42] they talk about the camaraderie, loyalty, and friendship of the team, and about the respect and sportsmanship received from opponents. However, they also recognize the overriding importance of victory and the loss of face that defeat brings in the eyes of the community. The bottom line is being a winner. This means sacrificing yourself for team victory. The highest respect is offered to the players who can give out and take physical punishment. Being able to inflict and endure physical pain is a badge of honor. As Foley notes, a true man can even overcome injuries and "play hurt."

> Players who consistently inflicted outstanding hits were called animals, studs, bulls, horses, or gorillas. A stud was a superior physical specimen who fearlessly dished out and took hits, who liked physical contact, who could dominate other players physically. Other players idolized a "real stud," because he seemed fearless and indomitable on the field. Off the field a stud was also cool, or at least imagined to be cool, with girls. Most players expected and wanted strong coaches and some studs to lead them into battle. They talked endlessly about who was a real stud and whether the coach "really kicks butt."[43]

Sexual and drinking exploits also are a common part of the athlete image. Players are straight and conformist in public, but, at least according to Foley, they learn how to use this public conformity to hide private nonconformity. Stories about athletes' rule-breaking behavior abound, especially in regard to drinking, sex, and drug use. Such exploits are used by athletes to support their macho image. True athletes, real men, can play even in spite of such distractions.

These macho activities also contain the important message that males and females should be judged by very different standards. It is ironic that sexual exploits are a mark of high status in male cliques, and at the same time characterize low status for females who are labeled "sluts." This double standard replicates the "traditional" power relations between males and females in our society.

Consider, for example, the powder puff football game described by Foley,[44] a ritual role reversal in which senior football players dressed as girls acted as cheerleaders for a football game played by the senior and junior girls. Usually such rites of reversal allow people to reverse cultural roles or satirize them without losing face. In this case the ritual reinforced male domination. Whereas the males parodied female cheerleaders in a burlesque manner, the females adopted a serious attitude about their game as if to prove they were equal to the males. According to Foley, this game was part of the "total football ritual" that "generally socialized both sexes to assume their proper traditional gender roles."[45]

What sport does seem to do among school males is to make legitimate a macho image. It is quite a paradox that the rituals of sports, in particular team sports, so important in the eyes of early twentieth-century educators for building respect for authority, the school, and American values, may actually reinforce a very different set of values among today's adolescents.

This is not to say that the image of the scholar/athlete, so popular among educators, and especially the National Collegiate Athletic Association (NCAA), has no basis in reality. Certainly jocks who are intelligent, studious, and less concerned with the image of machismo do exist in American schools. Such individuals may belong to high-status cliques and could serve as role models. Furthermore, the fact that sport usually is rejected by the low-status cliques such as the burnouts shows that, in the eyes of this group, it is associated with the official culture of the school. Burnouts are in revolt against the school's institutional values and see sport as just another form of regimentation and social control. However, the social life of adolescents tends to promote values that are different and sometimes opposite to the lofty goals of well-meaning adults, and high school athletics plays a prominent part in this social life.

Sport and School Life

For the school as an institution, sport serves important ritual functions. By marking the school calendar, sports function as rites of intensification. The weekly Friday football games give way to basketball season, which is followed by spring sports such as baseball and track. All educators and students are aware that the fall semester goes quickly, while the spring semester seems to drag on and on, especially after the end of basketball season. In most of America, football and basketball are the prestige sports that involve the most students. They serve to heighten interest, and the weekly or bi-weekly games and pep rallies give students and teachers alike events on which to focus their attention and interest.

In most schools, sports affect many more students than those who participate as athletes in the school's athletic programs. Consider the pep rally. In addition to athletes, cheerleaders, band members, and perhaps the members of a pep squad are all organized to contribute their time and talents to the athletic enterprise. Each of these is composed of individual students representing a variety of friendship cliques and ethnic and social-class elements. Those who perform at the pep rally are members of a wide social network that may crisscross the entire student body. It is for this reason that many students attend the pep rally, participate enthusiastically, and support the notion that sport builds school spirit and that this is good.

Sport events, like pep rallies, also serve as rites of intensification, promoting cohesion, reinforcing the common values of the institution, and reestablishing the school's authority structure. The mythology of sport provides a common agenda for all of the school's constituencies: community members, school administrators, teachers, and students.

Sport promotes attitudes and values beneficial to the social organization of the school as a bureaucracy. Varsity sport participation consistently and significantly increases positive attitudes toward school and decreases the level of independence and self-control. Thus sport promotes conformity to the rules and goals of school, and helps varsity athletes feel good about the school and themselves. Giving up some independence makes students more malleable and accepting of school authority.

Encouraging athletics as a means of unifying the school is not without risk. As Coleman has pointed out,[46] by using athletics to solve the problem of how to draw the energies of adolescents into the school, we run the risk of making athletics, not education, the school's central concern. Athletic-related rituals such as homecoming, sport banquets, and pep rallies are the heart of the social life of the school[47] and can preoccupy not just athletes, but also the many different support groups.

Recent ethnographic studies of high school sport[48] have shown how, during football season, the win-loss record of the school team is of great importance both to students and to teachers. Athletes may not be expected even to go to class, let alone to study. In Texas, for example, concern over the issue of the academic performance of athletes has sparked controversial no pass/no play reforms that are designed to insure that athletes maintain good academic standing while competing on school teams. In chapter 8 we shall see how these reforms have touched off a storm of protest. If the real message that students are receiving is that high school sport is more important than academic attainment, and that athlete-heroes are "dumb jocks," perhaps schools are paying too high a price for internal unity through athletics.

Summary

The relationship of sport and secondary education evolved quickly in the latter half of the nineteenth century, with educators, industrialists, and humanitarians all believing that sport would be beneficial in addressing perceived social needs. Once institutionalized, however, that basic relationship has not changed throughout the twentieth century.

Due to the historical links between morality and success in sport, involvement in athletics still is perceived as somehow making students better people. High school sport and the rituals and symbols that are attached to it give charisma to school leaders and help to legitimize their authority over the student body.

School administrators feel compelled to control the student body and enforce rules that inevitably restrict the personal freedoms of the students. However, the schools have to pay a price for this control. If the student body becomes oversocialized and begins to accept the ritual of athletics as the only game in town, much more important than the educational game of learning, then the school has failed in its fundamental role. Moreover, by co-opting athletes as a means of social control, the school alienates from sport a significant portion of the students. Some students reject the conformity required by the school and athletics, thereby rejecting another form of adult control. Another consequence of the control system is that many students come to accept inequitable gender roles as the norm.

What is the ideal character of a school? Is it a smooth running operation with high morale and pleasant environment where teachers and students do what is expected of them? Or, is it a highly productive organization that successfully conveys knowledge and socializes students with skills necessary for individual fulfillment and society's successful continuation? Sport, in its present form, has a clear place in the former; its role in the latter is not so clear. We shall discuss the role of sport in American education in later chapters, but before we can do that we shall examine the evidence for the idea that sport builds character.

Notes

1. James A. Mangan, *Athleticism in the Victorian and Edwardian Public School* (Cambridge, England: Cambridge University Press, 1981), p. 141.

2. Clifford Geertz, "Centers, Kings and Charisma: Reflections on the Symbolics of Power," *Local Knowledge: Further Essays in Interpretative Anthropology* (New York: Basic Books, Inc., 1983), p. 124.

3. James Alfred Montgomery, *The Development of the Interscholastic Athletics Movement in the United States, 1890-1940* (Ed.D dissertation, George Peabody College for Teachers) (Ann Arbor, Mich.: University Microfilms, Inc., 1960), p. 4.

4. Cited in Joel Spring, "Mass Culture and School Sports," *History of Education Quarterly* 14 (1974): 483-99.

5. Ibid., p. 485.

6. Benjamin G. Rader, *American Sports: From the Age of Folk Games to the Age of Spectators* (Englewood Cliffs, N.J.: Prentice-Hall, 1983), p. 157.

7. Ibid., p. 161.

8. For an excellent discussion of this, see Raymond E. Callahan, *Education and the Cult of Efficiency: A Study of the Social Forces That Have Shaped the Administration of the Public Schools* (Chicago: The University of Chicago Press, 1962).

9. Eric Hobsbawm, "Mass-Producing Traditions: Europe 1870-1914," in *The Invention of Tradition*, eds. Eric Hobsbawm and Terence O. Ranger (Cambridge, England: Cambridge University Press, 1983), pp. 294-95.

10. Benjamin G. Rader, *American Sports.*

11. Joel Spring, "Mass Culture and School Sports"; Timothy O'Hanlon, "Interscholastic Athletics, 1900–1940: Shaping Citizens for Unequal Roles in the Modern Industrial State," *Educational Theory* 30, no. 2 (1974): 89–103.

12. Christopher J. Hurn, *The Limits and Possibilities of Schooling: An Introduction to the Sociology of Education,* 2d ed. (Boston: Allyn and Bacon, 1985), chapter 5.

13. Ibid., p. 246.

14. Robert Lynd and Helen Lynd, *Middletown: A Study in Contemporary American Culture* (New York: Harcourt Brace, 1929), p. 214.

15. Willard Waller, *The Sociology of Teaching* (New York: J. Wiley and Sons, 1932), p. 112.

16. August B. Hollinshead, *Elmtown's Youth: The Impact of Social Classes on Adolescents* (New York: J. Wiley, 1949), pp. 193–94.

17. James S. Coleman, *The Adolescent Society: The Social Life of the Teenager and Its Impact on Education* (New York: The Free Press, 1961).

18. D. Stanley Eitzen and George H. Sage, *Sociology of American Sport* (Dubuque, Iowa: Wm. C. Brown, 1978), p. 82

19. Coleman, *The Adolescent Society,* p. 39.

20. D. Stanley Eitzen, "Sport and Social Status in American Public Secondary Education," *Review of Sport and Leisure* 1, no. 1 (1976): 110–18; Joel Thirer and Steven D. Wright, "Sport and Social Status for Adolescent Males and Females," *Sociology of Sport Journal* 2 (1985): 164–71.

21. Eitzen, "Sport and Social Status in American Public Secondary Education," pp. 110–18.

22. Ibid.

23. Ibid.

24. Thirer and Wright, "Sport and Social Status for Adolescent Males and Females," pp. 164–71.

25. David N. Suggs, *An Ethnographic Approach to the Ecology of Fourth Grade Peer Groups* (Masters thesis, Texas Christian University, 1981); Andrew W. Miracle, Brian Rowan, and David N. Suggs, "Play Activities and Elementary School Peer Groups," in *The Masks of Play,* eds. Brian Sutton-Smith and Diana Kelly-Byrne (Oakland, Calif.: Leisure Press, 1984), pp. 119–24.

26. Janet Lever, "Sex Differences in the Games Children Play," *Social Problems* 23, no. 4 (1976): 478–87.

27. National Federation of State High School Associations, 1990 news release.

28. Merrill J. Melnick, Beth E. Vanfossen, and Donald F. Sabo, "Developmental Effects of Athletic Participation among High School Girls," *Sociology of Sport Journal* 5, no. 1 (1988): 22–36.

29. Coleman, *The Adolescent Society,* p. 40.

30. Ibid., p. 41.

31. Ibid.

32. Ibid.

33. James S. Coleman, "Sport in School," *Sports and Education* 1 (1985): 7.

34. Coleman, *The Adolescent Society*, p. 8.

35. Andrew W. Miracle, "School Spirit as a Ritual By-Product: Views from Applied Anthropology" (Paper presented at the seventy-second Annual Meeting of the American Anthropological Association, New Orleans, November 1973.)

36. Joyce Caanan, "A Comparative Analysis of American Suburban Middle Class Middle School and High School Teenage Cliques," in *Interpretative Ethnography and Education*, eds. George Spindler and Louise Spindler (Hillsdale, N.J.: Erlbaum Press, 1987), pp. 385–406; Douglas E. Foley, "The Great American Football Ritual: Reproducing Race, Class, and Gender Inequality," *Sociology of Sport Journal* 7 (1990): 111–35; C. Roger Rees, "What Price Victory? Myths, Rituals, Athletics, and the Dilemma of Schooling," in *Sport and Physical Activity: Moving Towards Excellence*, eds. Trevor Williams, Len Almond, and Andrew Sparks (London: F. & E. N. Spon, 1992), pp. 74–84.

37. The regional variation in clique labels must be stressed. Terms can vary even among schools in close proximity. In addition to the terms for cliques mentioned in our discussion there are others which will be found in many schools across the country, e.g., "preppies" and "nerds." Still other terms may be geographically or culturally limited in their distribution, e.g., "ropers" or "goat-ropers" in Texas, those urban males who imitate cowboys in their dress and talk, and carry a can of snuff in the back pocket of their jeans. Ethnically defined cliques are common in many schools. Frequently, ethnic cliques tend to have a lower position in the adolescent pecking order. It is worth noting that even social analysts do not always agree on the use of clique labels. For example, based on her field work in Detroit suburban high schools, sociologist Penelope Eckert uses the term "jock" to describe all groups generally supportive of the school culture. She then identifies subgroups such as "jock jocks" and "band jocks." Penelope Eckert, *Jocks and Burnouts: Social Categories and Identity in the High School* (New York: Teachers College Press, 1989).

38. At the bottom of the status hierarchy are cliques of students called "burnouts" or "dropouts." They prefer heavy metal music, skip school frequently, and do not participate in school activities. Burnouts, who are typically from working-class families, feel little attachment to the educational system. They flaunt all rules and try to party all the time. The manifest function of the school, that of educating the student body, may be specifically rejected by these clique members who simply treat the school as a place to hang out until they are allowed to leave. Cf. Arthur G. Powell, Eleanor Farrer, and David K. Cohen, *The Shopping Mall High School: Winners and Losers in the Educational Marketplace* (Boston: Houghton, Mifflin, 1989).

39. Foley, "The Great American Football Ritual," p. 115.

40. Caanan, "A Comparative Analysis of American Suburban Middle Class Middle School and High School Teenage Cliques," pp. 385–406.

41. Ibid.

42. Foley, "The Great American Football Ritual," pp. 111–35.

43. Ibid., p. 127.

44. Ibid., pp. 118–19.

45. Ibid., p. 119.

46. Coleman, *The Adolescent Society*.

47. Jacquetta Hill Burnett, "Ceremony, Rites, and Economy in the Student System of an American High School," *Human Organization* 28: 1–10.

48. Foley, "The Great American Football Ritual," pp. 111–35. See also H. G. Bissinger, *Friday Night Lights: A Town, a Team, and a Dream* (Reading, Mass.: Addison-Wesley, 1990).

4

Evidence for the Myth

I am very doubtful that big-time sports, whether high school, college, university or professional, do much to alter the character of the young men who participate.

—James Michener (1976)[1]

We found no empirical support for the tradition that sports builds character. Indeed, there is evidence that athletic competition limits growth in some areas.

—Psychologists Bruce Ogilvie and Thomas Tutko (1971)[2]

There is little, if any, valid evidence that participation in sport is an important or essential element of the socialization process, or that involvement in sport teaches or results in learning of specific outcomes that might not be learned in other social milieu.

—Sociologists John W. Loy, Barry D. McPherson, and Gerald Kenyon (1978)[3]

Sports do not build character. They reveal it.

—Sports commentator Heywood Hale Broun (1976)[4]

James Michener did not include a chapter on sport and character in his book *Sports in America,* although he gave the "sport-builds-character" idea serious consideration as a fourth criterion to accompany his three basic principles that sports should be fun for the participants, that they should enhance the health of the individual and society, and that they should provide public entertainment. However, after reflecting upon the evidence of recent years, he concluded that the "sport-builds-character" belief was a myth. Most of the support for the myth came from athletic directors or ex-athletes who had a vested interest in perpetuating the belief. This does not mean that the personal experiences of these men and women were invalid, but that every success story could be balanced by one of failure. "The days of bland acceptance of sports are past," he wrote, and athletic programs would "have to be subjected to most careful scrutiny."[5]

Since the 1960s, the effects of participation in athletic programs have indeed been scrutinized by scholars with training in psychology and sociology. The examination of this "scientific" evidence is the concern of the present chapter.

The Scientific Approach

Scientists in general, and social scientists in particular, are very cautious when attributing cause and effect. How can it be proved, for example, that involvement in athletics caused some positive personality trait or a particular behavioral change? People are unique; they start with unique genetic blueprints and have unique upbringings. The interaction of these forces produces individuals who interpret their environment in unique ways. Social scientists cannot really do scientific experiments to test whether sport builds character. For one thing, all the factors other than sport that might change one's character cannot be held constant while the research project is taking place. For another, the individual is not passively accepting the "treatment" that the scientists are applying as part of the experiment, but is interpreting what is going on and acting on the basis of that interpretation. All this means that the usual way that scientists do research, that is, by looking at the effect of one thing on another within the controlled confines of a laboratory, presents some special problems for social scientists. They have to find other methods to test hypotheses such as "sport builds character." Consequently, they hesitate to say that one thing causes another.

This is not a problem for most of us. We rarely have to test our theories because we *know* that they are true. Thus we have the luxury of selecting evidence from our varied social experience that agrees with our point of view. For example, if it is believed that foreign cars are more reliable than domestic cars, consumers will be quick to notice American cars broken down by the side of the road. These incidents confirm the theory. However, when foreign cars are seen in the same predicament, these instances are more likely to be dismissed as "the exception that proves the rule." Consumers also are likely to disregard the fact that there are more American cars on the road than foreign cars, so that by the law of averages, there will be more American casualties irrespective of any mechanical differences between domestic and foreign cars.

The same is true in sport. If it is really believed that sport does build character, then situations will be remembered that are believed to support the theory and while incidents in which athletes lied, stole, cheated, or committed other antisocial acts are forgotten. Furthermore, since belief in the "sport-builds-character" myth is widespread, believers are more likely to have the positive view of athletics presented (indeed, sometimes shoved down their throats) by other individuals and the news media. In turn, athletes have learned that they are expected to be moral heroes, so many examples are observed of athletes subscribing to the "sport-builds-character" idea and playing that role in public. All this evidence "proves" the theory at the level of personal experience. It is likely that observers will be quite agitated by "stupid" social scientists for questioning the obvious fact that sport builds character.

If anecdotal evidence is inadequate and the traditional experimental methods are difficult to apply, how have social scientists tested the "sport-builds-character" relationship? Several approaches have been used with varying degrees of success in establishing cause and effect. Rather than present a detailed description of all the studies, we have chosen to describe these different techniques and illustrate them with several examples. We also present the conclusions of some detailed reviews of this literature within the field of sport sociology.[6]

Sport and Personality

The most common approach to studying the sport myth has been to examine personality differences between athletes and nonathletes, between athletes from different sports, or between athletes at different levels of ability. These studies have used many different measures of personality, and partly because of this have yielded mixed results. Some have found no difference between athletes and nonathletes; others have found differences, say, between team-sport athletes and individual-sport athletes. However, there is no clear pattern of evidence. In summarizing the results of these studies, Christopher L. Stevenson felt that the only generalizable finding was that athletes tended to be higher on the psychological factor of "dominance."[7]

An extension of the personality approach has been the study of the personality profiles of champion athletes compared to the norms for the general population. Reviews here are mixed. Psychologists Bruce Ogilvie and Thomas Tutko do not hesitate to endorse the existence of what they call "general sports personalities." Based on fifteen thousand personality profiles, they characterize successful athletes as high in need for achievement, respect for authority, psychological endurance, trust, and self-control, and low in anxiety and need for affiliation (i.e., association with a group).[8] However, other researchers are not so sure. In his more recent review, Stevenson described the evidence as contradictory.[9] For example, while one study might find significant differences between nonathletes and athletes from particular sports, the results of another study of a different sport would fail to support this conclusion.

Independent of the results, the methodology of this approach has great limitations for investigating the "sport-builds-character" myth. If team-sport athletes are different from individual-sport athletes or nonathletes, are they different because the experience of sport makes them different or because the demands of the sport require a particular type of person? Do high school athletes learn "character" from their experiences in interscholastic athletics, or are they selected because of already existing characteristics that are necessary for success?

This selection-versus-change dilemma is at the heart of the problem, and it cannot be answered by the methodological approach called *cross-sectional analysis*[10] characteristic of the research described above. For example, the champion athletes studied by Ogilvie and Tutko were described as high in psychological endurance and self-control. Was this because they had learned these through participation in sport or because those athletes with such characteristics have been "selected" by the demands of top-class sport, or because of a combination of both reasons? In order to isolate the selection and change effects one must observe groups of athletes and nonathletes over a period of time and compare the change in each group. This type of research, referred to as longitudinal research, is considerably more costly and time-consuming, and consequently less common than cross-sectional research, but some *longitudinal studies* on athletes have been completed.

One such study[11] measured personality change in 456 military cadets at West Point during their four-year program. In this study the personality changes of one group, which was classified as "nonathletic," were compared to those of another group labeled as "athletic." The research setting provided several advantages not often found in nonexperimental research. Due to the nature of the institution, West Point students live under very similar conditions so that the outside variations that might effect studies of students at most universities would be reduced. Furthermore, all students at West Point participate in an athletics program for the whole of their four-year stay. This makes West Point an ideal environment in which to study the effect of sport. Under these conditions, Werner and Gottheil found that, even though they had four years of regular athletic participation, the nonathletic group did not become more like the athletic group. They concluded that "no evidence was found to support the view that college athletics significantly influenced personality structure." This study was among the many reviewed by Stevenson in the 1986 update of his investigation of the effects of sport on character. In summarizing this review he says, "The basic conclusion must remain that there is little valid evidence that participation in college athletics has any effect upon the character of the athlete."[12]

High School Sport and Character

If college athletics do not build character, what about high school athletics? After all, high school programs usually are not subjected to the same professional pressure that are characteristic of some colleges.

Few longitudinal studies have been carried out on the effects of high school athletics, but those that have been done do not show many personality benefits. A study by Clayton Best[13] compared scores of male athlete and nonathlete high school students on academic achievement, social skills, physical development, religion, self-control, honesty, and independence. The results showed that there was very little difference between the groups. Although athletes scored higher on physical development and religion than did nonathletes, there was no difference on any of the other scales. These results were virtually identical, whether athletes were measured in their sophomore, junior, or senior year, and Best concluded that "male athletes seem to have the same values as their non-athlete counterparts."[14]

We reached a similar conclusion with our colleague Frank Howell, in a study in which changes in personality of sixteen hundred male high school seniors were analyzed.[15] We measured the effect of participation in varsity athletics on several different aspects of personality. There were affective states, which included such characteristics as independence, aggressiveness, and irritability; social feelings such as self-concept and school attitudes; and social values such as honesty and social responsibility. We found that participation in high school athletics increased self-esteem slightly and increased the value attached to academic achievement. On the other hand, it significantly increased aggression and irritability, and reduced the belief in the importance of being honest, as well as scores on self-control and independence. In general, however, the effects of high school varsity sports participation were small in absolute size and we concluded that high school sports did little to benefit or harm the social development of participants.[16]

Taken together, the results of these two studies make us seriously question the "sport-builds-character" myth, at least in the context of high school athletics. Both studies used large samples that were nationally representative. This means that the results could be generalized nationwide and were not subject to regional variations. Although it is a rather fuzzy concept and contains an array of different traits, some of the variables measured in these studies such as aggression, independence, honesty, and self-control seem to be prime candidates for inclusion under the umbrella concept of "character." That no positive change, and sometimes, a negative change, occurred in these measures indicates to us that high school sport is not building character in the active way that the adherents of the myth believe.

Both our study and the one by Best indicated that there was very little difference between the characteristics of athletes and non-athletes at the high school level. One possible implication of these results is that the "character development," if there is any, already has occurred before the students reach high school. The time frame for our study was from the sophomore year to just after graduation, while Best measured attitudes and values in the sophomore, junior, and senior years. Thus one might argue that sport already has had its effect. In response we would point out that research conducted on the effects of organized sport programs on young children does not give our critics much ground for optimism.

Organized Sport and Young Children

Although the research on the effects of participation in youth sport suffers from the same problems as the "sport-builds-character" research,[17] there have been results that make sociologists question the positive effects of organized programs on the sportsmanlike behavior of players. This research, primarily with young hockey players in Canada, has shown that the longer boys are involved in youth hockey, the greater they accept the importance of cheating,[18] the more they feel that violent behavior is legitimate and expected by the coach,[19] and the more they are likely to use illegal tactics learned through watching professional hockey players on television.[20] In one study of eighty-three high school hockey players in Toronto, it was found that the young athletes felt it was important to fight and the main concern of the coaches was that if they fought too much the penalties might cost them the game.[21] The players also felt that the spectators, usually their nonplaying peers, were eager to see violence in any form.

In another example, Douglas A. Kleiber and Glyn C. Roberts[22] conducted an experiment with 54 ten-to-eleven-year-old school children to test the effect of a sport experience on social characteristics. Boys and girls from two elementary schools were randomly assigned to either the experimental group, which played a "Kick-Soccer World Series" during recess for two weeks, or the control group that did not. This world series simulated the conditions of organized sport. The children in the experimental group were divided into two teams, scores were kept each day, and after two weeks the team winning the most games was declared the champion and those players were given trophies. All the children were measured on a social-behavioral scale before and after the experiment. This scale measured how people score on a continuum from rivalry to altruism. The results showed that the boys who had participated in the world series reduced their altruism compared to the boys in the control group. The scores of the girls were not different as a result of the experiment.

The researchers regarded this study as exploratory, but it has some interesting implications for the "sport-builds-character" discussion since it generated the conditions often associated with high-pressure sports. "Although the investigators did not intend to create an excessive amount of tension, crying occurred on three occasions, largely as a result of perceived failure or injustice, and quarreling took place at regular intervals with a fist fight even following one game."[23] That the boys became more rivalrous than the girls as a result of the experiment may be a result of the boys taking the activity (sport) more seriously. However, it also was noticed that boys and girls who previously had been involved in sport were more likely to act in a less altruistic manner than when they were originally measured on the pre-test. The researchers' comment on this finding is important. "Apparently, those children who were more experienced in competitive sports were more rivalrous than those with less sport experience. It still cannot be stated that organized sport necessarily forms and reinforces such tendencies—it may be that the more competitive children are merely the survivors in sport—but it does lead one to speculate that the emphasis upon winning in organized sport may lead children to become more rivalrous in social interactions with other children."[24]

This conclusion was virtually the same as the one made after a famous study of boys in a summer camp.[25] In this setting the researchers created two groups of ten- and eleven-year-old boys, and watched what happened when they interacted. They noticed that the main form of interaction, competitive sports, led to great intergroup conflict and hostility that transferred from the sport field to other situations in which the groups interacted. There were food fights and incidents of symbolic violence such as night raids on the other group's cabin and setting fire to the other group's flag. The researchers had to design special events that required the two groups to cooperate in order to achieve a goal that both groups valued before order could be restored. This study has important implications for how sport and other competitive activities might be structured so that competition does not get out of hand. In addition, it demonstrates the tensions and conflicts that sport can generate even with young children.

Of course the situation in hockey is not generalizable to the many millions of children involved in organized sport in North America, and the results of one experiment and one field study should not be used to condemn all organized sport programs for children. Obviously, there is a great need for more sophisticated longitudinal research.

Despite several interesting reviews critical of organized sport,[26] the consensus of scholars involved in youth sport research is that the experience generally does not have a negative effect on the participants. However, the picture is far from complete. At the present time, the most that cautious scholars will say is that the selection-versus-change issue has yet to be resolved, that scientific evidence of sport causing positive social development is scant, and that scientific evidence of a negative effect does exist.

It is the consensus among social scientists studying sport that whereas athletic participation per se is not good or bad, the environment of participation, or what has been called the social context of competition, is important.[27] If coaches stress that it is more important to win than to play fair, or that your opponent is to be hated rather than respected, then one of two things will happen. Either these values eventually will be internalized by the participants, or only those participants who had these values in the first place will remain involved in sport. Perhaps both these processes are going on at the same time. At any rate, most social scientists interested in sport cannot afford the large-scale longitudinal research necessary to isolate these effects. As an alternative approach, several scholars have turned their attention to the behavior of athletes in the context of sport, and the reasons they give for this behavior.

Athlete Behavior and Reasoning in Sport

One of the early approaches to the "sport-builds-character" question was to compare the attitudes toward sportsmanship of athletes and nonathletes. In his review, Stevenson was able to find six such studies and he summarized the results of them as follows.

These studies were consistent in concluding that, contrary to popular belief, athletes tended to be less sportsmanlike than nonathletes. Furthermore, the research showed that "major" sport athletes were less sportsmanlike than "minor" sport athletes, and that "starters" were less sportsmanlike than "substitutes."[28]

However, the variety of ways used to measure sportsmanship limited the degree to which the results could be generalized, and because sportsmanship scores of athletes and nonathletes were compared at only one point in time, the selection-versus-change issue could not be addressed.

Rather than comparing scores of athletes and nonathletes on sportsmanship scales, more recent approaches have concentrated on the reasoning used by them to justify actions in sport and other contexts. For example, sport psychologist John Silva has investigated the judgments of athletes and nonathletes about how legitimate it was to break the rules and to commit acts that would injure opponents. The 203 participants in Silva's study rated the legitimacy of slides showing body contact and fighting among male professional athletes. The results showed that those who rated dangerous acts in sport as more legitimate were males rather than females, males competing at higher levels of sport rather than at lower levels of sport, and those with more rather than less involvement in organized sport. He concluded that involvement in sport encourages athletes to see dangerous acts as legitimate. This is particularly true for male athletes in the sample, whom he called the *survivors* of the sport-socialization process.[29]

The special morality of sport has been explored in a series of studies by social psychologists Brenda Jo Bredemeier and David Shields.[30] They have presented fictitious moral dilemmas set in sport-specific and daily life contexts to high school and college athletes and nonathletes, and asked them to decide on appropriate ways to resolve these dilemmas. An example of a sport-related dilemma was whether Tom, a football player, should follow the instructions of his coach and intentionally injure an opponent so that his team would have a better chance of winning the game. A daily-life dilemma involved the question of whether someone should deliver some money to a rich man or use it to help feed his family. Bredemeier and Shields found that morality in sport was perceived differently from morality in everyday life. Sport was often viewed as an area of life in which moral issues were irrelevant. As one female high school basketball player said, "That's what I like about sports. You just play as hard as you can and try to win. You don't have to think about other people."[31] A female college basketball player said, "In basketball you don't think about whether or not hurting somebody is a moral thing unless that somebody gets hurt. Then you got to tell yourself it's necessary to play the game."[32] Other athletes use the idea that sport is different to justify violent behavior. One athlete reasoned as follows:

> If Tom looks at it as a game, it's OK to hurt the guy—to try to take him out of the game. But if he looks at the halfback as a person, and tries to hurt him, it's not OK. . . . When you're on the field, then the game is football. Before and after, you deal with people morally.[33]

The context of sport also was seen as one in which moral problems were resolved by the rules and the way the rules were interpreted by the officials and the coach. For example, one athlete thought that Tom should injure his opponent because these were the coach's instructions. "If the coach tells you to do something, you have to do it. You have to take orders or you'll get taken right out of the game. You can't play it your way."[34] This is a good example of the "how high" principle of sport, which was popularized in the Lombardi era: "The coach says jump and you say 'how high?' "

When athletes did think for themselves in sport they used what the authors called "game reasoning," which places the act in the context of the game. This means that in certain sports some behavior that is defined as illegal by the rules is really seen by athletes as a normal part of the game. Fighting in hockey is an example of such behavior. Game reasoning, say the researchers, "legitimates many acts that would normally be considered illegitimate. These 'legitimated' acts were inevitably advantageous to oneself or one's team."[35] With this type of logic, athletes are attempting to reconcile everyday morality with the demands of victory. Sometimes the line was rather vague and athletes endorsed violence as a legitimate response within some limits.

Most agreed that "cheap shots" were not legitimate, but some violence was part of the game.

For example, one athlete said, "Tom shouldn't try to hurt him. He should just hit him real hard, stun him, make him loose his wind, make sure he's too scared to run the ball again."[36] What happens if in hitting him "real hard" Tom does hurt him? Presumably this athlete is morally in the clear because he did not mean to hurt him.

In their research Bredemeier and Shields have measured the level of moral reasoning reached by the respondents and also their scores on the Continuum of Injurious Acts (CIA). The CIA depicts aggressive sports-acts that increase in seriousness. In general, the higher the athletes scored on moral reasoning, the lower they scored on the CIA. This relationship was greater for males than for females. When the CIA was readministered to athletes after an important game, college athletes judged a significantly higher number of acts as legitimate than did high school athletes. Bredemeier and Shields comment that high school and college athletes may hold similar beliefs about the appropriateness of intentional injury in sport, but the greater stress of college sport makes athletes at this level more willing to stretch morality when the need arises. They also note that athletes more often may have used game reasoning to justify their actual behavior in the game than in their answers to the hypothetical moral dilemmas.[37]

Finally, Bredemeier and Shields speculate on the implications of game reasoning for moral decisions in other nonsport situations. Since sport is held up as a reflection of society, athletes are seen as moral heroes, and the metaphors of sport are often used in other competitive situations. Following game reasoning, perhaps we shall have business reasoning or political reasoning. "Can the dirty tricks of politics be legitimated as if they were just a game?"[38]

While it does not seem fair to blame the socialization effect of sport for the Watergate and Irangate scandals, this research has brought us a long way from comparing athletes and nonathletes on sportsmanship scores. It is true that we do not yet know how much game reasoning is a product of the situation and how much is a product of the athlete. In other words, the selection-versus-the-change effect referred to previously has yet to be applied to athletes' moral decisions within and outside sport. Nevertheless, this research shows the inadequacy of the naive belief that participation in sport builds character. Morality in athletics, like morality in other contexts, is clearly a complicated process that is constructed socially by the individual within the situation.

Sport Builds Character: An Assessment

Assessing the "sport-builds-character" issue requires more than collecting anecdotes of athletes who believe that sport has taught them how to be successful or saved them from a life of crime or drugs. It also is not enough to compare groups of athletes with nonathletes or groups of athletes in different sports or at different levels of competition with each other. Any differences might as easily be the result of the rigorous selection process within the world of sport as the result of any change brought about by participation in sport. Even studies that examine the changes in the same group of athletes over a period of time have shown little support for the "sport-builds-character" myth. Some prosocial character changes may occur, for example, in self-esteem or valuing academic achievement, but these may be offset by increases in antisocial tendencies such as an increase in aggression or a decrease in self-control. At any rate, all of these effects are rather small.

Results of in-depth analyses of moral reasoning in sport have shown that athletes have a tendency to shrug off moral decisions as not their responsibility and that they also exhibit a self-serving bias when judging what violent behavior is appropriate. Moreover, athletes tend to adopt a less advanced form of moral reasoning to justify aggressive behavior than do nonathletes. Given the selection-versus-change problem, one cannot assume that athletes have developed these tendencies because of their experiences in sport. They may think this way prior to becoming involved. However, the belief that participation in sport leads to the development of prosocial personality traits, that it makes one a better person, and that it builds character in high school or any other context is in no way justified by the results of this review. On the contrary, the research reviewed in this chapter on youth hockey, the experiment by Kleiber and Roberts with ten- and eleven-year-old children, the large scale longitudinal studies of high school students, and the research on the moral reasoning of athletes tend to paint a negative, not a positive, picture. We find ourselves in agreement with previous reviewers and author James Michener that participation in sport does not build character.

This position is opposite to the one taken by social reformers and politicians. According to sport historian Donald Mrozek, they believed that "body and soul were inextricably bound together,"[39] that "moral power was directly transmutable into physical power,"[40] and that "actions formed character, rather than just reflecting it."[41] That sport helped to promote moral development was a matter of faith rather than science and there was no need to explain how personality changed as a result of participation. As Mrozek suggests,[42] the "sport-builds-character" myth should be viewed as part of the changing belief that human development was not predetermined, but was based upon social action. If correct actions were taken, for example, participation in sport and games during adolescence, as in the recapitulation theory of G. Stanley Hall, then moral growth would occur.

Given this reciprocal relationship between participation and morality, the "sport-builds-character" idea took on the characteristics of a self-fulfilling prophecy. "Once sport achieved a certain frequency and distribution, it tended to generate new conditions and advance its own acceptance."[43] If the actions of the athlete, in the process of winning, demonstrated moral strength, then it followed that athletes were moral people. Indeed, athletes both real and fictitious (e.g., Frank Merriwell), became moral heroes, even if the behavior of some of the most famous, such as Babe Ruth and Jack Dempsey, fell far short of the acceptable moral standards of the day.

As Mrozek points out, the sports-winning-morality theme carried with it the seeds of its own destruction. If victory was the way in which morality was demonstrated, then winning in sports became more important than merely participating in sports. Many athletes of yesterday and today have found the social demands of success and morality too difficult to fulfill. Biographical research has revealed the human failings of the athletic heroes of the past.[44] In the 1960s, when Paul Simon and Art Garfunkel sang, "Where have you gone Joe DiMaggio, a nation turns its lonely eyes to you," not only were they mourning the demise of the sports hero, but also the demise of morality in general.[45] Even today, the concept of victory in sport has elements of morality. The team that, after training, comes from behind to win shows character, and a local community, city, or country may experience a general sense of self-esteem when its team wins.

The "end-justifies-the-means" mentality is neatly captured in the Vince Lombardi dictum that "winning isn't everything, it's the only thing," and legitimizes the image of the player or coach who would literally do anything to win. Sports at all levels, from little league to professional, have been plagued by moral controversies rooted in this problem. High school sport does not exist in a social vacuum. Young hockey players learn illegal tactics from watching professional hockey players on television. High school athletes are told by commentators of professional football that you have to play with pain. If the high school coaches are following a professional win-at-all-costs model, and the local community lives and dies by the success of the high school team, then the message to the athletes is that they must win first and play fair second. By linking the concepts of morality and victory, the character development potential of sport is compromised.

Summary

The consensus of the research presented in this chapter, and the conclusion of other researchers who have reviewed the research in this area, is that there is no evidence to support the claim that sport builds character in high school or anywhere else. If this is indeed the case, we are intrigued by the power and longevity of the myth, and wonder why it has been defended so passionately throughout the twentieth century. In later chapters we develop an explanation of why the myth has survived so long.

A parallel issue also concerns us. Even the negative position that involvement in sport retards moral growth holds hope for the potential of sport to be a positive force in high school. If "antisocial" lessons are being learned through sport, then perhaps positive ones are possible. If high schools were committed to keeping interscholastic athletics for its character-developing potential and not for the other institutional benefits previously discussed, then the nature of interscholastic athletics ought to change. How sport should change in order to fulfill this function is the topic of a later chapter. Indeed, can sport change to fulfill a more important role in moral education?

The complexity of moral decision-making in sport implies that moral decisions in general are not the responsibility of one institution. Sport is part of a larger cultural context, and the high school football coach who tells Tom to put his opponent out of the game is only "doing what he has to do to win." If he does not win, his local community will fire him. Under those conditions, moral principles invariably will take a back seat to self-interest. We should not make the same mistakes as the play educators and politicians discussed in chapter 2 and lay the responsibility for the moral education of the nation's youth at the feet of sport. A concern for moral issues in sport cannot take place without a parallel concern for morality within other social institutions. High school sport may indeed become a medium for character development, but only when the school, community, and society value this more than being "Number One" in sports.

Notes

1. James Michener, *Sports in America* (New York: Random House, 1976), pp. 15–16.

2. Bruce C. Olgilvie and Thomas A. Tutko, "Sport: If You Want to Build Character, Try Something Else," *Psychology Today* 5, no. 5 (1971): 61–63.

3. John W. Loy, Barry D. McPherson, and Gerald Kenyon, *Sport and Social Systems: A Guide to the Analysis, Problems, and Literature* (Reading, Mass.: Addison-Wesley, 1978), p. 244.

4. Heywood Hale Broun, cited in Michener, *Sports in America,* p. 16.

5. Michener, *Sports in America,* p. 16.

6. Jay J. Coakley, *Sport in Society: Issues and Controversies,* 3d ed. (St. Louis, Mo.: Times Mirror/Mosby, 1986); Loy, McPherson, and Kenyon, *Sport and Social Systems*; Christopher L. Stevenson, "Socialization Effects of Participation in Sport: A Critical Review," *Research Quarterly for Exercise and Sport* 46 (1975): 287–301; Christopher L. Stevenson, "College Athletics and 'Character': The Decline and Fall of Socialization Research," in *Sport and Higher Education,* eds. Donald Chu, Jeffrey O. Segrave, and Beverly J. Becker (Champaign, Ill.: Human Kinetics, 1986), pp. 249–66.

7. Stevenson, "Socialization Effects of Participation in Sport."

8. Olgilvie and Tutko, "Sport."

9. Stevenson, "College Athletics and 'Character.' "

10. Cross-sectional analysis compares two separate groups (e.g., high school sophomores and seniors) on the same characteristics (e.g., self-confidence or social responsibility) at the same point in time in order to estimate changes that might occur over time in high school students. Contrastingly, longitudinal research collects data on the same group of individuals at different points in time (e.g., first as sophomores, later as seniors) to measure changes in individuals' characteristics. Being less approximate, longitudinal analysis is usually accorded more validity.

11. Alfred C. Werner and Edward Gottheil, "Personality Development and Participation in College Athletics," *Research Quarterly for Exercise and Sport* 37 (1966), pp. 126–31.

12. Stevenson, "College Athletics and 'Character,' " p. 264.

13. Clayton Best, "Differences in Social Values between Athletes and Non-athletes," *Research Quarterly for Exercise and Sport* 56 (1985): 366–69.

14. Ibid., p. 368.

15. C. Roger Rees, Frank M. Howell, and Andrew W. Miracle, "Do High School Sports Build Character? A Quasi-Experiment on a National Sample," *Social Science Journal* 27, no. 3 (1990): 303–315.

16. Ibid., p. 313.

17. See Coakley, *Sport in Society,* for a review.

18. J. K. Tyler and James H. Duthie, "The Effect of Ice Hockey on Social Development," *Journal of Sport Behavior* 2 (1978): 49–59.

19. Edmund W. Vaz, "The Culture of Young Hockey Players: Some Initial Observations," in *Training: Scientific Basis and Application,* ed. A. W. Taylor (Springfield, Ill.: Charles C. Thomas, 1972), pp. 222–34; Edmund W. Vaz and D. Thomas, "What Price Victory: An Analysis of Minor Hockey Players' Attitudes towards Winning," *International Review of Sport Sociology* 9 (1974): 33–56.

20. Michael D. Smith, "Social Determinants of Violence in Hockey: A Review," in *Children in Sports*, eds. Richard Magill, M. Ash, and Frank Smoll (Champaign, Ill.: Human Kinetics, 1978), pp. 294–309.

21. Michael D. Smith, "The Legitimation of Violence: Hockey Players' Perceptions of Reference Group Sanctions for Assault," *The Canadian Review of Sociology and Anthropology* 12, no. 1 (1975): 72–80.

22. Douglas A. Kleiber and Glyn C. Roberts, "The Effects of Sport Experience in the Development of Social Character: An Exploratory Investigation," *Journal of Sport Psychology* 3 (1981): 114–22.

23. Ibid., pp. 118–19.

24. Ibid., p. 121.

25. Muzafer Sherif and Carolyn W. Sherif, *The Robbers' Cave Experiment: Intergroup Conflict and Cooperation* (Norman, Okla.: University of Oklahoma Press, 1961).

26. For example, see Thomas Tutko and William Bruns, *Winning is Everything and Other American Myths* (New York: Macmillan, 1976).

27. Carolyn W. Sherif and Gillian D. Rattray, "Psychological Activity in Middle Childhood (5–12 Years)," in *Child in Sport and Physical Activity*, eds. J. G. Albinson and G. M. Andrew (Baltimore, Md.: University Park Press, 1976), pp. 97–132.

28. Stevenson, "College Athletics and 'Character,' " pp. 254–55.

29. John M. Silva, "The Perceived Legitimacy of Rule Violating Behavior in Sports," *Journal of Sport Psychology* 5 (1983): 438–66.

30. Brenda Jo Bredemeier, "Moral Reasoning and the Perceived Legitimacy of Intentionally Injurious Sports Acts," *Journal of Sport Psychology* 7 (1985): 110–24; Brenda Jo Bredemeier and David Shields, "Divergence in Moral Reasoning about Sport and Everyday Life," *Sociology of Sport Journal* 1 (1984): 348–57; Brenda Jo Bredemeier and David Shields, "Values and Violence in Sports Today," *Psychology Today* (October 1985): 23–26, 28–32; Brenda Jo Bredemeier and David Shields, "Athletic Aggression: An Issue of Contextual Morality," *Sociology of Sport Journal* 3 (1986): 15–28; Brenda Jo Bredemeier and David Shields, "Game Reasoning and Interactional Morality," *Journal of Genetic Psychology* 147 (1986): 257–75.

31. Bredemeier and Shields, "Athletic Aggression," p. 19.

32. Bredemeier and Shields, "Game Reasoning and Interactional Morality," p. 264.

33. Bredemeier and Shields, "Values and Violence in Sports Today," p. 28.

34. Bredemeier and Shields, "Athletic Aggression," p. 19.

35. Ibid.; Bredemeier and Shields, "Game Reasoning and Interactional Morality."

36. Bredemeier and Shields, "Values and Violence in Sports Today," p. 29.

37. Ibid.

38. Ibid., p. 32.

39. Donald J. Mrozek, *Sport and American Mentality, 1880–1910* (Knoxville, Tenn.: University of Tennessee Press, 1983), p. 40.

40. Ibid., p. 169.

41. Ibid., p. 226.

42. Ibid., pp. 226–27.

43. Ibid., p. 231.

44. See, for example, Randy Roberts, "Jack Dempsey: An American Hero in the 1920s," *Journal of Popular Culture* 8 (1974): 411–26.

45. See Gary Smith, "The Sports Hero: An Endangered Species," *Quest* 25 (1973): 59–70.

5

School Sport and Delinquency

The more athletics flourish in public schools, the less vice will be
found in them.

—J. C. G. Minchin (1901)[1]

Stay out for sports, and stay out of courts.

—Anonymous

He who flies with the owls at night cannot keep up with the eagles
during the day.

—Slogan from the walls of high school locker rooms[2]

The only thing I could come up with . . . I'd go back to school
days. Some of us were given so much freedom, breaking this rule
and that. I kind of felt like I was invincible, that no one would
do anything to me.

—Former high school football star Gary Edwards
trying to explain why he became a robber[3]

On September 22, 1989, Texas State District Judge Joe Kendall
sentenced ten teenagers to prison terms of up to twenty-five years

for a string of armed robberies. In itself this was not particularly newsworthy; it is a sad fact that teenage crime such as armed robbery is a common occurrence. What made this case different was that the youths were all current or former high school athletes. More than that, they were all football players for D. W. Carter High School in Dallas, Texas, and the Carter Cowboys had just won the state football championship. Several of the teenagers were fine athletes, likely to receive football scholarships from Division I schools. One was a consensus high school "All American."

How could it be that kids with so much going for them would jeopardize their futures by committing "more armed robberies than Bonnie and Clyde did in a lifetime"?[4] What about the values of truth, honor, and respect that athletics is supposed to teach? No one could figure it out, least of all one of the perpetrators of the crimes, Gary Edwards. As the above quote shows, to some extent he blamed the very institution that is reputed to instill values that make youth less susceptible to delinquency. His status as a football player in a high school, community, and state where winning football games is of paramount importance meant that normal school activities such as class attendance, studying, and test-taking did not apply to him. He was made to feel that he was "above" the rest of us, invincible, free to do as he chose.

The same impression was given by the members of the "Spur Posse" during their interviews on numerous talk shows. The Spur Posse, named after the San Antonio Spurs, the favorite team of several of the group's leaders, was a male clique at Lakewood High School in California. Boys in this clique gained status or "points" for the number of different girls with whom they had sex. The leaders of this group were star athletes who seemed to feel that their popularity meant that casual sex with girls was acceptable, even if, as in some cases, the girls were forced to have sex with several Posse members.[5] As one of the boys put it, "I don't consider myself a normal person you know. I think I'm a step above everyone else."[6]

Like the athletes of Carter High School, the Spur Posse members also saw themselves as being above the law, particularly the law of the school. For example, they did not always attend classes. One of their peers commented, "They ditch and then beg the teacher to pass them, because they have to have a C average to play on the teams."[7]

On one level these incidents show the danger of treating athletes as "superstars" and moral heroes at the same time. The "sport-builds-character" myth, or more precisely the myth that sport involvement for youth provides an alternative to delinquency, sets up athletes as "special." Young athletes become role models for the community and the country. When they get into trouble, as some of them do, their fall is greater because they have been built up. This is particularly true in the case of the Carter High School football players, since they were supposed to be winners, but acted like losers.

On another level these incidents illustrate the problems encountered when trying to decipher the relationship between delinquency and participation in high school athletics. As the previous chapter illustrated, anecdotal evidence of success and failure does not lead anywhere. It may be used by the promoters of or detractors from high school athletics who already have made up their minds about the social functions of sport, but it does little to reveal the underlying relationship between sport participation and delinquency, assuming any such relationship exists at all.

An investigation of the relationship between delinquency and participation in high school sport is the goal of the present chapter. First, we examine the research that shows a negative relationship, supporting the notion that sport can keep participants out of trouble. Afterward, we will discuss the reasons why this relationship could occur. We also review the opposite argument—that sport participation encourages delinquent behavior, particularly if delinquency is defined as activities like fighting, drinking, and drug use, especially illegal steroids. We will try to reconcile these opposite views by discussing the theory of "positive deviance," the idea that an overconformity to the athletic norms of physical strength, machismo, competitiveness, and winning may be responsible for some athletes behaving in socially unacceptable ways. Finally, we will make some suggestions about how high school athletics might play a more prominent "reform" role than it presently does, and so live up to the expectations of those who see it as a positive force in reducing delinquency rates.

School Sport and Delinquency Reduction

In chapter 2 the origins of the "sport-builds-character" myth were located in the philosophy of muscular Christianity. According to this philosophy, lessons in morality were learned on the sports fields of exclusive private schools in England and America. Through participation in team sports, upper- and middle-class children (boys in particular) would internalize the values of sportsmanship and fair play, and become so exhausted in the process as to have no energy for more devious recreational activities. In the words of one nineteenth-century headmaster: "I contend that athletic exercise is good not only for the bodily but also for the moral strength of a boy. I like every boy in my school to have so much exercise and fresh air that, when bedtime comes, he may soundly sleep till next morning without even dreaming."[8]

Aside from the veiled reference to nefarious nighttime activities (these were all-male boarding schools, after all), his statement would have been accepted by many contemporary leaders in education and sport in this country. As we have seen, a belief in the positive effect of high school sport has long been part of institutionalized thinking about education. For example, the Educational Policies Commission noted that "participation in sound athletic programs, we believe, contributes to health and happiness, physical skills and emotional maturity, social competence and moral values."[9]

An important component of the "sport-builds-character" myth is the belief that participation in athletics may provide a potent counteraction to antisocial activities such as theft, drunkenness, drug abuse and violence generally labeled as juvenile delinquency.[10] A number of reasons have been suggested to explain this "deterrent" effect depending upon which theory of delinquency is used to explain adolescent behavior.[11] For example, if delinquency among males is viewed as a result of the need to assert masculinity, then athletics may be seen as providing a socially acceptable context for this behavior. If delinquency is viewed as resulting from boredom, then athletics may be seen as filling the void.

It is thought that peer groups that place a high value on delinquent behavior may pressure juveniles to conform to these norms. In that case, it may be assumed that sport teams will have much more socially positive norms and will socialize juveniles into more socially acceptable behavior. To the extent that delinquency is viewed as a reaction to the frustration experienced by children because of their low social status compared to adults, sports may be seen as reducing this frustration. This is particularly true for children from lower socioeconomic backgrounds who are less likely to experience success in school. In such a case, it may be argued that membership on sports teams makes young athletes more willing to accept the constraints of education and may even provide a path for future educational success (see chapter 6). Finally, if delinquency is viewed as a result of weak social controls exerted on youth by the family or other institutions, then it may be assumed that the strict regimen of athletics and the discipline of the coach may provide the necessary antidote.

The confidence in athletics as a deterrent has been bolstered by research results that often showed athletes' delinquency rates to be lower than those of nonathletes, whether these rates were assessed through court records[12] or by self-report questionnaires.[13] This finding occurs for females as well as males,[14] and is consistent across different age ranges.[15] There are, however, some interesting inconsistencies depending upon which behaviors were designated as delinquent. For example, in one study[16] delinquent behavior such as neighborhood disturbances, petty theft, and drunkenness was found to be higher for the male athletes than for nonathletes, although what the authors called "severe crime" was lower. Another study[17] found a significantly higher rate of delinquency among female athletes than among nonathletes as measured by smoking, drinking, breaking school rules, cheating on tests, and getting into trouble with the law.

Findings such as these led to questions about the deterrent effect of sport.[18] If delinquency is a symbolic act of rebellion by youth against the limitations (e.g., rules, regulations, and authoritarian control) placed upon them by adult institutions, then rebellious youth are hardly likely to see conventional athletics as an alternative. On the contrary, rather than finding an alternative to delinquency in sport, they will find exactly the same constraints that caused their original revolt. Instead, nonconventional sports such as Outward Bound programs were offered as a legitimate alternative. These programs typically place delinquents in small groups in mountainous or wilderness environments. Here they are taught rock climbing, hiking, and survival skills in which they learn to test themselves and to depend upon each other. Success in these experiences would lead to feelings of mastery and self-worth, which subsequently would deter youth from the antisocial forms of behavior that previously had given them satisfaction. This theory was supported by studies[19] that showed lower rates of recidivism (i.e., readmittance to prison) for institutionalized delinquents who went through an Outward Bound program than for those who experienced more routine treatment.

Nonconventional sports such as rock climbing were seen as having a rehabilitative effect on delinquent youth, while the research showing a negative relationship between participation in conventional sport and delinquency rates was felt to support a deterrent effect. However, these generalizations need to be qualified. It is quite possible that we are dealing with two different groups: on the one hand, youth who tend toward "wild" or "antisocial" behavior, and, in the case of the Outward Bound studies, youth who have been institutionalized for criminal acts. Although this is not an either/or categorical difference, cheating on school tests or getting drunk is a very different matter from committing robbery. By definition, the institutionalized group cannot be involved in high school athletics if they are in jail, and it is realistic to expect that, even if they were high school athletes at an earlier time, their delinquent activity could mean an end to their athletic careers. In other words, could the different rates of delinquency between athletes and nonathletes cited in support of the deterrent effect really be the result of the coach throwing the delinquents off the team?

This problem is another example of the selection-versus-change issue discussed earlier. Like the character-development studies, most research on the relationship between delinquency and high school athletics has been of the cross-sectional variety that makes it misleading to attribute any change, positive or negative, to athletic participation. Most sociologists acknowledge the limitations of these research designs and are cautious in interpreting the results. Only one study[20] has looked at the effect of high school athletic participation upon change in delinquency rates over time, and the results have interesting implications for the deterrent/rehabilitation debate.

In this study the authors assessed the self-reported delinquency rates of over 2,000 tenth-grade boys on status offenses (i.e., school delinquency, running away from home, and trouble with parents), as well as serious delinquency (e.g., arson or assault with a weapon), interpersonal aggression, theft, and vandalism. Assessment was repeated at the twelfth-grade level and again after high school graduation when most of the sample were twenty-four years old. The results of this study showed no overall effects of participation in high school athletics until the sample was subdivided by race. Then the authors discovered what they called a reform effect for blacks. Initially, black sixteen-year-olds who took part in school sports were much *more* likely to be delinquent than blacks who were not on sports teams, but by eighteen years of age the black athletes were much less likely to be delinquent than their nonathlete peers. At age twenty-four the ex-athletes remained less likely to violate the law than the nonathletes.

In explaining why the reform effect was found with African Americans rather than with the full sample, the authors suggested that greater importance is attached to sport in the black community because it is a source of pride and because it is perceived as one of the few avenues of upward mobility for black youth.* To test this theory they reexamined the original relationship with a subsample of whites from small rural communities, arguing that here, as in black communities, high school sport is very important.† The findings were

---

*However, see chapter 6 on this point.

†See chapter 7 for a discussion of this issue.

similar to those for the black youth, prompting the authors to extend their reform theory. They suggested that sport does not select good boys but instead makes boys better. When sport fails to produce this effect it is because it does not count for enough, for example, in big cities where the mass media have reduced the importance of high school sport. For blacks and small-town whites, high school sport is the focus of intense community attention and interest. Therefore, it has the power to reform. "When sports are a focus of community solidarity they become invested with the capacity to reward athletes who conform to athletic ideals and to punish those who do not."[21]

It is possible that both a selection and a reform process are at work. An interest in athletics may remain in school youth prone to delinquency who feel no attachment to education.[22] If they are star athletes, they may indeed conform to socially acceptable behavior because it is necessary for maintaining athletic involvement rather than because they believe that it is the right thing to do. Even when sports are not linked to the school this conformity effect for elite athletes has been found. For example, one study of delinquency among fifteen- and sixteen-year-old hockey players in Montreal showed that the elite players had lower delinquency rates than nonathletes on self-reports of drug use, vandalism, and theft.[23]

In summary, there is some support for the idea that high school athletics can provide a deterrent and even a reform function to counter-act juvenile delinquency, although it is not clear why this might occur. High school athletes may be forced to conform to school norms by the threat of losing a valued activity, or they may want to conform because sport confirms the value of school culture. Interpersonal networks formed through athletics are less likely to be delinquent, and in this way athletes are protected from involvement in groups where committing delinquent acts may be given high status.

Nonconventional athletics (e.g., Outward Bound) also may have a rehabilitative effect on hard-core delinquents, but here, too, the explanations for the relationship are varied. The personal-challenge idea is one possible reason, but other possible explanations might include cutting delinquents off from their usual surroundings by isolating them in the wilderness, or introducing predominantly working-class youth to middle-class values.[24]

The tacit assumption behind all of the studies reviewed so far is that delinquency is an individual problem that can be "fixed" by exposing the delinquent to some sort of treatment (e.g., conventional athletics or Outward Bound). However, all behavior emerges out of social interaction. Some types of delinquency actually may be developed as part of the socialization process in sport.[25] This is the subject of the next section.

School Sport and the Development of Delinquency

The Carter High School athletes mentioned in the introduction were not reformed by their athletic experiences. Although athletic participation at high school is usually negatively correlated with serious crime, some studies already discussed show that high school athletes are more delinquent than nonathletes. Some of the research reviewed in the previous chapter shows that being violent is perceived to be part of a youth hockey subculture. Perhaps the demands of sport can lead to the glorification of violence and other forms of deviant behavior. If we are able to consider the possibility of sport providing a deterrent or a reform effect, we should certainly give attention to the opposite view. If high school sport has the potential to reduce delinquency then it also has the potential to increase it.

Some of the research reviewed in chapter 3 casts serious doubt on the theory that sport reduces delinquency. In particular, the results of the participant-observation studies of high school sport supported the idea that a subculture of deviance can exist below the facade of conformity. Despite their all-American outward appearance, some male athletes did see drinking, drugs, and sexual promiscuity as part of what it meant to be a man. The ethics of playing with pain and doing what it takes to win can lead to abuses that could be labeled delinquent if they were not in sport.

Where else but in sport can you escape prosecution if you hit someone with a stick, run into people with tremendous force, or pound an opponent into insensibility with your fists? Who but a sports fan can get away with verbal harassment of the representatives of justice (i.e., the officials), and public expressions of hostility and disdain for opponents? The research reviewed in chapter 4 showed that athletes had ambivalent attitudes on the issue of intentionally injuring an opponent. While accepting injury as part of the game, some athletes expressed concern about what they called "cheap shots." However, others felt little or no empathy for their opponents, and perceived intentional injury as just another tactic to be used if you wanted to win. To the extent that intentional injury is condoned in sport, it is being made legitimate. Many would agree that it is a form of delinquent behavior.

Just how physically dangerous are high school sports? The National Athletic Trainers' Association (NATA) estimates the injury total to be about 1.3 million per year.[26] This figure is based upon a three-year study of high school footballers, basketballers, and wrestlers. The study showed that 22 percent of the boys basketball players, 23 percent of the girl basketball players, and 27 percent of the wrestlers were injured at least once a year. Overall, 70 to 75 percent of these injuries were classified as minor, defined as having players sidelined for a week or less. However, one-third of all wrestling injuries sidelined the athletes for more than a week.

The results also showed that the high school football programs average 36 time-loss injuries per year, compared to 16 for wrestling and 16 for boys and girls basketball. The odds of sustaining an injury requiring surgery are 1 in 83 for wrestling, 1 in 90 for girls basketball, and 1 in 128 for boys basketball. For the girls, 89 percent of these injuries are to the knees. High school football programs average one surgery per year; 64 percent of the time this will be for a knee injury. The annual average of fatal or catastrophic injuries in high school football each year is 24, and the equivalent figure for all high school sports is 36.[27]

Readers will have to decide for themselves—we hope in discussions with their children—about the relative costs and benefits of participation, bearing in mind these statistics on injury. NATA officials point out that the data for their study could only be collected in schools where certified athletic trainers are employed, about 3,200 of 24,000 secondary schools in 1989. The goal of NATA is to have athletic trainers in half the nation's schools by the year 2000. Given that some degree of injury in high school sports is inevitable, having qualified athletic trainers on site seems a sensible suggestion, particularly if the trainer can counter the "play-with-pain" ethic and stop athletes from returning to competition too early (or being forced to return by coaches) and reinjuring themselves. The NATA report comments that reinjury is "an athletic trainer's nightmare," noting that the reinjury rate in the study was 15 percent for basketball and 9 percent for wrestling.

Trainers also might be able to give advice and guidance to athletes on diet, which might help to counter deviant dietary practices, some of which are built into training regimens. For example, the report notes with concern the "depletion" practices followed by many wrestlers to "make weight." This extreme restriction of food (and sometimes liquids) saps the energy and strength necessary for success and should be banned. The dietary and training habits of wrestlers have been the subject of several studies[28] that have documented frequent and rapid weight loss and gain cycles in this group of athletes. Wrestlers tend to do whatever it takes to lose weight, including wearing rubber sweatsuits in the sauna, restricting food and fluid intake, and sometimes vomiting and using laxatives and diuretics. Both the American Medical Association and the American College of Sports Medicine have issued position statements condemning the practice of weight-cutting in wrestling, and the state of Wisconsin has considered mandating a minimum level of 7 percent body fat for each high school wrestler before the beginning of the competitive season when weight-class membership is decided.[29]

Concern about eating disorders and extreme dieting practices is not limited to wrestling, but is widespread in athletics. Although results are varied, it has been estimated that 32 percent of female college athletes practice one or more pathogenic weight-control procedures.[30] Another survey showed that 25 percent of the college athletes polled reported using restricted food intake (less than 600 calories per day) to lose weight. Fasting was used by 11.9 percent, fad diets by 10.6 percent, and self-induced vomiting by 5.6 percent (more commonly among females than males). A total of 3.7 percent of the sample reported using laxatives and 3.2 percent used diuretics, while 10 athletes (1.4 percent) said they used enemas. When these results were compared to general college populations, extreme dieting practices were shown to be more prevalent among the athletes.[31]

Some experts point to the "athlete personality" as being one that is particularly prone to eating disorders. This argument suggests that athletes are compulsive, driven, and self-motivated—traits which characterize compulsive dieters in general. One study showed great similarities between compulsive runners and anorexic patients, but this finding has been hotly contested.[32] Less controversial is the idea that weight is a very salient factor in the lives of most athletes. Many coaches weigh athletes regularly and hold athletes accountable for their weight. Athletes can feel pressure to conform to the demands of their coach as well as the socially constructed image that athletes are physically fit, and fit people are thin. If this is the case, they can abuse their bodies in the quest for athletic success. Coaches should try to avoid this "get-thin-and-win" syndrome, counsel athletes about healthy eating habits, and make realistic goals for weight reduction if such reduction is necessary.

Information about playing with pain and bizarre dietary behavior tends to undermine the "clean-living" idea that is part of the deterrent theory already mentioned. Simply stated, this theory predicts that athletes will adopt a healthy lifestyle because they are trying to get the most out of their bodies. Alcohol and drug abuse will run counter to this goal and will be avoided. The clean-living ethic will be part of the culture of high school athletes so that any athlete who fails to conform to the norm will get pressure from his or her peers for not being a team player.

The small but growing volume of research on drug abuse among athletes also is relevant to this issue. For example, one study[33] involved indepth interviews of a sample of 100 adolescent drug users about their own and their peers' participation in sport and use (or nonuse) of drugs. About 60 percent of these adolescents were classified as being involved in either recreational or organized sports. A large percentage of organized sports participants said they were occasional, or regular users of beer, liquor, and marijuana (48.5 percent, 27.0 percent, and 33.3 percent, respectively). However, these percentages were higher for recreational sports participants (74 percent, 56.5 percent, and 43.5 percent), and even higher for the nonparticipants (77 percent, 71.8 percent, and 69.2 percent).

While these results may run counter to the idea that participation in sports encourages clean living, many of the youth in this study[34] did subscribe to the belief that sport involvement would cause drug use to decline. For example, some athletes gave involvement in sport as a reason for not using drugs, and some also believed that an anti-drug ethic in sport groups would have a rehabilitative effect and discourage drug use. Conversely, some athletes spoke of their drug use in relation to athletics, either as a mark of status (one youth mentioned a high incidence of drug use among pro-basketball and football players), or as an aid to athletic performance (e.g., codeine to mask the pain of injury and speed to get psyched up). Some athletes also felt that smoking marijuana helped them play better.

This study adds support to the picture being developed of a less clear-cut relationship between sports and delinquency among adolescence than the supporters of the deterrent or rehabilitation theories might like. Admittedly, the clean-living ethic is generally accepted by athletes. Part of this is the belief that sports and drugs do not mix. Even among adolescent drug users the incidence of beer, alcohol, and drug use was lower for the organized sport group than the recreational sport and the nonsport groups. However, some athletes view the recreational use of beer, liquor, and drugs as part of being an athlete, and sometimes athletes use drugs to enhance performance.

The performance-enhancing potential of drugs in sport is particularly true in the case of anabolic steroids (AS). These are synthetically derived compounds that simulate the effect of the male sex hormone testosterone and promote muscle growth. They can be taken orally or by injection, usually in a 6- to 12-week cycle.[35] It is estimated that 6.6 percent or between 250,000 and 500,000 adolescents of high school age use steroids.[36] Also disturbing is the fact that 38.3 percent of the boys said that they started at age fifteen years and younger. Almost 40 percent of the users reported five or more cycles of use, 44 percent reported that they practiced "stacking" (using more than one type of steroid at the same time), and 38.1 percent had used both the oral and the injectable method of administration. Of even greater concern is the evidence of heavy use. A total of 12 percent of the users reported *average* AS cycles of thirteen weeks. Adult power lifters with plenty of AS experience rarely exceed thirteen-week cycles.

The implications of this study are that a significant proportion of high school youth are experimenting with potentially dangerous drugs without medical supervision. Although experimental studies on the long-term health effects of regular steroid use have not been done, the results of case studies give cause for alarm. The possible physiological side effects of steroid use include heart attacks, strokes, increased LDL-cholesterol (the harmful kind) and decreased HDL-cholesterol (the beneficial kind), liver injury, damage to the reproductive system, and premature closing of the epiphyseal growth plates leading to shorter stature.[37] This last problem is particularly disturbing when high school and junior high school students use steroids, since bone growth is usually at a crucial stage during adolescence. Users also have reported significant personality changes as a result of steroid use, particularly increases in aggression, anxiety, tension, and anger.[38]

Not all of the steroid users are involved in interscholastic athletics. Some 35.2 percent of the users in the survey were nonparticipants and probably were motivated by cosmetic reasons. This means that they wanted a strong physique since this would give them high social status. Appearance was selected as the main reason for steroid use among 26.7 percent of the user group. However, athletic participation did figure prominently in the users' choices. The largest percentage of users (47.1 percent) reported that the main reason for using the drug was to improve athletic performance, while users were significantly more inclined than nonusers to be involved in school-sponsored athletics, particularly football and wrestling.

The results of this study show that a large number of adolescent athletes are experimenting with drugs that have dangerous side effects.

These effects can be compounded by the risk of hepatitis and AIDS if users share needles to inject the drug. Several approaches have been suggested to reduce steroid use among high school athletes.[39] The first area is drug enforcement. By classifying steroids as an illegal drug, the intent has been to reduce the available supply. The Anti-Drug Abuse Act of 1988 made distribution of steroids without a prescription a felony punishable by a six-year prison term, and twenty-five states have passed legislation designed to curb the nonmedical use of steroids. At the risk of sounding pessimistic, this policy has about as much chance of success as the more publicized nationwide crackdown on illegal drugs such as cocaine and heroin. As long as the demand for steroids is high, there will be entrepreneurs willing to take the necessary risks to supply the drug on the black market. It is a safe bet that steroids are readily available for the right price at your local gym if you know the right people.

The second approach has been an aggressive testing policy initiated by some high schools. Various problems confront school districts that favor the testing route. First, there is the privacy issue of an individual's rights against testing. Proponents of testing can argue that participation in extracurricular activities is a privilege for school children rather than a right,[40] and that the privilege can be withdrawn if students test positive for steroids.

It also has been argued that the ethical dilemma of steroid testing of athletes should be resolved in favor of testing because, without testing, athletes who do not want to take steroids are forced to do so to remain competitive with their steroid-taking opponents. Steroid testing helps to reestablish a more equitable basis for competition.[41] However, the question arises: Which students and which drugs? For example, why should male high school football players and wrestlers be singled out for steroid testing? What about all athletes, male and female, or all participants in extracurricular activities from the football team to the chess club? And why stop at steroids? Why not test for other drugs and alcohol?

A more practical consideration is the prohibitive cost of drug testing. When the Homewood-Flossmoor School District in the suburbs of Chicago decided to extend their drug-testing program to all interscholastic activities, they were faced with cost for basic screening of about $35 per student. A test that would be admissible in a court of law would cost about $75, while one to detect steroids would cost as much as $200. The school district also received notification from the American Civil Liberties Union of Illinois that it would probably challenge the legality of such tests.[42]

In contrast to, or rather in conjunction with, an aggressive detection program, a vigorous education program sometimes is advocated. The intent is to alert adolescents to the damaging side effects of steroid use and scare them away from the drugs. Faced with no hard data on long-term effects, the irrelevance of health risks in adulthood to the present lives of adolescents, the generally self-confident demeanor of high school athletes (the "it-won't-happen-to-me" syndrome), and the widespread perception that steroid use is a necessity for success at a high level in most sports, the effects of such education can be limited. One steroid education program that targeted a group of high school football players in Oregon is reputed to have caused an increase in steroid use as players learned more about the muscle-building capacity of the drug.[43] Furthermore, there is a certain hypocrisy in the strategy of telling kids to "just say no" to steroids while, at the same time, spending large sums of money to catch those who say yes. Adolescents, particularly high school athletes, can easily become confused by mixed messages that stress the importance of victory on the one hand, but on the other restrict what, from the perspective of the world of sport, may be perceived as a legitimate means of attaining the success that many adults seem to value so highly.

Steroid use is a major problem in international sport where the issue of fairness is paramount. While we may be willing to grant adults the right to do long-term damage to their own health in the name of victory, most of us are upset by the illegal advantage steroids gives to the user. Although the current testing policy of the International Olympic Committee has received much publicity by catching some famous athletes (e.g., Ben Johnson), how much money will have to be spent to eradicate steroid use at the highest levels of sport? Is such a goal even feasible given that there always has been cheating in sports?[44] At the level of the high school athlete the problem is compounded by the health issue. We will readily interfere to try to protect children from abusing their own bodies in the name of sport, but, as this section has shown, reducing steroid use is easier said than done.

We have presented several challenges to the theory that sport reduces delinquency. The image of a high school athlete injecting himself with adrenalin prior to a weight training session like a junkie shooting up in an alley is very different from the idea of the all-American boy learning the value of hard work, achievement, and group cooperation on the sports field. Given that athletes are often the most popular and highly respected members of adolescent communities, drug use, drunkenness, and promiscuity by them can make this behavior legitimate in the eyes of their peers. For example, the eight members of the Spur Posse who were arrested subsequently were cheered when they returned to school.

If such behavior is part of an athletic culture—how athletes perceive that they ought to behave—then athletics can be linked to the development of delinquency among athletes and nonathletes alike. Can there be some resolution to the opposing views presented in this and the previous section, where a largely negative relationship between athletics and delinquency was developed? An attempt at reconciliation, and the implications of this for the relationship between participation in sports and delinquency, is developed below.

Sport and Positive Deviance

By implication, steroid use and other deviant sport practices such as playing with pain and intentionally injuring an opponent are rooted in a philosophy of sport concerned more with the outcome than the process of competition. Where winning is valued above all else, playing with pain can be seen as a badge of courage. Steroid use, intentional injury, and pathogenic weight-control practices are all ways that athletes can show their total commitment to sport or, more particularly, to winning in sport. Similarly, sexual conquest is another way to score—with the girls and in the eyes of one's peers. It is all part of what it takes to be a real athlete. Sociologists have labeled this overconformity to the perceived goals and norms of sport as positive deviance.[45]

Sport sociologists Robert Hughes and Jay Coakley have stated,

> We argue that a significant portion of deviance among athletes does not involve disregarding or rejecting commonly accepted cultural goals or means to those goals, nor does it result from alienation from society. Instead, it is grounded in athletes' uncritical acceptance of and commitment to what they have been told by important people in their lives ever since they began participating in competitive programs; in a real sense, it is the result of being too committed to the goals and norms of sport.[46]

The concept of positive deviance can encompass most of what has been presented in the previous section and explain how athletes "do harmful things to themselves and perhaps others while motivated by a sense of duty and honor."[47] It can explain why athletes can support an ethic of clean living and morality and yet indulge in behaviors that are classified as delinquent by those outside the athletic culture. The conformity by athletes to this culture helps to create very strong bonds that can form the basis of negative behavior, especially among athletes who have low self-esteem and are vulnerable to group demands, or among athletes who see sport as their only opportunity for success in life.

According to Hughes and Coakley, the leading advocates of the positive deviance theory in sports:

> In the case of athletes in highly visible sports, this process of developing fraternity, superiority, and disdain for outsiders might also lead some of them to naively assume they are somehow beyond the law, and the people outside the athletic fraternity do not deserve their respect. This could lead to serious cases of negative deviance including, for example, assault, sexual assault, and rape (including gang rape), the destruction of property, reckless driving, and alcohol abuse.[48]

The theory of positive deviance might be used to explain the crimes of the Carter High School football players mentioned at the beginning of the chapter, and the feeling of invincibility expressed by Gary Edwards. In addition, it could provide insight into the activities of the Spur Posse and other incidents of sexual abuse by male athletes. Positive deviance also suggests a way out of the dilemma created by conflicting research findings, and it has an interesting message for those who would like to make sport a more positive force in the lives of adolescents.

Recall that the most powerful study of the effect of high school athletics on delinquency found support for a reform effect among black male athletes and white high school athletes in small rural communities where "sports are a focus of community solidarity."[49] It is in these communities where high school athletes are treated like young gods and the winning ethic is strongest.[50] It is difficult to see sport teaching such moral values as fairness, respect for others, and self-control under conditions in which the community is addicted to winning. In these circumstances athletes are expected to pay the price, even if it includes playing with pain and taking steroids. Some parents reacted to their sons' actions as members of the Spur Posse with blasé "boys-will-be-boys" acceptance. According to one father, his son's behavior would be expected of any "red-blooded American boy."[51]

Some teachers and coaches argue that positive deviance will continue until the philosophy of sport is reshaped to focus more on the thrill of competition and less on the fixation with winning.[52] Obviously such a philosophical change will not be adopted quickly, but support for this view comes from research in which sport programs have been reorganized so that the teaching of moral responsibility, not winning, has been the principal goal.[53] For example, in one experiment a group of thirteen- to seventeen-year-old males classified as delinquent were divided into three groups matched on aggression and personality adjustment. One group received traditional training in a martial arts form called Tae Kwon Do. During this training, the philosophical component of Tae Kwon Do, which includes maintaining a sense of responsibility, emphasizing respect for others, and the building of confidence and self-esteem, was stressed. Physical skills and meditation also were included. The second group practiced a modern form of Tae Kwon Do in which only the fighting and self-defense components were taught. The third group (the control) received no martial arts training but played basketball and football instead. After six months, the youth in group one were no longer classified as delinquent, and showed lower aggression and anxiety levels and higher scores in self-esteem and social skills. The members of group two had higher delinquency scores and were more aggressive and less well-adjusted than before. Those in group three showed no change in delinquency scores.[54]

Although recently elaborated in the context of sport, the theory of positive deviance helps to explain a number of puzzling inconsistencies in the world of sport that are particularly relevant to the high school athletics and delinquency debate. Implied in the theory is the simple idea that athletic programs can help reduce delinquency to the extent that they are organized with this goal in mind. All too often, while delinquency reduction might be a stated aim, it is one to which we pay only lip service. The real emphasis is on winning.

Summary

This chapter began as a seemingly simple examination of the effectiveness of high school athletics in the battle against juvenile delinquency. When delinquency is characterized as a state of being that can be cured by having youths pass through some program, the deterrent or reform effect of athletics seems a feasible issue. One of the strengths of myth is that the behavior that is "mythologized" is passed off as common sense (i.e., "Of course high school sport helps to reduce delinquency, only a fool would think otherwise").

As usual, the problem is more complex than it seems on the surface. Below the outward conformity of sport lies a culture in which behavior labeled deviant in the outside world is sometimes highly valued. Athletes have to learn appropriate behavior in order to gain access to this culture and become part of the world of sport. This world is often characterized by positive deviance, a strict adherence by athletes to a code of ethics that sometimes runs counter to societal norms. At its extreme this ethic can include serious criminal behavior. This aspect of the theory—the relationship between athletics and crime—has yet to undergo scientific testing, yet it offers a tantalizing explanation for why some athletes break the mold of conformity. We build athletes up as the symbolic protectors of school and community pride, treat them like demigods, sometimes place them above the laws of the school and the community, and then shake our heads in confusion and disbelief when they occasionally call our bluff.

The theory of positive deviance points the way for high school athletics to play a more positive social role than it has in the past. The usual assumption has been that athletes pick up moral values automatically as they continue in their athletic careers, but this assumption has been challenged by evidence presented in this chapter, the previous one, and elsewhere in this book. We can only make high school sport a moral force in the school and community if we coordinate efforts toward such a goal. To the extent that high school athletics occurs in a hostile atmosphere, where the pride of the team, the school, and the community rests on beating the opponent, and the community solidarity symbolized by our team depends on seeing their team (or community) as the enemy, positive deviance may be the norm.

High school athletics could be a medium through which participants learn to respect rules and honor their opponents. It could provide common ground in which communities of different racial or ethnic backgrounds learn to accept their differences and coexist peacefully.[55] However, this will not happen by chance or if we continue to invent the traditions of delinquency reduction and character building to justify sport while in reality concentrating on winning, "whatever the cost."

Notes

1. J. C. G. Minchin, *Our Public Schools* (London: Macmillan, 1901), cited in Malcolm Tozer, "From 'Muscular Christianity' to 'Esprit de Corps': Games in the Victorian Public Schools of England," *Stadion* 7, no. 1 (1981): 117–30.

2. Eldon E. Snyder, "Athletic Dressing Room Slogans as Folklore: A Means of Socialization," *International Review of the Sociology of Sport* 7 (1972): 89–102.

3. Roger Campbell, "Prison Life Dims Glory Days," *Fort Worth Star-Telegram,* December 24, 1989: Section 1, p. 1.

4. Associated Press, *New York Times,* September 24, 1989: Section 1, p. 29LA.

5. Joan Didion, "Trouble in Lakewood," *The New Yorker* (July 26, 1993): 46–50, 52–60, 62–65; Jill Smolowe, "Sex with a Scorecard," *Time* (April 5, 1993): 41.

6. Didion, "Trouble in Lakewood," p. 59.

7. Ibid., p. 52.

8. Report of the Meeting of Head Masters of Schools, Winchester, England (1883), p. 56; cited in Tozer, "From 'Muscular Christianity' to 'Esprit de Corps.' "

9. Educational Policies Commission, "School Athletics: Problems and Policies," (Washington, D.C.: U.S. Government Printing Office, 1954): 1.

10. Although there are many definitions of juvenile delinquency, the one most used by sport sociologists in the past has been: "behavior that violates institutional expectation, i.e., expectations which are shared and recognized as legitimate within a social system." See A. Cohen, "The Study of Social Disorganization and Deviant Behavior," in *Sociology Today,* eds. Robert Merton et al. (New York: Basic Books, 1959), p. 62. More recently sociologists have been less willing to assume societal consensus on such behaviors and have concentrated on how institutions enforce conformity, or how the label "delinquent" is used to protect the status quo. See Jeffrey O. Segrave and Douglas N. Hastad, "Future Directions in Sport and Juvenile Delinquency Research," *Quest* 36, no. 1 (1984): 37–47.

11. Jeffrey O. Segrave and Donald Chu, "Athletics and Juvenile Delinquency," *Review of Sport and Leisure* 3, no. 2 (1978): 1–24.

12. For example, Donald Landers and Donna Landers, "Socialization via Interscholastic Athletics: Its Effect on Delinquency," *Sociology of Education* 51 (1978): 299–303.

13. For example, Segrave and Chu, "Athletics and Juvenile Delinquency," pp. 1–24; Jeffrey O. Segrave, Claude Moreau, and Douglas N. Hastad, "An Investigation into the Relationship between Ice Hockey Participation and Delinquency," *Sociology of Sport Journal* 2, no. 4 (1985): 281–89.

14. Hans G. Buhrmann and Robert D. Bratton, "Athletic Participation and Deviant Behavior of High School Girls in Alberta," *Review of Sport and Leisure* 3, no. 2 (1978): 25–41.

15. See Douglas Hastad, Jeffrey O. Segrave, Robert Pangrazi, and Gene Peterson,

"Youth Participation and Deviant Behavior," *Sociology of Sport Journal* 1, no. 4 (1984): 366–73.

16. Segrave and Chu, "Athletics and Juvenile Delinquency."

17. Buhrmann and Bratton, "Athletic Participation and Deviant Behavior of High School Girls in Alberta."

18. For example, John Sugden and Andrew Yiannakis, "Sport and Juvenile Delinquency: A Theoretical Base," *Journal of Sport and Social Issues* 6, no. 1 (1982): 22–30.

19. For example, J. Kelly and J. Baer, "Psychological Challenge as a Treatment for Delinquency," *Crime and Delinquency* 17 (1971): 437–45.

20. Rodney Stark, Lori Kent, and Roger Finke, "Sport and Delinquency," in *Positive Criminology*, eds. Michael R. Gottfredson and Travis Hirschi (Newbury Park, Calif.: Sage Publications, 1987), pp. 115–24.

21. Ibid., p. 124.

22. Jeffrey O. Segrave and Douglas N. Hastad, "Interscholastic Athletic Participation and Delinquent Behavior: An Empirical Assessment of Relevant Variables," *Sociology of Sport Journal* 1 (1984): 117–37.

23. Segrave, Moreau, and Hastad, "An Investigation into the Relationship between Ice Hockey Participation and Delinquency."

24. See Segrave and Hastad, "Future Directions in Sport and Juvenile Delinquency."

25. See Segrave and Hastad, "Future Directions in Sport and Juvenile Delinquency," for a discussion of this and other approaches.

26. Athletic Training, "3-Year Study Finds 'Major Injuries' Up 20% in High School Football," *Journal of the National Athletic Trainers' Association, Inc.* 24, no. 1 (1989): 60–69; Athletic Training, "Injury Toll in Prep Sports Estimated at 1.3 Million," *Journal of the National Athletic Trainers' Association, Inc.* 24, no. 4 (1989): 360–73.

27. Athletic Training, "Injury Toll in Prep Sports Estimated at 1.3 Million," pp. 360–73.

28. See James S. Thornton, "Feast of Famine: Eating Disorders in Athletics," *Physician and Sportsmedicine* 18, no. 4 (1990): 116–22.

29. Ibid.

30. Ibid.

31. David R. Black and Mardie E. Burckes-Miller, "Male and Female College Athletes: Use of Anorexia Nervosa and Bulimia Nervosa Weight Loss Methods," *Research Quarterly for Exercise and Sport* 59, no. 3 (1988): 252–56.

32. See Heyward L. Nash, "Do Compulsive Runners and Anorectic Patients Share Common Bonds?" *Physician and Sportsmedicine* 15, no. 12 (1987): 162–67.

33. M. Stuck and M. Ware, "Sport and Substance Use/Non-Use among Adolescent Athletes and Non-athletes" (Paper presented at the Fifth Canadian Congress on Leisure Research, Halifax, Nova Scotia, May 21, 1987).

34. Ibid.

35. See Terry Todd, "Anabolic Steroids: The Gremlins of Sport," *Journal of Sport History* 14, no. 1 (1987): 87–101; Charles E. Yesalis, "Steroid Abuse in Secondary Schools," *National Association for Sport and Physical Education (NASPE) News* 25 (1989): 1, 3; Charles E. Yesalis, James E. Wright, and Michael S. Bahrke, "Epidemiological and Policy Issues in the Measurement of the Long Term Health Effects of Anabolic-Androgenic Steroids," *Sports Medicine* 8, no. 3 (1989): 129–38.

36. William E. Buckley, Charles E Yesalis, Karl E. Friedl, William A. Anderson, Andrea L. Streit, and James E. Wright, "Estimated Prevalence of Anabolic Steroid Use Among Male High School Seniors," *Journal of the American Medical Association* 260, no. 23 (1988): 3441–45.

37. Yesalis, Wright, and Bahrke, "Epidemiological and Policy Issues in the Long Term Health Effects of Anabolic-Androgenic Steroids."

38. See Todd, "Anabolic Steroids."

39. See Yesalis, "Steroid Abuse in Secondary Schools."

40. For example, the Texas Supreme Court has ruled that participation in extra-curricular activities is not a right. See the discussion on no pass/no play in chapter 8.

41. Warren Fraleigh, "Performance-Enhancing Drugs in Sport: The Ethical Issue," *Journal of the Philosophy of Sport* 9 (1985): 23–29.

42. Dirk Johnson, "Illinois School to Extend Drug Tests to All Interscholastic Activities," *New York Times,* August 30, 1989: 94.

43. Yesalis, "Steroid Abuse in Secondary Schools."

44. Todd, "Anabolic Steroids."

45. Robert Hughes and Jay Coakley, "Positive Deviance among Athletes: The Implications of Overconformity to the Sport Ethic," *Sociology of Sport Journal* 8, no. 4 (1991): 307–325; Keith Ewald and Robert M. Jiobu, "Explaining Positive Deviance: Becker's Model and the Case of Runners and Bodybuilders," *Sociology of Sport Journal* 2, no. 2 (1985): 144–56.

46. Hughes and Coakley, "Positive Deviance Among Athletes," p. 308.

47. Ibid., p. 311.

48. Ibid., p. 314.

49. Stark, Kent, and Finke, "Sport and Delinquency," p. 124.

50. See H. G. Bissinger, *Friday Night Lights: A Town, a Team, and a Dream* (Reading, Mass.: Addison-Wesley, 1990).

51. Jill Smolowe, "Sex with a Scorecard," *Time* (April 5, 1993): 41.

52. Yesalis, "Steroid Abuse in Secondary Schools."

53. Brenda Jo Bredemeier, Maureen R. Weiss, David Shields, and Richard R. Schewchuk, "Promoting Moral Growth in a Summer Camp: The Implementation of Theoretically Grounded Instructional Strategies," *Journal of Moral Education* 15 (1986): 212–20; Thomas Romance, Maureen R. Weiss, and Jerry Bockoven, "A Program to Promote Moral Development through Elementary School Physical Education," *Journal of Teaching in Physical Education* 5 (1986): 126–36; Michael

E. Trulson, "Martial Arts Training: A Novel 'Cure' for Juvenile Delinquency," *Human Relations* 39, no. 12 (1986): 1131–40.

54. Trulson, "Martial Arts Training."

55. C. Roger Rees, "Beyond Contact: Sport as a Site for Ethnic and Racial Cooperation," in *Sociological Perspectives of Movement Activity*, eds. Edith H Katzenellenbogen and Justus R. Potgieter (Stellenbosch, South Africa: Institute for Sport and Movement Studies, University of Stellenbosch, 1991), pp. 24–33.

6

Sport and the Education Pay-Off

It would have been impossible for my father to have put all seven of us children through college without the existence of athletic scholarships as we know them today.

> —Heart surgeon Fletcher Johnson of Nyack, New York

I always told our kids three things. The first was "make as much money as you can." I forget what the other two things were.

> —Attributed to former college basketball coach Al McGuire

There is little evidence to support the "rags to riches" account of athletes rising from impoverished backgrounds to attain elite status.

> —Sport sociologist Susan Greendorfer[1]

The skill, mastery, and discipline that the student realizes from sports competition can be transferred to the classroom and translated to other students by student athletes.

> —State Senator Emil Jones of Chicago, Illinois[2]

As role models, student athletes could encourage greater effort among non-athletes, not only to become athletes, but to develop the work habits that lead to academic success.
> —Larry Hawkins, Director of Special Programs, University of Chicago[3]

Sports alone do almost nothing to enhance a person's career—unless that career is in sports.
> —Social historian Allen Guttman[4]

The individuals quoted above—coaches, politicians, and educators—share an interest in one of the greatest myths of school sport. It is the belief that athletics can be used to improve one's financial and social standing in society, in other words, that participation in school athletics "pays off" later. Many of us believe that participation in interscholastic athletics sets boys, and, more recently, girls, on the road to eventual economic success. The paths to the board room, the operating room, and the State House supposedly lead through the locker room. In sports, it is argued, students learn motivation and dedication, which can be transferred to other goals and to education, the high cost of which can be financed through athletic scholarships. For the lucky few, high school sport is seen as a direct path to success, via college, to professional athletics, the pot of gold at the end of the athletic rainbow.

Here we discuss the myth that school sport helps young people get ahead in life. We examine the ideas that make the myth legitimate, the research that tests it, and the controversy that surrounds it. We contrast the anecdotal evidence with the results of research studies, and examine factors that may intervene to reduce or augment the pay off. For example, is there a separate "athletic effect" that sets athletes on the fast track for success in any field they choose, or does success depend upon access to a college education? Can athletic ability in high school help provide the skills necessary for successful college graduation, or do athletics merely raise educational aspirations for high school athletes, aspirations that cannot be achieved because of intellectual shortcomings and/or the demands of quasi-professional sports programs at college? Does the pay-off phenomenon differ depending upon whether we are talking about male or female athletes? Specifically, do athletics open the door to college for more males than females? Do college athletic programs demand less time from female rather than male athletes, or is this view an example of gender stereotyping? Finally, special attention will be paid to the fate of black and other minority athletes since they make up a relatively large proportion of college athletes in the highly visible sports of basketball and football. Here we are concerned with a special case of the pay-off myth, that high school athletics is particularly valuable for male minority students as a ticket out of the ghetto. We begin with the direct route to money and fame for the aspiring male high school athlete, the ultimate dream for many starry-eyed adolescents—not to mention their aging fathers—the dream of being a professional athlete.

High School Athletics and Professional Sports

If the ultimate American dream is to be rich and famous, then, on the face of it, professional athletes make that dream real. Names like Michael Jordan (basketball), Nolan Ryan (baseball), Bo Jackson (football/baseball), Wayne Gretzky (hockey), and Jack Nicklaus (golf) are well known in most American households. These men are public icons, symbols who epitomize the American values of competitiveness, hard work, and success. They, like many other professional athletes, are cited as role models for our nation's youth, the epitome of the best that we can be. They also make a great deal of money from sports.

Superstars in sports may make as much as $5 million or more per year. Of course, such figures are very much the exception rather than the rule. According to sport sociologist George Sage,[5] the average 1989 salaries in the "big four" team sports were $577,200 (National Basketball League), $490,000 (Major League Baseball), $212,000 (National Football League), and $156,000 (National Hockey League).

The public perception is that this is a great deal of money to pay young men for participating in what many of us do for fun in our leisure time, and it is certainly a great deal more than most of us make.

However, if the salaries of superstar athletes are compared to Michael Jackson ($65 million in 1989), or Sylvester Stallone ($38 million in 1989), or other well-known entertainers, they are not spectacular. The average professional career in the "big four" sports has been estimated to be approximately five years.[6] There is going to be considerable variation in this figure depending upon the sport and the position played, but, in general, professional athletics is a risky and short-lived career.

Nevertheless, the salience of professional sport to the lives of adolescents may make them dream of such a career and may affect the time and effort they put into high school and college sport. It is a sobering exercise in reality to calculate the probability of that dream coming true. Various odds have been offered to represent the probability of a high school athlete realizing the career goal of becoming a professional athlete. Using 1980 U.S. census data and 1986 and 1987 team rosters, two sociologists[7] calculated the probability of achieving professional athlete status for different male and female ethnic groups in various sports. They estimated that opportunities for a professional career in sports are highly restricted—for all sports 4 of every 100,000 white males achieved professional status, while 4 of every 1,000,000 white females reached the professional ranks, and 4 of every 100,000,000 black females did. They calculated the probability for black males to be 2 in 100,000 and for Hispanic males to be 3 in 1,000,000. The chances of success are hardly more encouraging when calculated for the four major team sports. In football the odds per one million are 16 for white males and 21 for black males (they are 4 in 10,000,000 for Hispanics). In baseball the odds per million are 12 for whites, 3 for blacks, and 2 for Hispanics. Only 28 out of every 10,000,000 white high school basketball players will make it in the pros along with 65 out of every 10,000,000 blacks. Golf and tennis, the only major professional sports currently available to women, offer odds of 19 and 23 per 10,000,000 for white females.

The equivalent number for black females in tennis is 5 in 100,000,000. There are currently no black female professional golfers.

No matter how the probabilities are calculated, they are extremely low. The message is that school athletes should not put all their career aspiration eggs in the professional athletic basket. They should understand that the chances of achieving, let alone maintaining, a career in professional sports are very slim. These low percentages should be set against the media hype of sport as a means of upward mobility. This is particularly important in the case of black male students who are exposed to many black athletic role models, reinforcing the erroneous assumption that professional sport—or rather professional basketball, baseball, or football—provides a realistic career opportunity for blacks. As sociologist Harry Edwards has noted,[8] if they try to emulate O. J. (Simpson), Reggie J(ackson), Dr. J. (Julius Erving), Kareem Abdul-J(abbar), or Magic J(ohnson), black youth are more likely to end up with "no J," that is, no job at all, after completing their playing career at high school or college. The same could be said for white males. At least female high school athletes are not seduced by this myth, given the paucity of opportunities for women in professional sports.

Most people realize that the odds against becoming a professional athlete are enormous. Consequently, the direct route to fame and fortune for the high school athlete is but a small part of the "high-school-sport-pays-off" myth. Much more widely accepted is the belief that participation in sports at the high school level somehow teaches lessons and values that can be put to use later in life in the job market. Proponents of the pay-off idea see two general processes at work here. The first concerns the belief that athletics teaches teamwork and other interpersonal skills. That is, through experiences in high school, athletes gain advantages over nonathletes in jobs that require interactional skills. The second process concerns the indirect effect of high school athletics: access to college education leading to greater occupational prestige and remuneration. High school sport is seen as an integral part of the school culture through which athletes increase their commitment to educational goals and raise their educational aspirations. These aspirations are turned into educational attainment (i.e., a college degree) as a result of athletic scholarships. Detractors from the pay-off myth are skeptical about the positive effects of high school athletics in both of these processes.

High School Sports, Interactional Skills, and Earnings

Proponents of the interactional skills argument[9] make the claim that high school athletes in team sports learn how to get along with peers in a highly structured, goal oriented, competitive environment. It is assumed that these athletes learn how to adapt their egocentric needs to the team effort and stay cool under the pressure of public scrutiny. This constant public exposure creates maturity and self-confidence. Thus, athletes think of themselves as winners and bring a "can do" attitude to other competitive situations after they have graduated from high school.

Furthermore, it may be argued that the aura of athletic achievement affects their peers. Male athletes are among the most popular students in the school and are idolized by other students (see chapter 3) and by adults in the local community (see chapter 7). Whether the high school athletic experience changes the athletes or not, community leaders may think that it does. The label "athlete" raises the visibility of participants in the eyes of the community and gives them the inside track for hiring and promotion, providing a classic case of the self-fulfilling prophecy. Finally, contacts through "old boy" networks developed by athletes as a result of participation, or used by well-wishers on the athletes' behalf, are instrumental in establishing and maintaining the careers of ex-high school athletes, especially in service professions that place a premium on dealing with people.

The bulk of this argument applies to male rather than female athletes and most of the research on the relationship between athletic participation in high school and subsequent career success has been done with males. If there is a relationship, we would expect it to be stronger for males than for females. Status differences between male and female high school athletes usually exist (see chapter 3), more often in favor of the males than the females. Also, "old girl" networks, if they exist at all, will be less developed than their male counterparts in the business world.

Critics skeptical of the interactional-skills argument point out the lack of evidence for the "sport-builds-character" myth (see chapter 4). They argue that there is nothing in the high school sport experience per se that prepares either males or females for the world of work,[10] that athletics can teach independence or dependence or nothing at all, and that if athletes care only about sport they will find little success outside sport. Finally, they raise the image of the "dumb jock" to counter the image of the "winner."

What evidence can be applied to this controversial issue? Several studies[11] have identified a definite "pay-off" effect of high school athletic participation. That is, the earnings of high school athletes are higher than those of nonathletes some years after graduation, a finding which is independent of social class, socioeconomic status, and all the other factors that usually affect salary differences. For example, one study[12] with a sample of students from the southern United States found that being an athlete in high school had a significant pay-off effect on earnings eleven years after completing high school. On average, former high school athletes earned $252 per month more than non-athletes, but this figure varied depending on athletic subgroup membership (black male athletes made an additional $116 a month and white females an additional $71 a month, when compared to their nonathletic peers).

These findings are interesting and support the interactional-skills argument. However, in a similar study on a nationally representative sample of high school males five years after high school graduation, we found no support for this earlier finding.[13] There was no athletic effect on the earning power of high school graduates who did not attend college, a fact which causes us to question the suggested relationship between playing high school sport and subsequent success in the world of work. Specifically, if athletes do learn interpersonal skills, why does this effect not occur in the early career of the athlete? If a labelling effect is at work, surely this would be greatest immediately after graduation when the memory of the athlete would be fresh in the minds of community members. Likewise, the benefit of a network would likely be greatest early in the athletes' career, before they developed other contacts independent of athletics.

However, there was a major difference between these two studies. Because of the relatively short time span in our study (data were collected five years after graduation compared to eleven years in the previous study), we removed college students from the results. Their earnings would be depressed relative to noncollege graduates who had a four-year head start in the labor market. Thus it is possible that the interactional effects being discussed do not work independently of intellectual ability and that ex-jocks need something more than high school stardom to achieve later job success. That the pay-off from high school sport is dependent upon educational success after high school is discussed in detail in the next section.

School Sport, Educational Aspirations, and Attainment

The idea that the high school athlete—usually a male from a blue collar family—can use an athletic scholarship to complete a college education that he otherwise would have not been able to afford is one of our great cultural myths. One sociologist has referred to it as "an almost sacred belief."[14] It is particularly powerful myth because we like to think of our society as "open" in the sense that we all have an equal opportunity to attain the American dream no matter what our social origins. We also believe in the importance of a college education as the foundation of this opportunity and realize that the cost of such an education is already high and still rising.

This particular cultural myth was reinforced some years ago in the film *All the Right Moves*, in which Tom Cruise plays the part of Stef Georgeovich, the son of a western Pennsylvania steelworker, and the linebacker for the Ampipe High School football team. Stef is a bright student and wants to be an engineer. Football is his way out of Ampipe and into the best engineering program in the country. Only his coach stands in his way. Coach Nickerson is a stereotypical "win-at-all-costs" high school football coach: autocratic, demanding, and dictatorial. He figures Georgeovich is a "wise ass" who won't do as he is told. After a heartbreaking final-second loss to archrival Walnut Heights, Georgeovich has an argument with the coach and is thrown off the team. The incident confirms to Nickerson that Stef has an "attitude problem," and the coach warns off all the college recruiters. It looks as if Stef will be doomed to a life in the steel mill like his brother, father, and grandfather until, in the final reel, Coach Nickerson, on his way to Cal Poly as the new defensive backfield coach, has a change of heart and offers Stef a full scholarship to the university, which happens to have one of the best engineering programs in the country.

All the Right Moves is the stuff of which myths are made. On the other hand, Hollywood did not make a movie about Kevin Ross.[15] His athletic story, although true, does not portray the American dream. Kevin Ross was a 23-point, 20-rebounds-a-game high school basketball star from Wyandotte High School in Kansas City. Like Stef Georgeovich, he was going to use sport to get a college education, but unlike Stef he was not a great student. Despite shaky academic credentials he received a basketball scholarship to Creighton University but was not successful, and, in four years, started fewer than ten games. He also had academic problems and "majored in eligibility," taking non-academic courses in an attempt to maintain a grade point average high enough to play college ball. That he experienced academic difficulties is not surprising because, although he had sixteen years of schooling, he had never learned to read or write. Creighton University, feeling some responsibility for Kevin yet ill-equipped to handle his problem (traditionally universities are not expected to teach students how to read and write), paid for him to enroll in Westside Prep in Chicago, where he joined the eighth-grade class.

There are many real-life Stef Georgeoviches and, unfortunately, there are also plenty of Kevin Rosses. What is the relationship between high school athletics and educational success? In the next section we examine the research behind the myth, first as it pertains to performance in high school and then the extent to which athletes are able to use their ability to get a college degree. We begin with the relationship between participation in athletics and the high school grade point average, a popular measure of academic achievement.

School Sport and the GPA

Grade point average has often been used (and abused) in the argument over the actual relationship between athletics and academics in high school.[16] Nonbelievers in the value of high school sports (the skeptics) point to early studies[17] showing that athletes' grade point averages were lower than nonathletes. The skeptics subscribe to the "dumb jock" image of high school athletics, which holds that participation in high school sports distracts the athletes from their academic goals. On the other hand, believers in the educational value of high school athletics (the believers) can cite research showing that athletes have the same, and sometimes a higher, GPA than nonathletes,[18] and can explain this difference in a number of ways that place high school athletic performance in a positive academic light.

Believers in the myth might assume that athletes could be motivated to keep their grades up so that they could remain academically eligible to play. Athletics could teach them positive values that could transfer into positive study habits. Athletes could be forced to budget their study time because of the demands of their various sports. Or, the self-esteem gained from athletics could create a higher level of aspiration in other areas, including academics.

In turn, the skeptics counter by pointing out that athletes may be graded more leniently than nonathletes, may take easier courses than nonathletes (in order to maintain eligibility), and may get extra help to compensate for the class time missed as a result of athletic participation. Moreover, if they were too dumb to keep their grades up, they might have become athletic dropouts, and consequently be counted in the nonathlete group.

It is hard to choose between the opposing positions in this debate. First, both sides are making assumptions that go well beyond the results of the studies. Implicit in the believers argument is the assumption that the outcome of high school athletics is positive. Whereas self-esteem may increase as a result of participation in sport, it may also decrease. There is nothing in the athletic experience that inevitably leads to positive outcomes. Nevertheless, this myth is still being espoused by the proponents of athletics in our nation. Consider the recent Knight Foundation report on intercollegiate athletics: "Games and sports are educational in the best sense of the word because they teach the participants and the observer new truths about testing oneself and others, about the enduring values of challenge and response, about teamwork, discipline and perseverance."[19]

The assumption that athletic involvement automatically detracts from academics is equally erroneous. Grade point averages cannot be used to support or refute the "sports-are-educational" myth. For one thing, understanding the relationship between high school athletic performance and GPA is impossible unless the athletes are categorized into subgroups based on parents' occupation, socioeconomic status, race, and gender—all of which are variables of academic performance in their own right. In addition, a GPA is only as good as the academic status of the courses upon which it is based. The need to remain eligible for high school sport and a possible athletic scholarship to college provides an extra incentive for some athletes to find relatively easy courses to pad their GPA. This practice has been recognized recently by the National College Athletic Association and is built into Proposition 48, the eligibility rule for freshman entering college. In order to play in his or her freshman year, the incoming student must have a minimum cumulative GPA of 2.00 in eleven academic units.[20]

Clearly, differences in grade point average between athletes and nonathletes do not tell us very much. To argue that a higher GPA for high school athletes than nonathletes is evidence that athletes' grades do not suffer as a result of participation in sports oversimplifies the picture.[21] Calculating an overall GPA for athletes and nonathletes, one study of male basketball players in public and private schools in the Washington, D.C., area showed that black athletes got lower grades in school than did white athletes even though there was no difference in the degree to which the groups value academic or sports success.[22] Ironically, blacks were more likely than whites to see basketball as a positive influence on their lives, helping them to keep grades up. The author of the study felt that since blacks tended to come from less wealthy backgrounds than whites they had fewer resources available to use in the competitive academic environment at school, particularly in private school, where blacks often were recruited for their basketball skills.

To summarize, we are suggesting that overall comparisons between GPA scores for athlete and nonathlete groups does little to explain the educational pay-off myth of high school sports. Kevin Ross got Cs and Ds at Wyandotte High School. His principal remembers him reading and writing below grade level, but this did not stop him from getting a college scholarship. To understand how this happened it is necessary to look at the relationship between participation in high school sport, educational aspiration, and educational attainment, of which GPA is but a part. The effect of sports on the educational aspirations of high school athletes is the subject of the next section.

School Sport, Educational Aspirations, and College Entrance

One of the most consistent findings in the research on the relationship between high school sport and education is that athletics increases participants' educational aspirations. This means high school students' expectations of acquiring a college education are increased as a result of playing high school sport. This is particularly true for male students from low socioeconomic backgrounds who normally would not view college attendance as a realistic post-high school option.[23] Some studies also have identified a positive athletic effect on the educational aspirations of female athletes, but a recent analysis of the responses of over 6,500 female students as high school sophomores and again as seniors failed to confirm this result.[24]

A study of almost 12,000 male high school seniors in 1980 with follow-up interviews in 1982 showed that participation in high school athletics also has a positive effect on college attendance.[25] However, when the researchers controlled for the effects of race, socioeconomic status, and cognitive development, some interesting trends were discovered. The positive effect of participating in sport on potential college attendance was most evident among students who had lower cognitive development, that is, the students who were least suited to college entry. This relationship held for whites, blacks, and all but one subcategory of Hispanics (those with high social status, good parental relations, and high cognitive development). In other words, no matter what the race, high school athletics opens the doors of colleges to those students who are *least* qualified to pass through them.

The believers explain the finding that high school athletes have high educational aspirations by emphasizing the positive interpersonal contacts made through sports, particularly for lower-class male athletes. Through high school athletics these boys gain access to the "leading crowd," the social elite of the school. This latter group usually comprises children of educated and wealthy parents who see college attendance as a natural progression after high school graduation. The athletes internalize these values of the "leading crowd" and raise their sights toward a college education. Furthermore, because of their star value in the community, they receive special counseling from teachers, coaches, and other significant community members about how to realize these academic dreams. Access to such information would have been denied them without the positive exposure of high school athletics.

In addition to the personal-contact hypothesis, believers of the myth also might employ the "athletic-involvement-helps-academic-success" argument. This belief holds that high school athletes improve their academic performance, grades, and overall self-concept as a result of participation in sport, which in turn increases their expectations of college attendance and ultimate graduation.

Those skeptical of sport's educational pay-off would not deny that participation in high school sport increases the educational aspirations of the athletes, but they would disagree with the believers on the interpretation of this finding. Rather than see athletes' aspirations for a college education as a positive step on the road to upward mobility, the skeptics would see it as a cruel hoax. From the skeptics' viewpoint, high school athletes, particularly those from nonacademic backgrounds without the necessary "educational capital" that can later be translated into educational success, are being set up for eventual academic failure at college. After being used for four years (or five if they are "red-shirted"*) by colleges in the quest for the fame and fortune that winning sports is reputed to bring, they will be returned to society with no degree, no education, and very few job prospects.[26] This is a valid point since it is with students of low cognitive abilities that the positive effect of sports participation on college attendance is the greatest.

A 1989 report by the Women's Sport Foundation focusing on the effect of high school varsity participation on the social, educational, and career mobility of minority students found that sport was neither a dead end nor a road to success. This study reported on the progress of a nationally representative sample of African-American, Hispanic, and white youth from their sophomore year in high school to four years after high school graduation. It found that athletic participation in high school enhanced the athletes' popularity and their involvement in school and in the community. Minority athletes did better academically than nonathletes, not because of sports, but because they already were more academically inclined than their nonathlete peers. The report also found that sport was not associated with minority success in the work force after graduation. The study concluded that "our findings run counter to the popular view that sport provides an automatic pathway to upward mobility for minorities."[27]

The Women's Sport Foundation study did not report on the college graduation rates of minority athletes although it did show that black male athletes from urban high schools were almost four times more likely than nonathletes to report having worked toward a bachelors degree after high school. The contentious issue of athlete

---

*Being "red-shirted" means that college athletes sit out a year of athletic participation usually because they are injured in the pre-season practice or in the early part of the season.

graduation rates is reviewed in the next section as the final step in the "sport-pays-off" myth.

School Athletes and College Graduation: The Jock Trap

The focus in this section is the degree to which college athletics can provide a realistic opportunity for athletes to attain their educational aspirations, which, as we have seen in the previous section, have often been fostered as a result of involvement in sports at the high school level. Although the research is almost exclusively on schools classified by the NCAA as Division I, it is at this level that the results are most important, since Division I schools provide the athletic scholarships which are the means to the ends of educational success in the educational myth scenario. Furthermore, examination of the different academic success rates for male and female athletes or for athletes in different sports in these institutions may shed more light on the opportunity/exploitation debate. To the extent that gender and type of sport differences exist, this may be a reflection of the extra pressure placed on athletes in the "revenue-producing" sports.*

The believers of the "education pay-off" myth may take support from the generally positive view of intercollegiate athletics presented in the 1991 report of the Knight Foundation Commission. This report gave a vote of confidence to the educational credibility of the vast majority of the 828 athletic programs at colleges and universities catering to over 254,000 student-athletes that comprise the National Collegiate Athletic Association.[28] The report was, however, less sanguine about the state of big-time athletics, which characterizes a highly visible minority of programs in the NCAA. Of particular concern to the members of the commission were the admission and graduation statistics for athletes in such programs. For example, at half of all Division I-A institutions, basketball and football players not achieving minimal university entry requirements are accepted as "special admits" at a rate ten times higher than that permitted in the rest

---

*Namely, football and basketball

of the freshman class. Also, in a typical Division I college or university, only 33 percent of male basketball players and 37.5 percent of football players graduate within five years.[29]

Clearly, the majority of athletes entering basketball and football programs at Division I schools are unlikely to turn their aspirations of graduation into reality. Their initial academic deficiencies are exacerbated by the demands of these high-powered programs which require that they devote about thirty hours a week in season to their sport.[30] Critics estimate the time spent in sports in big-time programs to be much higher than that: fifty to sixty hours a week in-season if travel time is included, and eighteen hours a week in the off-season.[31]

A study[32] of the academic performance of athletes from one NCAA Division I school over a four-year period underscores the problems. College athletes' GPAs vary relative to the athletes' race, gender, and type of sport (revenue versus nonrevenue) and their high school academic performance. This study showed that minority athletes tended to enter the university less well-prepared academically than whites, and that these discrepancies continued at the university level. Yet minority athletes received a higher proportion of scholarship assistance than whites because they were playing predominantly in the revenue-producing sports. The authors concluded that academic performance was the price athletes had to pay for involvement in the revenue sports. White female nonrevenue sports participants as a group had the highest academic performance.

That the academic survival of some athletes at college is a legitimate concern was reinforced by an in-depth study of 167 male student-athletes participating in football and basketball at one NCAA Division I school.[33] Based on several indicators of academic performance measured over one academic year, the study found 19 percent of the athletes "passing easily." By the end of the academic year these students had passed an average of 15.3 credit hours per semester with a GPA of 3.222. Most of the student-athletes (55 percent) were classified as "getting by." This group of athletes maintained a GPA slightly above the NCAA requirement of 2.0 but only through dropping courses in which their grades were low. The remaining student-athletes (26 percent) were classified as "struggling along." In the fall semester these athletes registered for an average of 13.6 credits but passed only 5.1 credit hours with a GPA of 1.791. Although their performance was better in the spring semester (passing an average of 10.1 hours of the original 13.6 registered, with a GPA of 1.778), they fell far short of the NCAA requirement of a 2.00 average for 24 credit hours for the academic year.

The demands of big-time college sports are in part responsible for these results. A 1987 NCAA report on the responses of over 4,000 college students showed that football and basketball players spent more time on sports than on classes. Student-athletes also reported that they had less time to participate in other student activities than nonathletes and were more isolated.[34] However, many athletes enter the university with sport rather than education uppermost in their minds.

Another recent NCAA study assessed the reasons given by 344 male and 261 female undergraduate student-athletes from fifteen Division I baseball and twenty-two softball teams for their choice of university.[35] Both baseball and softball players placed the "amount of scholarship" choice very high on the list (first for the baseball players and second for the softball players). Clearly most of these athletes see some sort of financial aid as essential to their college choice. It was also interesting to note the differences between the male and female athletes. Indicators of the colleges' scholastic attributes, i.e., "academic program" and "curriculum/major," were ranked seventh and ninth on a list of ten by the baseball players, but third and seventh by the softball players. In the authors' view, some baseball players may attend college simply to gain the experience necessary for professional baseball. Female softball players, without the professional opportunities of the male athletes, are more concerned with academic factors. This study did not assess the athletes' aspirations for a professional career, but in the NCAA survey referred to above, about 23 percent of the football and basketball players, as well as 30 percent of the athletes in other scholarship sports, reported in their freshman year that they intended to become professional athletes after graduation.

If students enter the university with the career goal of professional athletics, however unrealistic that goal may be, they are in danger of suffering academically. In one of the early studies on athletes' educational aspirations and attainment, sociologist William Spady[36] showed that athletic ability alone did not lead to college graduation. He divided his sample of male high school students into subgroups based upon other extracurricular activities such as student government. Following the academic fortunes of these subgroups through college, he found the lowest graduation rates among the "athletes only" group, those whose only extracurricular activity was athletics.

More recent in-depth studies of the "lived experience" of university athletes confirm the conclusions of the survey research reviewed above. In one case study[37] the authors lived for four years with male college basketball players in the dormitory of a Division I university and became intimately associated with the athletic and academic experiences of the athletes. The players, mostly from lower- and middle-class backgrounds and mostly black (70 percent), entered the program as freshmen believing in the "educational pay-off" myth with dreams of college graduation and a good job. One freshman said, "If I can use my basketball ability to open up the door to get an education, hopefully I can use my degree to get a good job."[38]

However, the dual pressures of big-time athletics and the demands of college work were too much to handle for most of these athletes. Over the four-year period their early idealism was replaced by an attitude of pragmatic detachment toward academics. The players' priorities were transformed as they became disillusioned by the demands of college work, which were often beyond their intellectual ability, were advised by coaches who were under pressure to win, and reinforced by a peer culture which devalued academics and reinforced sport. In general, the athletes grew increasingly cynical about and uninterested in academics and accepted their marginal status as students. Some became preoccupied with maintaining eligibility rather than graduating, while others had abandoned any educational aspirations by their senior year and pinned their hopes on a professional basketball career.

However, a more optimistic picture was painted of women's college athletics.[39] In-depth interviews with senior basketball and volleyball players at one Division I school indicated that the female athletes generally strengthened their academic resolve as their college education progressed. One athlete said, "I put more emphasis on [education] as I get older. First of all I realize how lucky I am to get a free education, and I better start taking advantage of it. And I want to be as smart as I can be, and I don't want to be a dumb shit, so I can get a good job and people will say, 'That girl has her stuff together, she knows what she is doing.' "[40]

The author of this study, Barbara B. Meyer, cited the lack of professional athletic outlets for women, the lack of public recognition for women's sport, and the lack of a "jock" mentality by the female athletes generally as reasons why the women maintained their commitment to education. She also noted a difference in socioeconomic background between the women she interviewed and the male basketball players in the previous study.

Clearly the educational fortunes of college athletes are mixed. The skeptics would see the material presented in this section as a ringing indictment of the whole system of big-time college athletics, and might view the Knight Commission as a form of "damage control" to prop up this hypocritical system.[41] Critics also would question the Commission's blanket endorsement of the majority of NCAA programs without any evidence for or against. On the other hand, the supporters of college athletics could respond that college graduation rates are generally higher for athletes than for nonathletes. The five-year graduation rate for all Division I athletes entering college in 1984 was 56.1 percent compared to 47.9 percent for all students in general.[42] However, as we have seen in the case of the high school GPA, general measures may mask specific differences. For example, the Southeastern conference had a graduation rate of 46 percent for the student body compared to 36.4 percent for athletes. Sixty Division I schools did not graduate any basketball players from the class of 1984.

The material presented in this section shows that although high school athletes receive college scholarships, in many cases they find it difficult to use these scholarships to achieve a college degree. The myth of the "athletic free ride" obscures the reality that in most Division

I schools athletics is a business run primarily for the benefit of the schools. Colleges give scholarships to athletes for athletic, not academic, performance and it is not surprising that the demands of college sports interfere with academics. This is especially true if the athletes are marginal students in the first place, but conflict can occur for all student athletes. For example, tailback Robert Smith quit the Ohio State football team at the beginning of the 1991 season claiming that the coaches were less concerned with the education of athletes than with keeping them eligible to play. Besides being an outstanding college football player, Smith was a gifted student who found it impossible to combine the demands of a pre-med major with big-time college football.[43]

The reality of college athletes seems to fall somewhere between the believers' and the skeptics' positions. Some athletes, particularly those who have authentic academic credentials, will be able to balance the often conflicting demands of athletics and academics to graduate in four or five years. Others will struggle and face the choice of dropping athletics for educational reasons or giving up on academics and concentrating on sports. The latter choice is often made by athletes who are not educationally oriented or have no alternative to an athletic scholarship as a means of financing their education. They are caught in the "jock trap" of college athletics. To the extent that black male athletes as a group are primarily in the time-consuming commercial sports of basketball and football, they are in greater danger of falling victim to the "jock trap" than are others.[44] Female college athletes are more likely to be able to translate academic aspirations into college success.

Summary

If the believers of the "high-school-sport-pays-off" myth were to write the script for *All the Right Moves II,* a follow-up on the career of Stef Georgeovich four years after high school graduation, they would adopt a positive scenario. We would see Stef as an academic all-

American in his final year at Cal Poly about to graduate in engineering after a successful college football career. There would be the probability of a good job in engineering waiting for him after graduation, or, if the job market were tight, the possibility of a career in coaching. Coach Nickerson, just promoted to the head coaching job at Cal, would offer him a graduate assistantship, the first step on the long road of sponsorship in the college coaching profession. In his capacity as a college football coach, Stef could then help other high school students like himself use football to get an education and make a success out of life.

On the basis of evidence presented in this chapter we could offer two other scenarios for *All the Right Moves II,* one of them "professional," the other "educational." In the "professional" scenario Stef becomes progressively more involved in football the longer he stays at Cal Poly. By the end of his junior year he has lost interest in engineering and transfers to communications so he will have more time to devote to his sport. Realizing that his size limitation will definitely hurt his prospects of becoming a linebacker in the NFL, he begins to use anabolic steroids and the growth hormone in combination with a intense weight-lifting program during the off-season. By the end of his senior year he is a 250-pound "monster" back who stands a good chance of winning the Outlands trophy for the best college defensive player, and is very likely to be picked in the first round of the NFL draft, and make millions of dollars playing professional football. An alternative plot for this scenario would be for Stef to sacrifice his college education for football, only to have his professional hopes dashed by a career-ending injury in his senior year.

Under the "educational" scenario, the old interpersonal problems that dogged Stef's relationship with his high school coach resurface in his freshman year of college ball. After disagreeing with Coach Nickerson over a defensive assignment, he loses his starting job to the big junior college transfer from Texas. Generally disillusioned by the conflict of juggling the demands of big-time college football and an engineering major, he quits the team to concentrate on his studies. With the help of student loans and part-time jobs he is able to offset the educational costs incurred by the loss of his football scholarship, and graduates "summa cum laude" with a degree in engineering after four years.

This chapter has dealt with the possibilities of all three scenarios as part of the "high-school-sport-pays-off" myth. We have found little support for the belief that participation in athletics in high school teaches skills that can be used to the athletes' advantage in the job market after graduation. Some high school athletes eventually will become professional athletes, but the very low probability of this makes it an extremely unrealistic career choice.

The most popular element of the "high-school-sport-pays-off" myth is the belief that athletes can use sport to get an education. Based upon results of large-scale surveys of high school athletes over their high school and post high school academic career, as well as in-depth studies of athletes' college experiences, the validity of this myth also must be challenged. Participation in high school sports may raise educational aspirations and provide access to college via athletic scholarships, but college graduation is a different matter, especially for male athletes in the "revenue-producing" sports, and especially if these athletes are from black or other minority groups.

High school sport may open doors to college for athletes, but it does little to guarantee that they will walk out of those doors four or five years later with a degree. If athletes are deficient in academic skills in high school, they are not likely to gain those academic skills at college. Indeed they are much more likely to major in academic eligibility at college and take courses only to maintain the required GPA. In this situation the only chance of a pay-off is a pro contract, and the odds against this are very great.

On the other hand, there is hope for athletes who have solid educational credentials in high school and who participate in college athletic programs that do not monopolize their time and commitment. The message of this chapter is that the "pay-off" myth may raise aspirations, but high school athletes need to keep their eyes on the prize of education rather than sport. We should be believers and skeptics at the same time.

Notes

1. Susan L. Greendorfer, "Psycho-Social Correlates of Organized Physical Activity," *Journal of Physical Education, Recreation, and Dance* 58, no. 7 (1987): 60.

2. *Sport and Education* 1 (Winter 1985): coverleaf.

3. "Publisher's Statement: A Rationale for Action," *Sport and Education* 1 (Winter 1985): 2–3.

4. Allen Guttman, *A Whole New Ballgame: An Interpretation of American Sports* (Chapel Hill, N.C.: University of North Carolina Press, 1988), p. 137.

5. George H. Sage, *Power and Ideology in American Sport: A Critical Perspective* (Champaign, Ill.: Human Kinetics, 1990), p. 160.

6. Wilbert M. Leonard II, *A Sociological Perspective on Sport* (New York: Macmillan, 1988).

7. Wilbert M. Leonard II and Jonathan E. Reyman, "The Odds of Attaining Professional Athlete Status: Refining the Computation," *Sociology of Sport Journal* 5, no. 2 (1988): 162–69.

8. Harry Edwards, "The Collegiate Athletic Arms Race: Origins and Implication of the 'Rule 48' Controversy," *Journal of Sport and Social Issues* 8, no. 1 (1984): 14.

9. Luther B. Otto and Duane F. Alwin, "Athletics, Aspirations, and Attainments," *Sociology of Education* 42 (1977): 102–113; J. Steven Picou, Virginia McCarter, and Frank M. Howell, "Do High School Athletics Pay? Some Further Evidence," *Sociology of Sport Journal* 2, no. 1 (1985): 72–76; Norman R. Okihiro, "Extracurricular Participation, Educational Destinies, and Early Job Outcomes," in *Sport and the Sociological Imagination*, eds. Nancy Theberge and Peter Donnelly (Fort Worth, Tex.: Texas Christian University Press, 1984), pp. 334–49.

10. Jay J. Coakley, *Sport in Society: Issues and Controversies,* 4th ed. (St. Louis, Mo.: Times Mirror/Mosby, 1990), pp. 83–84.

11. For example, Otto and Alwin, "Athletics, Aspirations, and Attainments"; Picou, McCarter, and Howell, "Do High School Athletics Pay?"

12. Picou, McCarter, and Howell, "Do High School Athletics Pay?"

13. Frank M. Howell, Andrew W. Miracle, and C. Roger Rees, "Do High School Athletics Pay? The Effects of Varsity Participation on Socioeconomic Attainment," *Sociology of Sport Journal* 1, no. 1 (1984): 15–25.

14. William G. Spady, "Status, Achievement, and Motivation in the American High School," *School Review* 79 (1971): 380.

15. Edward Menaker, "Former Wyandotte Star Tries to Make Up for System's Failure," *Kansas City Time,* October 5, 1982: Sec. D.

16. See Barry D. McPherson, James E. Curtis, and John W. Loy, *The Social Significance of Sport* (Champaign, Ill.: Human Kinetics, 1989), pp. 69–72 for a review.

17. For example, Elwood C. Davis and John A. Cooper, "Athletic Ability and Scholarship," *Research Quarterly for Exercise and Sport* 5, no. 4 (1934): 68–78.

18. Richard A. Rehberg, "Behavioral and Attitudinal Consequences of High School Interscholastic Sports: A Speculative Consideration," *Adolescence* 4 (1969): 69–88; Walter E. Schafer and J. M. Armer, "Athletes Are Not Inferior Students," *Transactions* 5 (1968): 61–62.

19. Knight Foundation Commission on Intercollegiate Athletics, *Keeping Faith with the Student-Athlete: A New Model for Intercollegiate Athletics* (Charlotte, N.C., March 1991), p. 3.

20. Ibid., p. 15.

21. Donald F. Soltz, "Athletics and Academic Achievement: What Is the Relationship?" *NASSP Bulletin* (October 1986): 20–24.

22. Othello Harris, "Athletics and Academics: Contrary or Complementary Activities?" in *Sport, Racism, and Ethnicity*, ed. Grant Jarvie (London: Falmer Press, 1991), pp. 124–49.

23. See Eldon E. Snyder and Elmer Spreitzer, "Sport, Education, and Schools," in *Handbook of Social Science of Sport*, eds. George F. Luschen and George H. Sage (Champaign, Ill.: Stipes, 1981), pp. 119–46 for a review of these studies.

24. Merrill J. Melnick, Beth E. Vanfossen, and Donald F. Sabo, "Developmental Effects of Athletic Participation among High School Girls," *Sociology of Sport Journal* 5, no. 1 (1988): 22–36.

25. Eldon E. Snyder and Elmer Spreitzer, "High School Athletic Participation as Related to College Attendance among Black, Hispanic, and White Males: A Research Note," *Youth and Society* 21, no. 3 (1990): 390–98.

26. See, for example, Edwards, "The Collegiate Athletics Arms Race"; Sage, *Power and Ideology in American Sport*, pp. 182–84.

27. Women's Sport Foundation, *Minorities in Sport: The Effect of Varsity Sports Participation on the Social, Educational, and Career Mobility of Minority Students* (New York: 1989): 5.

28. Knight Foundation, *Keeping Faith with the Student Athlete*, p. 3.

29. Ibid., p. 16.

30. Ibid.

31. Edwards, "The Collegiate Athletics Arms Race"; Sage, *Power and Ideology in American Sport*, pp. 183–84

32. Gary Kiger and D. Lorentzen, "The Relative Effects of Gender, Race, and Sport on University Athletic Performance," *Sociology of Sport Journal* 3, no. 2 (1986): 160–67.

33. Richard M. Brede and Henry J. Camp, "The Education of College Student-Athletes," *Sociology of Sport Journal* 4 (1987): 245–57.

34. Irvin Molotsky, "For College Athletes in the Major Sports, Games Come First," *New York Times,* November, 30, 1991: 1A, 28D.

35. Carrie A. Doyle and Gary J. Gaeth, "Assessing the Institutional Choice

Process of Student-Athletes," *Research Quarterly for Exercise and Sport* 61, no. 1 (1990): 85–92.

36. William G. Spady, "Lament for the Letterman: Effects of Peer Status and Extra-Curricular Activities on Goals and Achievements," *American Journal of Sociology* 75 (1970): 680–702; Spady, "Status, Achievement, and Motivation in the American High School," pp. 379–403.

37. Peter Adler and Patricia A. Adler, "From Idealism to Pragmatic Detachment: The Academic Performance of College Athletes," *Sociology of Education* 58 (1985): 241–50.

38. Ibid., p. 243.

39. Barbara B. Meyer, "From Idealism to Actualization: The Academic Performance of Female Collegiate Athletes," *Sociology of Sport Journal* 7, no. 1 (1990): 44–57.

40. Ibid., p. 47.

41. Shannon Brownlee and Nancy Linnon, "The Myth of the Student-Athlete," *U.S. News and World Report* (January 8, 1990): 50–52.

42. Mike Lopresti, "Universities Have a Weak Record with Basketball, Football Players," *USA Today,* March 27, 1991: 6C.

43. Austin Murphy, "Goodbye Columbus," *Sports Illustrated* (September 9, 1991): 46–49.

44. A 1992 survey showed that while blacks comprised only 6 percent of all the students at the 245 Division I colleges, they held 42.7 percent of the football scholarships and 59.9 percent of the men's basketball scholarships. See Douglas Lederman, "Blacks Make Up Large Proportion of Scholarship Athletes, Yet Their Overall Enrollment Lags at Division I Colleges," *Chronicle of Higher Education* 41, no. 1 (1992): 1, A30–A34.

7

School Sport and the Community

There is nothing to replace it. It's an integral part of what made the community strong. You take it away and it's almost like you strip the identity of the people.
  —Brad Allen, president of the Permian High School booster club
    on the impact of high school football in Odessa, Texas[1]

I think it gives them a shot in the arm on Friday night and Saturday night, because they can forget all their worries about, I've got to pay the electric bill on Monday.
                —Oregon-Davis coach Dan Warkentien on the effect of
                high school basketball on the town of Hamlet, Indiana[2]

The Senior Ceremony

It was the last day of football practice for the season at Jefferson High School. Parents, members of the booster club, cheerleaders, and even a few band members were present. At a signal from the head coach, the normal routines of practice ceased and all players

153

ran to the center of the practice field. Then, an assistant coach, with all the senior players following, ran off the field and out of sight. The other players assembled in front of the goal posts on one end of the field as all of the visitors watched from the sidelines.

Trumpet players, excused from the marching band's regular practice, began playing taps as the seniors reemerged and ran a gauntlet of underclassmen before symbolically hitting the blocking sled, which had been positioned at the goal posts, for the last time. The head coach stood on the sled as pairs of players took turns blocking the sled's padded arms.

Following this, each senior made a brief farewell speech. Representatives from the junior and sophomore players, as well as each assistant coach, then saluted the seniors who would be leaving the team forever after the next night's game. The head coach was the last to speak. Almost as soon as he began, he broke into tears. He cut his speech short and began hugging the senior players before shaking each one's hand. At this point, most of the seniors also were crying, as were all of the cheerleaders and many of the visiting parents.

The seniors then formed a huddle and gave a cheer. The underclassmen cheered the seniors as a parent consoled the head coach, who was still wiping tears from his eyes. All of the players ran the full length of the field and were joined by the coaching staff. Parents left the field talking in soft voices about the beauty of the ceremony and how proud they were of the team and the coach. In the background, practice resumed.[3]

The individuals participating in this ceremony—players, coaches, cheerleaders, band members, parents, and booster club members—faced a common crisis. The team's seniors, those players and sons, were soon to leave the team and assume new status positions, new roles. The void they would create in doing this would result in stress for the individuals and a crisis for the team. The senior ceremony described above was intended not only to honor the seniors for their contributions to the team, but to enable the participants to cope better with the stresses related to this change.

Additional by-products of the ceremony included the promotion of common values and cohesion among group members, and the shuffling of roles and status positions within the group. For example, the juniors present were elevated to high-status positions within the team. For the first time all season, a junior, not a senior, initiated the action of calling a team meeting after practice that day.

Finally, the attendance of parents and community members, at the invitation of the head coach, demonstrates the reciprocal relationship between school and community. An event as important as this one demanded the presence of community representatives. In turn, the community members added to the perceived importance of the event for the team and the school. Moreover, those community representatives left the event with renewed commitment for football, the school, and the value of athletics.

The senior ceremony described above, along with other sport-related activities such as homecoming or post-season tournaments, is an example of a complex cultural ritual, an event that can be understood on a number of different levels, but overall seems to have a symbolically unifying effect. For example, the Olympic Games serve as a source of inspiration for individual athletes, as a forum for political protest for some nations and for others as a means of gaining international recognition and prestige. Overall, the Olympic Games provide the world with a sense of unity.[4]

In the senior ceremony, high school athletics serves as a rite of passage for the students and provides a shared sense of unity for the community. As we shall see, high school sport is the principle source of such feelings in many communities throughout the country. Particularly for small cities and rural communities, high school sport may be the only game in town. When the school team wins, the community feels good about itself, even if economic or social conditions are bleak.

Successful teams symbolize a successful school, and the community can be proud of the character that is being built in its youth. However, a community should not lose sight of the fact that winning football does not guarantee a quality education or a unified community. It is victory in sport that creates community spirit, and that victory may be at the expense of the community down the road. For example, incidents in high school sports may initiate or perpetuate local rivalries which unite "us" against "them."

Moreover, since high school sport has an intergenerational element (i.e., grandfathers and sons may have played for the same school team), it helps to create the impression of cultural continuity rather than cultural change. However, community ethnic or racial tensions caused by the attempts of minority groups to take a more active role in community politics may find their way into high school sports. While a winning team may temporarily allay or cover up these tensions, it is no substitute for community reform. Communities are always in a state of change and sometimes high school sport is symbolic of the status quo, especially in the eyes of the "disenfranchised."

School Sport as a Celebration of Community

High schools in America tend to represent communities, that is, towns, small cities, or neighborhoods in large cities. Frequently the name of the school is the name of the community (e.g., Scarsdale [New York] High School or Western Hills or Northside High School in Fort Worth, Texas).

James Coleman has noted that seldom do most communities experience common goals[5]; there are few events, such as a natural disaster, to "engender a communal spirit and make members feel close to one another by creating collective goals." Games or contests between communities or between the athletes that represent them are one of the few mechanisms to provide a common goal. Sometimes this function is served by professional teams, but more often it is accomplished with school-aged athletes. Most towns and cities do not have professional teams to represent them, and even in those cities which do have professional teams, many citizens find it much easier to identify with high school sports. Professional players seldom seem as though they are real members of the community. Moreover, given the distances between cities with professional teams, few professional games bring members from the competing communities together except electronically via television.

It is different though with high school sports teams. "The community supports the team, and the team rewards the community when it wins. The team is a community enterprise, and its successes are shared by the community, its losses mourned in concert."[6] It has been this way since the 1920s (or earlier) in most towns and small cities across the United States. A number of early sociological studies of American communities noted that the success of high school sports teams was a source of prestige in the community as well as in the school.

In towns and cities across America, on billboards and especially on water towers, whose contents are necessary to sustain life, are displayed symbols of pride necessary to sustain the spirit. The simplicity of the statements and their similarity from one community to the next are testaments to their power. "Lorena Leopards State Champions 1985" (seen along Interstate 35 in central Texas) means "We're number one." As does the sign on Highway 49 south of Jackson, Mississippi, which proclaims Magee "3A State Football Champs, 1984," and the one which states matter of factly, "Farmington, NM Scorpions, 1986, 1984 Baseball State Champions."

In Broken Bow, Oklahoma, the local "Savages," who have been state champions nine times, are celebrated on the water tower and several signs and buildings around town. A few miles down Highway 259 there is a green-and-white sign looking much like a state highway information sign that declares Idabel as the "Oklahoma Track Capital" and lists the championship seasons. There are hundreds, probably thousands, of similar signs across America proudly announcing for all who pass their way that the residents of this place are special, that the athletes here are champions, and that in this community "We are number one."

For many people, high school athletics helps to fill a void. Local sports teams can provide a tremendous sense of accomplishment, even for those who have done nothing more than sit in the bleachers and cheer. A team, especially a winning team, is more than the players and coaches. The power of a team seems directly proportional to the number of fans who support the team and to the level of the fans' unwavering support. Fans believe they are an important element in the team's success. If the fans don't cheer them on, the team is less likely to win. This belief is reflected in the popular reference to the fans as the "12th man" on an eleven-player team.

Sport symbolizes the school and the school remains the single most important symbol for many communities across America. Thus when a school athletic team wins, the entire community can bask in the reflected glory of its young gladiators. When the team wins, it can cast the entire community in a positive light and community members feel proud. They believe that victory is important, and they assume that others—especially those neighboring communities they have beaten—feel the same way.

If you think football is important and you support your school's team, and if our team beats your team, then our school beats your school, our community beats your community. Our team has made us the victorious and you the vanquished—and we won't soon let you forget it. We *are* number one.

Victory by our high school team makes us feel good. Moreover, we believe that it correctly demonstrates that we are worthy. Therefore we can be justifiably proud of our accomplishment, of our abilities as fans and spectators.

It is not surprising, then, that communities are less interested in what high school sport does for the participants and more interested in what it does for the fans. A dozen or so young athletes can make thousands of fans feel good about themselves and their community. Lest anyone question the use of young gladiators for this purpose, there are always principals and coaches and a few former hero-players to remind everyone that sports are good for the athletes because "sport builds character."

While boys' athletics, especially football and basketball, are usually noted as the primary bearers of the community's prestige,[7] that has not always been the case. For example, in 1926 the Palatka High School girls basketball team won the state championship. Palatka is a small city on the St. John's River in northern Florida. The community was so proud that the local Rotary Club, over the objections of the principal who feared it would interfere with their studies, sponsored the team on a trip to Philadelphia and Washington, D.C.[8] These female athletes served as ambassadors for this small southern city while beating northern basketball squads and thereby further enhancing the city's reputation. Today, the role of girls basketball continues to function in a similar fashion in communities across the state of Iowa.

In 1925 girls high school athletics was forced out of the Iowa High School Athletic Association (IHSAA) by men who felt that "competitive sports before crowds that paid admission was good only for the boys."[9] As one man argued, "I coached girls basketball once, and my conscience has bothered me ever since for the harm I might have done the girls."[10] As a result of the action by the IHSAA, supporters organized the Iowa Girls' High School Athletic Union, which now provides athletic competition for 29,000 girls in thirteen sports. These include five-player and six-player basketball, tennis, golf, swimming, softball, indoor and outdoor track, cross country, gymnastics and volleyball for girls, as well as coed tennis and golf. Girls basketball, however, may be the premier high school sport in the state.

The state championship tournament is over eighty years old. In some families, four generations of athletes may be present at the tournament, which boasts a tourney attendance of 90,000 annually with over $300,000 in ticket sales. In addition, television and radio broadcasts carry the games and tournament spectacle across Iowa and to surrounding states.

Iowa is the only state with a separate association for high school girls athletics, and the only state where it is never said that revenues from boys sports pay for girls athletics. That girls can function as gladiators for local communities has been recognized by Jim Enright in writing about high school athletics in Iowa.[11] "If a school is well-known for a winning tradition, the sport for which it is well-known will usually be girls' basketball first, wrestling second, and girls' softball third."[12]

High school athletics can serve as a celebration of community. "A local team is not only an expression of the moral integrity of a community; it is also a means by which that community becomes conscious of itself and achieves its concrete representation."[13] While this statement originally was made in reference to professional sports, it is obvious that it applies even more strongly to high school sports where the athletes are homegrown sons and daughters of local citizens who participate in the full range of the community's structures, organizations, and activities. For example, it may be known where the left tackle goes to church, where he gets his hair cut, where he works during the summers, who his girlfriend is, and what all of the members of his family are like. There is no question that this left tackle is part of the community. When he excels, the whole community can be proud, for through him it also has excelled. "The team acts in many ways as the symbolic community that unites belief systems and authority structures with peoples' everyday lives."[14]

At games, students and other members of the community come together for a common purpose. They are united, at least for the duration of the contest. Personal differences, politics, even business matters may be put aside. Those gathered view themselves as the community, united against another community. Everyone pulls together, and in so doing the community generates uncommon energy and commitment. With community members acting in unison with the force of passion, for the very dignity of the community is at stake, the whole is more than the sum of its parts.

These generative effects are greater in some communities than in others. Hence it may be surmised that the role of high school athletics is greater in some communities than in others. It might be expected that the effects are greatest "in communities in which residents have a greater sense of community identification, and which have fewer alternative outlets for expression of community pride."[15] Generally this would mean that smaller communities and those with stable populations (i.e., not much in- or out-migration) would more likely experience the beneficial generative effects of high school sports.

With the possible exception of an unusual period of demographic growth, it has been difficult for the citizens of most towns and cities to measure their civic worth. A high school sport team's record can give a community such a sense of accomplishment, and thereby add meaning to its collective life.

Small communities in particular can cherish the dream of receiving recognition and prestige when the local high school team "knocks off" a larger and more favored opponent in post-season competition. In the case of the Oregon-Davis Bobcats of Hamlet, Indiana (population 640), this chance came in March 1988, when the high school basketball team reached the play-offs in the Indiana State Basketball Tournament. This was an example of life copying art, or rather film, since the true story of Milan High School winning the same championship in 1954 was the subject of the popular film *Hoosiers.*

Although the Bobcats lost their bid to reach the quarter finals in a game against a school with a student body over ten times larger than their own, the event was the subject of articles in the *New York Times* and *USA Today,* as well as an ABC News "Nightline" program. In this program, the picture was presented of a small town that had fallen on hard times being held together by its high school basketball team.

High school sports may serve an additional function for American communities—they can help glue such communities together across socioeconomic divisions and across generational divisions. Sports have been called the coin of social interaction.[16] Sports are the common idiom that links Americans, whether friends or strangers. As a topic of conversation sports are safe, even expected, especially of males: with a cabby in a taxi, in a hotel bar, by the office water cooler, with a convenience store clerk or shoeshine stand operator, sports are the best initial topic of conversation. Within a community marked by a single high school, that school's sports programs become the single best topic for conversation.

High school sports also serve to link generations within communities. Traditionally this is especially true for males, but with the growth in participation by girls, school sports may become equally important for females, just as girls basketball has in Iowa. Within a community, young and old will be familiar with the high school's teams, past and present. Not only athletes can share experiences of games from former times. Everyone is expected to remember the big games or those with unusual or special circumstances. With the athletes, however, there may be a special bond—that which pertains to those who have undergone common rites of passage, who now have special status and share secret knowledge.

In 1973 and 1974, anthropologist Walter Precourt studied a small Appalachian community of 800 people in southeastern Kentucky. In his description of high school basketball, Precourt provides a good example of how high school sport can integrate a community across generations.[17]

Basketball serves as the locus of interactions among members of all identity groups in this Kentucky community, as defined by age, sex, kinship affiliation, social status, or occupation. Basketball organizes the diversity within the community while maintaining a continuity of experience.

High school games are important. At such times, there are more community members assembled in one place than at any other community event. However, informally organized basketball events are critical in linking the generations. No one in this rural town grows too old for basketball. Games are played at homes or on small plots of farmland, using rims attached to trees, telephone poles, or the side of a building. Especially significant are the games played at a local gas station.

Participants may include fathers and sons, brothers and sisters, or peer groups of varying sizes and ages. Adult males, particularly those who formerly played high school basketball, are frequently involved in these activities. High school alumni also may assemble in the school gym for informal games, with high school and elementary school students participating with them or watching from the sidelines. At the school's homecoming there is a regularly scheduled game between members of the high school team and an alumni team.

The idea presented in this illustration is that high school sports provide a source of identity for local communities. Perhaps because different ethnic, racial, and socioeconomic populations are represented in schools, particularly in smaller communities, high school sports sometimes can provide a rallying point for all community members. Support for the local high school team can reach across race, ethnic, and class differences, seeming to unite the community in a sense of harmony.

However, this image of the community, united behind the ritual of high school athletics and the myth that "sport builds character," is a rather simplistic picture. The term "ramified" has been used to describe the different cultural interpretations of sport.[18] This term literally means "branches" or "offshoots," as from a plant. If the image of a tree is used to characterize the cultural significance of high school sport, then the trunk of the tree represents the image of community solidarity. (In earlier chapters we identified the roots of the tree as muscular Christianity, and showed how "new growth" in the form of "American" values were grafted onto old stock imported from Britain.) Branches of this tree may have different meaning and represent different forces or tensions in the community. They can be looked at separately from the trunk. One such branch is entertainment.

School Sport and Community Entertainment

Entertainment is a very important function of high school sport and the community is often willing to pay for the opportunity to celebrate itself through athletics. This is especially true when high school sport is the only game in town. Competition with other sports, as well as nonathletic forms of inexpensive entertainment, is experienced in most large cities. However, even small towns are not immune from these effects of competitive entertainment outlets. Consider the case of Breckenridge, Texas, population 7,000.

Breckenridge is a small oil boomtown in west Texas where high school football has built a winning tradition and fierce community pride.[19] The school has captured four state football championships outright and tied for the championship in two other years.

In a newspaper article, Louise Bloxom, owner of a local feed store, said, "Our football heritage goes back to oil boom days. The oil companies would hire men to work for them who had husky sons, so we always had good teams. . . . Football was a wonderful thing. It held the town together. We were special. We were from Breckenridge."[20] However, in the past few years Bloxom has noticed that enthusiasm for football is not as strong as it used to be, except when the team goes on a winning streak.

In the same article, Pat Ward, editor of the *Breckenridge American,* said almost everyone in the community is a fan. "It is the biggest event in the city. Residents are proud of the team and that pride is handed down from generation to generation."[21] Besides, there is little other entertainment in town. "The football games give people something to do," Ward says. "It furnishes entertainment and involvement. People are doing things together."[22]

On the other hand, James C. Rominger, president of Citizens Bank and a member of the Boosters Club, says, "Used to, we didn't have anything but high school football, so we devoted a lot of attention to it."[23] However, he thinks television has made a difference. "Going to a college game was a big deal several years back," he says, and "television has made a difference in the degree of enthusiasm for high school football. We can see college and professional football on television and the Dallas Cowboys are big in west Texas now."[24]

A high level of high school sport as entertainment also can result in big business. In Valdosta, Georgia (population 38,000), a perfect football season, i.e., one with no defeats, will result in ticket sales of about $250,000.[25] While this may be exceptional, many school districts, and their local communities, do well with the business of high school sports, especially football.

Consider the case of the suburban Birdville Independent School District in north central Texas.[26] There are two high schools in the district, which has a total population of about 70,000. In 1977, the Birdville Stadium had revenues of $83,730 in eleven weeks of football, in spite of bad weather on four of those Friday nights. School Superintendent W.G. Thomas has said, "A shower Friday afternoon about 7 o'clock could take $2,000 or $3,000 off your income."[27]

While most of the income is used on the football programs, a small "profit" ($3,031 in 1977) can be used to help finance other sports, including junior high school football and other nonrevenue-producing sports.

The economic effects of high school football are not limited to the school district; football is a source of income for the sixty adults who work at each of the varsity games. At Birdville, these include eight officials, four to eight police officers, twelve or thirteen parking attendants, thirteen to sixteen concession workers, eight ticket sellers, four ticket takers, two ambulance attendants, a doctor, and four persons who work in the press box. An electrician and a stadium manager also are on duty for each of the games.

Booster clubs, sometimes called athletic associations, quarterback clubs, or groups named after the local school's mascot, are the common means for community involvement in high school athletic programs. While the specific roles and activities of such organizations vary, generally booster clubs, composed of parents and other adult community members, provide financial assistance for school sports in addition to official support from property tax revenues allocated by the school system.

Booster clubs may build new playing fields or practice areas, donate and equip weight rooms, donate labor and materials to construct or repair facilities, even supplement coaches' salaries with gifts of money, cars, boats, expensive shotguns, or other material expressions of their gratitude for the coaches' efforts with the community's youth, usually as manifested by winning seasons.

For example, consider the Touchdown Club, the forty-year-old high school booster club in Valdosta, Georgia.[28] The Touchdown Club has about 1,200 members, but the school has no parent-teacher association. The club raises around $40,000 each year which is used to pay for pregame meals and two weeks of football camp for team players.

Community members, as individuals or collectively through booster clubs, exert influence on many aspects of high school sports. They can influence the youthful athletes, the coaches, and the school as a community institution.

The influence of the community on young athletes primarily is through the establishment of norms. Communities set the expectations for participation. For example, in many small communities, every able-bodied boy is expected to play football.

In Valdosta, where the Wildcats are consistently ranked among the top teams in the nation, boys begin their football training in the spring of sixth grade, or as early as the fourth grade if they participate in the football programs run by the Boys Club or the YMCA. Jane O. Hansen has described the Valdosta system: "Through a sophisticated machine, four junior high programs feed into the high school program with coaches at all levels teaching the same plays and number system. By the time they reach high school, the youngsters are well trained."[29] The high school coach already knows who will likely be his starting quarterback four years from now.

Coach Nick Hyder spends a lot of time watching the sixth-graders practice, and gets to know all his future prospects. "I want to know them, I want to know their teachers, I want to know their parents. And I want them to know I care about them."[30] He is a frequent speaker at the sixth-grade football banquets. Hyder rationalizes this by saying, "It's like the people in New England. Harvard is the tradition there. Here, it's football."[31]

Communities also determine the rewards for athleticism. Those who clearly lack athletic talent may be ridiculed while praise is publicly heaped on those who excel. Recognized star athletes may be rewarded materially as well. Cushy jobs or gifts may be given to local sports heroes. In addition, the prestige awarded to star athletes is its own reward, often creating special, exceptional rules. Authorities—for example, teachers or police—may look the other way or be more tolerant or exempt the athlete from normal sanctions. Absences, tardiness, rudeness, school pranks, lost or incomplete homework, or low grades may mean one thing for the average student and something quite different for the athlete.

The community's influence on the coach probably correlates directly with the amount of financial resources it provides the sports program. It is not unheard of for a large contributor to give a coach advice about strategy, specific plays, or even starting lineups. Nor is it considered exceptional when the son of a large contributor gets the nod over another youth of roughly equal ability to quarterback or captain a team.

The way the community influences the school as an institution is evident in the way salaries are established in many communities.

School boards typically pay coaches more than other teachers, even when they require them to teach fewer classes than other teachers, or even require them to teach no classes. Moreover, when there is a search for a new principal, it is common for a coach to be promoted to the position. After all, a respected coach has many of the requisite skills to be a good principal. Not only do coaches tend to become principals, but later they may become superintendents.

In our experience, a respected coach is often a stern authoritarian with students and a person with whom civic leaders feel comfortable. In many traditionally oriented communities, it is not required that coaches or principals have a superior command of English grammar, mathematics, pedagogical techniques, or be knowledgeable in educational philosophy.

It is not surprising that schools—or at least their administrators, principals, and coaches—often attempt to manipulate the community by giving citizens what they seem to want most from schools—winning athletic programs. Conventional wisdom among these educators holds that it is easier to obtain tax increases or get bond issues passed if the community is pleased with the job that schools are doing with sports.

Of course, communities may take direct action in such matters. For example, James Coleman has reported[32] that in Paris, Illinois, which won a state basketball tournament in the 1950s, the community voted funds for a large, new gymnasium even though the school remained without a library. In another school, Coleman reports[33] that around 1960 the school built a new gym and a new reading room; money for the gym was donated by a community member while the reading room was constructed with school building funds from taxes.

Vernon is a rural west Texas town. The sign says the population is 12,001; the school stadium really does seat 5,400.[34] The $19,000 scoreboard was donated by a local business. The high school boasts an indoor multipurpose workout facility 120 x 60 feet. The building is 25 feet tall and carpeted with Super Turf. Construction costs were $63,000; it was built entirely with contributions from local businesses and the booster club. In 1987, in spite of a depressed economy in west Texas, weight facilities were added at a cost of $27,000; again, no tax dollars were needed.

School Sport and Community Division

The identification and entertainment function of high school sports can put a lot of pressure on the players and coaches. In towns with proud traditions of victory, a losing season is an insult. In the extreme, a community's fixation with sports can elevate high school athletics to unbelievable heights. According to author Buzz Bissinger,[35] the Permian Panthers of Odessa, Texas, perennial winners in Texas high school football, were the most sacred icon of the town. "Football stood at the very core of what the town was about, not on the outskirts, not at the periphery." Permian football was "as intrinsic and sacred a value as religion, as politics, as making money, as raising children."

Bissinger reported that after the team lost in 1988 by one point to archrivals Midland Lee (after being favored by three touchdowns), people had trouble looking head coach Gary Gaines in the eye. "It seemed as if he had violated some sacred public trust."[36]

When a town has so much feeling invested in the fortunes of thirty or so adolescents who play football, the unity it so desperately wants exacts a heavy price. Often the community down the road is the common enemy. As Odessa attorney Michael McLeaish put it about the relationship between the people of Odessa and the people of Midland, a few miles to the east: "I don't like people from Midland. They don't like us and we don't like them. I just can't stand those bastards and they feel the same way about us."[37]

Interscholastic rivalries do nothing to reduce these tensions; in fact, they may increase them if the community emphasizes victory, and through victory the belief that you are better than your opponent. High school basketball playoffs in Nassau County, Long Island, New York, occasionally fall victim to such intergroup rivalries. The fear of violence at the games can become so great that they sometimes have to be played at a neutral site without any audience. The location of the game is kept a secret from the communities for fear that the contest will spark rioting by rival fans.

It is because high school sport represents the community that tensions within the community will be reflected in sport. Anthropologist Douglas E. Foley has noted this in his study[38] of high school football in a southwest Texas town, where the community was not only split between Anglos (non-Hispanic whites) and Hispanics, but the Hispanics were divided between those who sought accommodation with Anglo institutions and those who chose political confrontation as the best means of dealing with Anglo society. In such a situation, the pressures on students and players were significant and compounded by racial tensions.

For example, the head coach, who was Hispanic, was placed in an impossible situation. Part of the moderate group of Mexican Americans in the town, he was perceived as a "sellout" to the Anglos by the more radical Hispanic activists. On the other hand, some of the more conservative Anglos were upset that a Hispanic coach had been chosen over a conservative Anglo candidate. Since his coaching style was easy going, he was also criticized for not being a strong disciplinarian and for not conforming to the stereotypic image of the authoritarian coach. Foley concludes that, "The coach had the double jeopardy of being neither manly enough nor white or brown enough to lead North Town youth into battle. He was constantly challenged to prove himself, both to the Hispanic activists and to the more redneck Anglos."[39]

Racial stereotypes dominated the discussions of many aspects of high school football in this town, from coaching style to who should play. Should the coach start the "strong-armed Mexican boy" or the "all-around smart Anglo boy" at freshman quarterback? Racial tensions also affected the homecoming ceremony, one of the traditional rituals of community solidarity. The homecoming king and queen, typically considered to be the best of the future generation of the community, were elected by the student body. According to tradition, the queen and her court, dressed in evening gowns, would be transported to the football game in convertibles. The queen would be crowned as the centerpiece of the half-time ceremony. On this occasion, however, the queen and her retinue all were Hispanic and the usual convertibles did not appear. The queen had to suffer the indignity of walking to her own coronation, amid charges of discrimination and racism.

Perhaps the most dramatic recent example of high school sports splitting a city and its school is that of Conroe, South Carolina.[40] In 1989 the Conroe Tigers were a pre-season favorite to win the state championship. Then, before the beginning of the season, the returning senior quarterback, who had led the Tigers to an 8 and 4 record the previous year, was moved to defensive back. The former quarterback, who is black, was replaced by a white, who happened to be the son of an assistant coach.

This reassignment of a player to a different position led to a series of political confrontations that spread from the team to the school to the community. It resulted in thirty-one of the team's thirty-seven black players joining a boycott; the local head of the NAACP, who was a middle-school teacher, being fired by the school board; and the previously highly touted Tigers finishing the season 1 and 11 while being outscored 42 to 332.

Discrimination, not football, became the issue. For example, in a county where 30 percent of the population is black, only 10 percent of the teachers are blacks. Large numbers of blacks began attending school board meetings, demanding change. The confrontations continued for months after the football season had ended. In fact, the initial controversy seemed almost forgotten.

This case, which received national media coverage (e.g., *Sports Illustrated,* "ABC Nightly News," and "Nightline"), demonstrates that sports can undermine a community as easily as they can build one. The ritual effects of sports can serve as a multiplier. Where there are shared values, common traditions, and a sense of community, these may be enhanced by high school sports. Do not expect, however, that sports can work miracles where there is divisiveness or distrust.

The most that can be hoped for is that team members and community members may learn to work together for the accomplishment of a common goal that requires the cooperation of everyone in order to assure success. There is no evidence, however, that such cooperation will change people's values or their perceptions of others. The existing data indicate that even under the best of circumstances, there is no apparent carry-over from the playing field to other spheres of life.[41] Such changes are likely to take generations and require changes of social structure as well as individuals' experiences in sport.

Incidents at homecoming and disagreements about who should play or start on high school football teams seem relatively small matters when set against the larger issues of racial and political struggle in society. That they are of great significance within the communities in which they occur is understandable; that they make the news outside these communities attests to the significance of high school sport as public ritual. Community solidarity may provide the trunk of the tree that represents high school sports as a cultural symbol, but a different picture of that performance is seen from the branches. Myth is a conservative force in any society and a hedge against social change that seems too rapid. The conclusion of the anthropological study of one southwest Texas community was that it showed

> how deeply implicated community sport—in this case high school football—is in the reproduction of class, gender, and racial inequality. The white ruling class and the town's patriarchal system of gender relations are preserved in spite of concessions to new ethnic challenges.[42]

Summary

Schools continue to change, albeit slowly, and the role of sport in schools also continues to evolve. Traditionally sport has symbolized school for many Americans, and schools continue to symbolize communities. Since the professionalization of schooling in the early decades of this century, sport has been the primary avenue for community participation in the schools. High school sports can be a source of civic pride, and sports also can be good business in local communities.

Moreover, school sports help unite community members at various stages in the life cycle.[43] For many it is a common experiential bond, a set of behaviors and related sentiments in which they have or will have participated at one level or another, in one or more roles, at various points in the life cycle.

As the Iowa Girls' Basketball State Tournament demonstrates, the ritual of the event, as much as the play of the games, "fulfills a collective need for entertainment, allows for reaffirmation of traditional values, acts as an acceptable vehicle for changing social status, ensures the continuation of the organizational structure, and lastly, in the eyes of the viewers and participants, proclaims Iowa's superior high school girls' sport program."[44]

Sport is more than entertainment. It is a cultural performance— a cross between a medieval morality play and the Roman *circus*. Thus, simultaneously, high school sport can provide a common goal and be a celebration of community. Participation in the ritual of high school sport helps reinforce a sense of community as well as a collective identity.

However, like the Roman *circus*, high school sport runs the risk of becoming more an entertainment spectacle and less like a community festival. Sometimes athletes feel like gladiators fighting for their lives and, symbolically, for the honor of the community. In fact, this image was used by Jerrod McDougal, starting offensive tackle for the 1988 Permian High School Panthers, to describe high school football. "It's like the gladiators. . . . It's like the Christians and the lions, like Caesar standing up there and saying yea or nay."[45]

If high school sport becomes too much "entertainment" and not enough "community," then performance criteria such as victory take precedence over process criteria such as celebration of community unity. The message of rituals such as the senior ceremony described at the beginning of this chapter get lost in the bigger message that our team (or school or community) is better than yours. This "in-your-face" style of community relations has its down side.

As we have tried to show, high school sport sometimes generates too much tension within and between communities. It certainly reflects the tensions and disagreements which already exist in the community that it symbolizes. Since high school sport is seen as an institution, an "invented" tradition that makes the status quo legitimate, it often is used as a conservative force in society.[46]

Rather than bringing immigrant minority students, in this case Mexican and Vietnamese, into the mainstream of school life in Garden City, Kansas, sociologist Mark A. Grey found that the rituals of sport increased their isolation.[47] Participation in athletics, particularly football, was an important way for lower-class students to gain status. However, most immigrants found this a difficult proposition since they had no background in the game. Furthermore, their failure to make the team was seen by some residents as evidence of their unwillingness to become part of mainstream American life.

When the victory of adolescents in sport becomes the principal, if not the only, measure of community worth, then the "sport-builds-character" myth has been blown out of proportion. As we shall see in the next chapter, the power of high school sport is such that it can blind a community to the realities of education and the need for educational reform.

Notes

1. H. G. Bissinger, *Friday Night Lights: A Town, a Team, and a Dream* (Reading, Mass.: Addison-Wesley, 1990), p. 43.

2. ABC News "Nightline," "The Oregon-Davis Bobcats," ABC News Transcript 1780 (March 18, 1988).

3. Taken from field notes; Andrew W. Miracle, "Talent, Task Orientation, and Ritual in a High School Football Program" (Paper presented at the Seventy-second Annual Meeting of the American Anthropological Association, New Orleans, November 1973); Aidan Dunleavy and Andrew W. Miracle, "Understanding Ritual and Its Use in Sport," in *Sport and the Humanities: A Collection of Original Essays*, ed. William J. Morgan (Knoxville, Tenn.: Bureau of Educational Research, University of Tennessee, 1979), pp. 21–22.

4. John J. MacAloon, "Olympic Games and the Theory of Spectacle in Modern Societies," in *Rite, Drama, Festival, Spectacle: Rehearsals Toward a Theory of Cultural Performances*, ed. John J. MacAloon (Philadelphia: Institute for the Study of Human Issues, 1984), pp. 241–80.

5. James S. Coleman, *The Adolescent Society: The Social Life of the Teenager and Its Impact on Education* (New York: The Free Press, 1961), p. 42.

6. Ibid.

7. August B. Hollingshead, *Elmtown's Youth: The Impact of Social Classes on Adolescents* (New York: J. Wiley, 1949).

8. *The Palatka Daily News*, March 3, 23, 25, and April 27, 1926.

9. Chris Lage, "Iowa Girls' Basketball" (Unpublished paper, Department of Sociology, Texas Christian University, 1987), p. 3.

10. Ibid.

11. Jim Enright, *Only in Iowa* (Des Moines, Iowa: IGHSAU Press, 1976), cited in Lage, "Iowa Girls' Basketball."

12. Ibid., p. 9.

13. Barry Schwartz and Stephen F. Barskey, "The Home Advantage," *Social Forces* 55 (1977): 657.

14. Richard Lipsky, "Political Implications of Sports Team Symbolism," *Politics and Society* 9 (1979): 68.

15. Mark S. Mizruchi, "Local Sports Teams and Celebration of Community: A Comparative Analysis of the Home Advantage," *The Sociological Quarterly* 26 (1985): 516.

16. Gregory P. Stone, *Games, Sports, and Power* (New Brunswick, N.J.: Transaction Books, 1972).

17. Walter Precourt, "Basketball, Social Structure, and Cultural Transmission in an Appalachian Community" (Paper presented at the Annual Meeting of the American Anthropological Association, Washington, D.C., 1976).

18. MacAloon, "Olympic Games and the Theory of Spectacle"; Roberta J. Park, "Sport, Gender, and Society in a Transatlantic Victorian Perspective," in *"Fair Sex" to Feminism: Sport and the Socialization of Women in the Industrial and Post-Industrial Eras,* eds. James A. Mangan and Roberta J. Park (London: Frank Cass, 1987), p. 73.

19. Orville Hancock, "Football Obsesses Them: At Breckenridge, Buckaroos are in the Blood," *Fort Worth Star-Telegram*, September 7, 1985: 1A–2A.

20. Ibid.

21. Ibid., p. 2A.

22. Ibid.

23. Ibid.

24. Ibid.

25. Jane O. Hansen, "Football 'the Biggest Show' in Some Georgia Towns," *Atlanta Journal and Constitution*, December 28, 1986: 1A, 10A.

26. Kara Rogge, "The Business of High School Football," *Fort Worth Star-Telegram*, Evening, November 1, 1977: 1B.

27. Ibid.

28. Hansen, "Football 'the Biggest Show' in Some Georgia Towns."

29. Ibid., p. 10A.

30. Ibid.

31. Ibid.

32. Coleman, *The Adolescent Society*, p. 42.

33. Ibid.

34. Whit Canning, "Emotion, Devotion, Resurrection," *Fort Worth Star-Telegram*, Morning, September 13, 1990: Section 3, p. 9.

35. Bissinger, *Friday Night Lights*, p. 237.

36. Ibid., p. 240.

37. Ibid., p. 207.

38. Douglas E. Foley, "The Great American Football Ritual: Reproducing Race, Class, and Gender Inequality," *Sociology of Sport Journal* 7, no. 2 (1990): 111–35.

39. Ibid., p. 120.

40. Hank Hersch, "Choosing Sides," *Sports Illustrated* 71, no. 22 (1989): 42–44, 46, 63.

41. Andrew W. Miracle, "Factors Affecting Interracial Cooperation: A Case Study of a High School Football Team," *Human Organization* 40, no. 2 (1981): 150–54; C. Roger Rees and Andrew W. Miracle, "Participation in Sport and the Reduction of Racial Prejudice: Contact Theory, Superordinate Goals, Hypothesis or Wishful Thinking?" in *Sport and the Sociological Imagination*, eds. Nancy Theberge and Peter Donnelly (Fort Worth, Tex.: Texas Christian University Press, 1984), pp. 140–52.

42. Foley, "The Great American Football Ritual," p. 111.

43. Precourt, "Basketball, Social Structure, and Cultural Transmission in an Appalachian Community."

44. Janice A. Beran, "The Iowa Girls' High School Basketball Tournament Viewed as an Institutionalized Ritual," in *Play as Context*, ed. Alyce Taylor Cheska (West Point, N.Y.: Leisure Press, 1981), p. 157.

45. Bissinger, *Friday Night Lights*, p. 7.

46. Foley, "The Great American Football Ritual," p. 31.

47. Mark A. Grey, "Sports in Immigrant, Minority, and Anglo Relations in Garden City (Kansas) High School," *Sociology of Sport Journal* 9, no. 3 (1992): 255–70. Also see Douglas E. Foley, "Mesquaki Sports Participation as an Adolescent Rite of Passage," *Journal of Ritual Studies* 7, no. 1 (1993) for a description of the disenfranchisement of Native Americans and high school sports.

8

School Sport, Education, and Corporate Needs

Manufacturers and men of affairs have noted the marvelous strides Germany has made in recent years in the industrial world, and have studied the reasons and have found them not in the advantages which Germany possesses in raw material, in means of transportation, or in other of the material things which we possess to a degree far in excess of any other country in the world, but in the development of the educational system of Germany on technical and industrial lines, and they are demanding a modification of our educational system on similar lines.

> —L. D. Harvey, Superintendent of Schools,
> Menomonie, Wisconsin (1907)[1]

I came at the education problem as an economic and global competitive issue. I'd been traveling to Japan a lot in the late seventies and early eighties and [had] been thinking about our competitive situation, which was dire. It hit me that by the year 2000 we'd be out of qualified workers. . . . Businesses change because competition forces them to. But institutions don't change without outside

pressure. So business must make clear its requirements, push the schools for structural change.
—David T. Kearns, former CEO of Xerox Corporation, appointed Deputy Secretary, U.S. Department of Education in 1991[2]

We're not going to sit idly by and let Texas become a backwater state. The issue is not no-pass/no-play. The issue is no-learn/no-earn. . . . We must have an educated work force in Texas in order to attract the business, industry, and jobs to our state that are vital to keeping Texas a leading economic force.
—Mark White, Governor of the State of Texas (1986)[3]

Nothing in either our state constitution or statutes entitles students to an absolute right to participation in extracurricular activities.
—Texas Supreme Court (1985)[4]

By now it should come as no surprise to see criticism of our schools by leaders of business and education alongside statements about the proper emphasis on sports in high school. In the past, business leaders have viewed sport as a way of instilling the discipline and loyalty in youth necessary for their future roles as workers in American society. They also subscribed to the "sport-builds-character" myth and the belief that it demonstrated the "American" spirit of competitiveness and dedication to victory. That is why business leaders such as J. P. Morgan, John D. Rockefeller, and Andrew Carnegie helped to finance the Public School Athletic League (PSAL) in New York. At the turn of the century, victory in sport was symbolic of America, a nation newly arrived on the world scene and destined to be number one, if it had not already obtained that status. In the words of one historian of the period, "The teamwork and intense specialized training needed to prevail in games such as football also clearly reflected the commercial competitive dictates of the new corporate-industrial order."[5]

The leaders of American industry felt that their workers needed to be loyal and punctual, but not necessarily good academically. Critics of this policy[6] have argued that high school sport actually has socialized youth into a passive acceptance of the status quo and the need to be controlled by autocratic leaders. The status of athletes in adolescent cliques is based on athletic ability, not academic ability, and often the two characteristics are seen as mutually exclusive. For example, the rather unkind saying exists that football players need to be bright enough to learn the plays and dumb enough to think they matter.

The evidence shows that being an athlete does not improve one's chances of being a good student and that sport does not make poor students good students or good students even better. A great deal of emphasis is placed on the athletic performance of athletes but much less on their academic performance. In our universities, for example, some athletes major in "maintaining eligibility," particularly in football and basketball. Some, like Kevin Ross (see chapter 6), leave college after four years of athletics without being able to read or write. At the high-school level the community demands for entertainment sometimes preempt the demands of education.

What happens when business leaders perceive that the educational needs of the nation have changed? When America is obviously no longer number one, either in international sport or in international business, what happens to the "sport-builds-character" myth? Can high school sport be adapted to fit the new educational model or will it lose its significance as a national symbol? This chapter reviews the historical links between education, sport, and the changing needs of the American corporate economy. We present a recent case study that illustrates the symbolic role of high school sport in the struggle for contemporary educational reform.

The Evolution of the Modern School

During the industrializing era from the end of the Civil War through the early years of the twentieth century, schools in nonurban America were viewed as the center of a community's social life. The school offered a site for entertainment, and much of that entertainment nominally focused on the community's children. School picnics, poetry readings, and ice cream socials were open to the entire community and were not intended just for the families of students.

Commonly such assemblages had important political and social functions in addition to entertainment. Local politicians and civic leaders were featured prominently at many of these events. Moreover, since many high schools required subscription fees and since only affluent families could afford to do without the labor of their teen-aged children, frequently only students from the top of the social hierarchy were able to attend high school. This added to the social importance of school functions, which tended to reinforce the local status quo.

By the 1890s, the agenda of urban schools already differed considerably from that of schools in the rest of the United States. Urban schools were the focus of attention for social and educational reformers who sought to remedy the problems of youth resulting from immigration and industrialization. Calls for laws restricting child labor accompanied those demanding compulsory education.

Starting around 1900, following the municipal reform movement, the reorganization of American education began. Control of schools was placed in the hands of a few local business and civic leaders to oversee the expenditures of school funds raised through local property taxes.

The reorganization of schools was required because educational needs had changed. Between 1865 and 1900, fourteen million immigrants entered the United States, and following the turn of the century another one million persons immigrated annually. It was necessary to enculturate these masses of immigrants, especially the children, so that they could be productive members of American society. The immigrants were poor, unskilled, and spoke little English; schools were a natural institution for providing skills and inculcating values.

Child-labor laws and compulsory education were instituted between 1890 and 1910. These laws marked the beginning of the custodial nature of American schooling. Partly in response to the growth of labor unions, children could no longer be employed in the place of adults. Anxious citizens demanded that these poor and unemployable children be taken off the streets and institutionalized.

The period between 1911 and 1925 saw the gradual professionalization of teaching and educational administration.[7] It was pre-
dictable that the model for schools in this rapidly industrializing society
would be the factory. The first quarter of this century was marked
by a tremendous growth in the number of schools and the size of
the student population. Schools utilized double and even triple sessions.
Departmentalization was implemented, along with efficiency surveys,
the use of standardized tests to measure productivity, and the use
of records and reports to demonstrate efficiency.

The emerging industrial base of the American economy in the
early decades of this century required workers trained to accept
punctuality, dependability, obedience to authority, good health habits,
and above all, the notion of hard work as the means to success.
Success, of course, became synonymous with financial success.

Public schools were to provide workers for the assembly line.
Local school boards were to insure that this goal was met as efficiently
as possible. Managers and professionals would come from the middle
and upper middle classes who could send their children through private
preparatory or public high schools and even on to college.

Industrial magnate Andrew Carnegie was a proponent of educational reform that would result in more practical education for
students. Fully congruent with prior and subsequent anti-intellectual
traditions in American education, Carnegie wanted schools to provide
a better work force for American industry. Carnegie's concern extended
to higher education, for he believed that men had been sending their
sons to colleges

> to waste energies upon obtaining a knowledge of such languages
> as Greek and Latin, which are of no more practical use to them
> than Choctaw. . . . They have in no sense received instruction. On
> the contrary, what they have obtained has served to imbue them
> with false ideas and to give them a distaste for practical life. I
> do not wonder that a prejudice has arisen and still exists against
> such education. In my own experience I can say that I have known
> few young men intended for business who were not injured by
> a collegiate education. Had they gone into active work during the

years spent at college they would have been better educated men in every true sense of that term. The fire and energy have been stamped out of them, and how to so manage as to live a life of idleness and not a life of usefulness has become the chief question with them. But a new idea of education is now upon us.[8]

In 1912, an editorial in the *Springfield Republican* called for a system of educational accountability.

New York City spent last year nearly $35,000,000 for education, and hardly a dollar of it was spent for measuring results. Are educators supposed to be such experts that their methods cannot be improved? Lately we have had a striking demonstration of what experimental science can do by reducing the motions in laying brick and the fatigue in handling pig iron. It can hardly be pretended that scientific efficiency is of less consequence in the schools.[9]

As an institution that was to serve all American youth, it was deemed essential that those charged with responsibility for schools be held accountable by higher political authorities.

From the second decade of this century through the end of World War II, schools across America increasingly adopted an emphasis on industrial arts, training, and preparation for occupations, just as an increasing percentage of youth continued their education past the age of mandatory compulsory attendance.

The emphasis on practical training was not the only change in the academic curricula of twentieth-century high schools. There also was a new emphasis on inculcating common values in students. Those values that schools emphasized included patriotism, undoubtedly owing to the two world wars in the first half of the century and to the perceived need to infuse a sense of national identity into immigrants and first-generation Americans. Other values taught by schools were those compatible with the industrial, corporate fabric of the United States: values that would make for good workers.

Since the end of World War II, schools have experienced several crises which demanded public attention. The first of these was the baby boom. It resulted in the necessity of increased school construction, the training and hiring of masses of new teachers, and increases in taxes and the passage of local bond issues to pay for these. A new awareness of education also was promoted by the GI bill of rights, which enabled many parents of baby boomers to get a college education and thus to raise the level of educational expectation for future generations. Another measure of general concern for education was the growth of parent-teacher organizations such as the Parent-Teacher Association (PTA).

This democratization of American education, however, presented schools with new problems. More community members were demanding a voice in the education of their children, and those voices were now more heterogeneous. High schools, staffed by middle-class professionals, were faced with the responsibility of educating most of the entire community's children—lower class, blue collar, middle class, and upper middle class. The resulting mix of social-class values and educational expectations meant difficulties for students, parents, and teachers.

The Sputnik reaction was another crisis affecting modern education. When the USSR initiated the space race, Americans responded with curricular initiatives and special programs for gifted students. At first these emphasized mathematics and the sciences, but eventually much of the traditional curriculum of American schools was changed. It is significant that many of these changes alienated local bases of support from schools. While professional educators could see the value of such changes, many parents and less progressive laypersons frequently could not. New math, which prevented parents from helping their children with homework problems because the concepts were unfamiliar to the older generation, is one example. Programs dealing with moral judgments, such as values clarification, are examples of communities' inability or unwillingness to accept changes introduced by professional educators.

The desegregation of American schools resulted in tremendous educational changes. Schools in black communities which had been sources of pride in the South since Reconstruction were closed. Black teachers, trained differently and teaching different content with different pedagogical techniques, were forced to adapt to white standards or leave the profession. Black principals and coaches were demoted, displaced by whites in the newly integrated system.[10] Black students experienced great difficulty trying to deal simultaneously with the culture of white schools, white pedagogical practices, and racial prejudice.

White communities faced an equally difficult task of transition. However, what often is overlooked is that drastic change in the form of social heterogeneity already was underway in American high schools before desegregation affected most communities. This social change, the presence of increasing numbers of students from lower-class and blue-collar backgrounds, was less visible than the mixing of black and white students. Moreover, the allegiance given to the American myth of social equality tended to blind many to this changing reality. Blacks in formerly all-white schools were highly visible, they were predominantly not middle class, and they were bearers of a different subculture. Attention in education was focused on the highly visible minority rather than the broader social changes affecting schooling in America.

The responses to desegregation varied. The federal government made money available. Local schools often diverted that money for purposes other than those for which it was intended. Professional educators devised educational innovations that often functioned to resegregate students, usually for the benefit of teachers.[11] Some local communities were quite successful in staving off the brunt of desegregation through one means or another. Many parents moved to the suburbs or placed their children in private schools.

A consequence of desegregation was the alienation of many citizens, black and white, from the educational process. The era of local control over neighborhood schools had finally come to an end. Professional educators, after almost seventy-five years of struggle, had gained a virtual monopoly over the control of American schools.

Just as it seemed that American education might be run by professional educators and bureaucrats, a new voice was heard. More accurately, an old player in the educational game reemerged—the industrialist. In the 1980s, the successors to Andrew Carnegie began to demand public attention with the push for new educational reforms that, to historians and those with long memories, have a familiar ring.

Those whom we have called industrialists are business interests with the resources to influence the political process to a much greater extent than the average citizen. All of us have a tendency toward self-interest; it should not be surprising therefore that industrialists tend to work for goals that favor their own needs or that will effect the vision they have of America. Moreover, for industrialists, whose decisions about employee levels and plant locations can dramatically impact the local or state economy and tax base, the desire for a more highly educated pool of employees is likely to be weighed heavily when reconsidering the educational needs of the community.

As America enters a period of economic transition, regearing for a new postindustrial economy, industrialists and business leaders are again urging educational reform. This time, with state and national educational structures already in place, these economic leaders are taking their appeals directly to politicians and bureaucrats in Washington, D.C., and each of the state capitals. In the process, local communities are often being circumvented or ignored.

School Sport and Corporate Needs

That sport could provide an important means of unifying the conglomeration of different nationalities and ethnic groups that immigrated to America already has been discussed. In sport an earlier generation of political and economic leaders saw the development of "American" traits of leadership, competition, and victory, as well as an exciting source of entertainment for their labor force. The echo of muscular Christianity espousing the importance of action in character development is heard in Andrew Carnegie's call for education to be practical. High school sport could build character among children, especially the sons of immigrants, and give the students who were seen as nonacademic a way of becoming involved in the culture of the school. The excitement of watching the victories of local high school teams could instill a sense of pride in the community, especially when high school athletics was the only game in town.

For many communities throughout the United States, having winning sport teams remains a major priority. It may be football in Georgia, or basketball for girls in Iowa or for boys in Kentucky. Elsewhere it may be wrestling, soccer, or gymnastics. Interscholastic athletics can provide exciting and fulfilling experiences for students and adults alike. However, if providing winning teams becomes the *raison d'etre* of the school, our priorities are seriously out of order. When this happens, high school athletics can work as a reactionary force against educational reform. Consider the following example.

In 1984 Texas Governor Mark White appointed a blue ribbon panel known as the Select Committee on Public Education. The committee was chaired by Dallas-based industrialist H. Ross Perot, a leading proponent of educational reform. The work of the committee resulted in the passage of legislation dubbed "no pass/no play." While this measure was a small part of the total educational package passed by a special session of the state legislature, it received a great deal of publicity and became one of the most hotly debated political issues in Texas. Other educational reforms in 1984 included teacher competency tests, pay raises for teachers, 70 percent as the minimum passing grade, and the replacement of the elected twenty-seven-member state board of education with a smaller appointed board.

Political compromise resulted in the committee forfeiting some of its suggested reforms. For example, the committee had recommended extending the length of the school day and the school year. It also wanted to bring the University Interscholastic League (UIL),[12] the agency established to regulate high school athletics in Texas, under the control of the state board of education. Necessary compromise rendered both of these measures political casualties. There were, however, some early unexpected victories.

While debate raged over Perot's charge that far too much time and money were spent on extracurriculars, the director of Texas's school athletic coordinating board proposed substantive changes in sport programs, including tougher academic standards for players, fewer coaches, and a curtailment of junior high and elementary school sport programs. Also, the state board of education—even while Perot was calling for their replacement—approved sweeping curriculum changes for Texas schools: increasing the number of credits necessary for graduation, calling for additional study in basic courses, and limiting the amount of class time students could miss to participate in extracurricular activities.

None of these actions, however, had the effect of thwarting the momentum behind Perot and the Select Committee on Public Education. A special session of the legislature was called in the summer of 1984 to consider educational reform. After a great deal of posturing and lobbying, Governor White succeeded in getting most of the committee's recommendations included in House Bill 72, which was passed and signed into law.

Under no pass/no play, a student must pass all classes with a grade of 70 percent or better in order to participate in any extracurricular activity. Another reform affecting athletics is the 8-20 rule. This rule limits a student's practice time to no more than eight hours per week in any one activity and no more than twenty hours per week in all of a student's activities combined. Furthermore, school districts cannot schedule or permit students to be absent from class more than ten times during the 175-day school year. In addition to the five absences granted all students, five more absences can be granted by a local school board to allow students to take part in UIL-approved extracurricular activities.

Proponents say the effect of the new legislation is to emphasize academics in order to strengthen the state's educational productivity. This, it is assumed, will attract new industry to the state and provide the educated workers needed by the increasingly high-tech economy.

A New Mythology Rationalizes Change

Thus, it might be said that a new mythology has arisen in Texas. First publicly espoused by H. Ross Perot, other industrialists, local and state politicians, leaders of higher education (though not so many in secondary education), media authorities, and most of the more formally educated middle and upper middle classes have accepted the new mythology. Simply stated, it is believed that Texas must have excellent schools and an educated work force in order to attract new businesses to move to the state; this is necessary because high-tech firms require excellence in education since they rely on skilled employees.

Former Governor White expressed his belief that Texas must have an educated work force in order to attract business, industry, and jobs. White stated that those who run the highly mobile, high-tech industries want to go somewhere with a good quality of life where their children can get the educational opportunity they enjoyed. Without quality education, White has said, societies—their economic and governmental structures—will fail.[13]

This mythology, and the implementing strategies that accompany it, is not limited to Texas. For example, New Mexico's Governor Toney Anaya came to Austin in July 1985 to pick up tips on getting controversial education revisions past a reluctant legislature in his own state. Anaya congratulated White on his successful campaign to change from an elected to an appointed state board of education, saying that was a key to ensuring that improvements in education take place. "I think all the eyes of America are on Texas," Anaya stated.[14] Anaya said he wished he had thought of bringing prominent business leaders, typified by H. Ross Perot, into the educational revision process earlier. "What we're attempting to do is bring them on board at this point. In retrospect, and looking at the success in Texas, that was a mistake on my part."[15]

An article in the *New York Times*[16] stated that with respect to educational reform Texas was a model for other states, but that most politicians were waiting to evaluate the political consequences of the strategy before implementing plans in their own states.

The political consequences of Texas's educational reform are not easy to evaluate. In the wake of the 1984 legislation, public opinion polls indicated that there was widespread support for all of the provisions of House Bill 72, including no pass/no play. In addition, there is some evidence that support for no pass/no play increased among Texans after its implementation. A survey conducted by Texas A & M University in October 1985 found that 70 percent of 1,000 adults surveyed statewide supported no pass/no play, while 25 percent said it should be less restrictive, and 5 percent had no opinion.[17] In March 1986 Governor White said his poll showed 77 percent favored no pass/no play, and 68 percent even supported the tax increase to put more money into education.[18] As recently as 1993, there were attempts to weaken provisions of the legislation, but popular support deterred legislators from responding to pressure from special-interest groups, especially the Texas High School Coaches Association.

It is clear now that as the perceived needs of the national corporate economy change, i.e., from labor and resource-intensive heavy industry and manufacturing to specialized service and technology-dependent industry, the corporate interests will promote changes in education, including changes in high school sport. This relationship between economic interest and attitudes toward high school sport may be illustrated by the fact that many of the strongholds of Texas high school football are in areas where the "old" type of industry dominates the economy. An example of this is the steel town of Daingerfield.

Daingerfield is a town of 3,000 in Morris County in northeast Texas. The Daingerfield Tigers, which set a national record for fourteen consecutive shutout games in 1983, won the state 3-A championship for three consecutive years. The town's enthusiasm for its high school football team has been characterized as "excessive even for East Texas."[19]

Daingerfield's largest employer, Lone Star Steel, which had employed 7,000 workers in 1981, let go its last 2,100 employees in March 1986. It is estimated that 3,000 people left this county of 14,000 between 1982 and 1986. In 1986 unemployment in Morris County was reported at 30.8 percent, down from a high of 36.3 percent, but still the highest in Texas. The high school principal said that the football team gives the town something to rally around, something to tie it together. "There's nothing else that everyone has in common . . . unless it's unemployment, and nobody wants to focus on that."[20]

The "importance-of-sport" legacy continues in many towns and small cities similar to Daingerfield. It is a phenomenon that also can be found in inner-city minority communities and the schools that serve them. Yates High School in Houston is one such example.

Yates, Houston's oldest black high school, is located in an inner-city neighborhood called the Third Ward, which is 97 percent black. Tucked beneath the freeways of the state's largest city, the ward's economy is depressed and almost devoid of chain businesses.[21]

In 1981 Yates lost in the state finals to Dallas Lake Highlands, but Yates's principal said the fact that Yates got to the final game "created a positive atmosphere" in the Third Ward. In 1985 Yates won the state 5-A championship by beating Odessa Permian 37–0 at Texas Stadium in Irving, home of the Dallas Cowboys.

One newspaper article described the results of that game: "The delirium has died down on Sampson Street, but deep down, old-timers in this city's Third Ward are still choking back pride. In the 'Cuney Houses'—a sprawling housing project that runs along both sides of a street called Cuney—gray-haired black men can be seen wearing old Yates High School letter sweaters and talking about football."[22]

Yates's defensive line coach commented, "What we fight in the Third Ward is totally different from what the small schools do. This is a bigger environment. The biggest problem here is keeping a kid's mind on just one thing at a time. And it's the same on the football field or in the classroom."[23]

The head football coach at Yates said, "You cannot deny that football affects the community in a big way. When we get between 12,000 and 20,000 people on the road to go to a ballgame, there's a lot of gasoline and oil bought, there's food bought. You'd be surprised at the number of caps, shirts, and other items with slogans on them that have been bought in the last month."[24]

A Yates guidance counselor also was positive about the football championship. "Because of winning in football," she said, "we now have a chance to tell people that, hey, 85 percent of our juniors passed the language arts part of the [Texas high school skills proficiency test] and 75 percent passed the mathematics part."[25]

Individuals in communities such as the Third Ward are even less likely than the residents of Daingerfield to benefit from today's changing economic base. Inner-city residents traditionally have served as the cheap pool of labor essential for heavy industry and manufacturing. The pool was cheap because it was filled with under-educated laborers who had few employment options. Today such a pool is unnecessary for emerging industries that rely on lasers and microchips instead of furnaces and welding machines, and require employees with technical competence rather than strong backs.

It is not surprising that many Texans have ambivalent feelings about no pass/no play, and that a minority of Texans has resisted all attempts at reform. There are three recognized constituencies that have demonstrated the most resistance to educational reform and no pass/no play in Texas.

Texas educators, specifically school teachers, opposed parts of the educational reform package. However, few voiced great opposition to no pass/no play, since most of their concern centered on teacher competency testing, which they opposed. All public school teachers were required to take a standardized test, and all of the organized teacher groups except the American Federation of Teachers energetically opposed this measure.

Coaches were an exception to the general response of educators to no pass/no play. The Texas High School Coaches Association was concerned enough to form a political action committee to work against Governor White's reelection. The reactions of individual coaches varied, of course, but there was a general lament for high school sports. As one coach put it, "The golden era for high school football is gone and we are never going to get it back."[26] Though it is debatable whether it has passed or not, the golden era to which that coach referred is symbolized by coaches such as Tim Edwards at L. D. Bell High School in the Hurst-Euless-Bedford Independent School District. Edwards was quoted in *Time* magazine and appeared on ABC's "Nightline" in the wake of the no pass/no play ruling. Not only does L. D. Bell enjoy a junior high school feeder system,* but Edwards, as football coach and athletic co-ordinator, is exempted from all teaching responsibilities. According to a recent report, Edwards's salary is over $63,000 a year.[27] This may be the "golden era" of Texas high school football that the coaches want to preserve.

Some parents, socialized under the old myth and hoping to see their own children serve as highly valued ritual performers, also have resisted the recent reforms. The degree of this resistance is best indicated by the parent-initiated litigation that occurred in the spring of 1985, the first semester of enforcement for no pass/no play.

By May 1985, the University Interscholastic League and the Texas Education Agency faced at least forty-five restraining orders related to no pass/no play. In many cases, a suit was filed and a judge immediately granted a temporary restraining order, good for ten days. This would allow a student to participate in a hog show at the county fair or some other activity; then the suit would be dropped. One case, however, went further.

In early May 1985, Houston Judge Marsha Anthony ruled that no pass/no play was unconstitutional. However, a week later in a separate case, the Fifth U.S. Court of Appeals found that participation in interscholastic athletics is not a constitutional right protected by due process and that courts are not "super referees over high school athletic programs."[28]

All of this came during the state's Class 5-A high school baseball playoffs because one school, Aldine, had used academically ineligible players to defeat West Orange-Stark in the opening round series of the playoff games. The UIL was subsequently caught between two court orders, one telling the UIL to let the Aldine players continue to play and the other stating that the playoffs could not continue with Aldine as a participant.

Judge Anthony had ruled that the no pass/no play law "is not rationally related" to its purpose of improving students' education; furthermore, it penalized only those in extracurricular activities and

---

*The athletes from junior high schools become the pool from which the high school teams are selected.

gave principals "unguided discretion" to exempt students in advanced or honors courses.[29]

The attorney for one group of students in the case said the no pass/no play law led to arbitrary exclusions of students from educational extracurricular activities. "It hurts education if you remove someone from student government, computer club, or the debate team. . . . They make no exceptions. They say all of this is play."[30]

Subsequently, Texas school officials pointed out that there was no evidence the law violated free-speech rights of students wanting to take part in student government or the school newspaper. They said that at the time of the court action two students had been barred from band activities and the rest were disqualified from track, football, basketball, and other sports.[31]

Judge Anthony's ruling was canceled by the Texas Supreme Court on May 24, 1985. This cleared the way for the continuation of the 5-A baseball championship playoffs. Then, on July 10, the Texas Supreme Court ruled unanimously in a separate case that public school students have no inherent right to take part in extracurricular activities.

On February 24, 1986, the U.S. Supreme Court, citing the lack of a "substantial Federal question," rejected an appeal by students who said the law violated their constitutional rights. Their attorneys argued that the law was arbitrary and capricious because it may single out students who fail one course and get straight As in all other courses, while a student with all Ds is not prevented from taking part in extracurricular activities.[32]

Thus, resistance to the proposed changes in high school sport in Texas can be attributed primarily to the reluctance of the educational bureaucracy to yield control to the very interests, i.e., business interests, which created it in the first two decades of this century[33] and to the inherently conservative nature of public ritual.

It should be noted that the no pass/no play aspects of House Bill 72 have not been changed. In fact, this legislation is no longer controversial. There have been attempts to weaken some of the provisions of the law, as it pertains to extracurricular activities, but the existing law has such widespread support that all such attempts have been stymied in the legislature. No pass/no play is the new status quo.

Educational Accountability and the Myth of School Sport

H. Ross Perot, as a spokesperson for corporate America, has made it clear that "the business of Texas schools is education."[34] Today this does not mean that schools merely should inculcate corporate values in students in order to produce obedient, healthy, prompt, cooperative laborers. While that may have been sufficient for the needs of corporate, industrializing America early in the twentieth century, it is no longer sufficient. The emerging economy demands something else. What is lacking are literate, technically competent skilled employees who are as dependable as their grandfathers but who can function more independently in the workplace.

No one can doubt the abilities of corporate America to effect changes in public education and its related athletic programs. Economics, however, is not the only force affecting high school sports. Sport has functioned as public ritual in North America for a century, and high school sports have been an important part of that ritual system at least since 1920. The Texas example shows that high school sport continues to perform this function in a powerful way.

Sport was born out of the crisis created by the initial phase of industrialization. High school sport developed as industrialization reached a mature and stable phase. Now it appears that high school sport will change as the perception of an impending new economic crisis spreads.

However, it also is clear that economic arguments alone are insufficient to explain sport as a social institution. The contention offered here is that while the initial impetus for sport may have been economic, the power of sport has resulted from its adoption as public ritual with a powerful supporting mythology.

The new emerging educational mythology is one that is functional for a high-tech economy. Designing schools to prepare literate, mathematically competent students for jobs in such an economy is being viewed as a serious civic responsibility. At stake, it is widely believed, is America's ability to triumph over foreign industrial competitors. This new mythology utilizes aggressive symbols from the world of business with strong ties to the traditional work ethic. There is, however, little room for sport with a higher priority than academics and its associated dumb-jock imagery. The Gipper can't win the battle for America's economic future. Only an intelligent, well-educated, and creative work force can do that.

That the myth of school sport can be adapted to meet changes in technological demands is implied by the no pass/no play example. However, in some of the middle-class suburban neighborhoods of the Northeast (e.g., metropolitan New York), the interest in high school athletics is less intense than it was twenty years ago. Coaches complain about a lack of dedication among students, but behind this is the realization that interscholastic athletics, in its present state, cannot compete successfully for students' time with activities such as studying, dating, part-time work, car, computer games, or a host of other leisure activities available to the affluent adolescent. Perhaps the no pass/no play rule does not go far enough. A well-educated football team does not guarantee a well-educated student body or local community in the same way that a winning football team does not guarantee a winning student body or local community. They are both, after all, only symbolic.

It requires cultural upheaval to replace one mythology and its accompanying ritual system with another. The majority of Americans believe strongly in the value of sport; only a minority (perhaps those marginal to the traditional sport status system) are likely to oppose high school sport actively. This is especially true since high school sport is no longer primarily a male domain—witness the increased numbers of female athletes in high schools in recent years.

However, the traditional mythology concerning the role of sport in character-building and educational functions has been shown to lack scientific support. In an age where science is crucial, this calls the institution of school sport into question.

The impetus for recent reforms comes predominantly from the

leaders of large industrial corporations and politicians in federal and state government, especially governors looking to expand the tax base of their home states. The message is succinct: American public schools are failing to provide the corporate world with the labor pool it requires.

The reasons for this are twofold. First, the change to a high-tech service economy requires employees with different educational preparation than the assembly lines and steel mills of the past. The number of low-skill jobs is declining dramatically.[35] Second, there is a predicted shortage for white-collar and managerial positions by the year 2000.[36] These positions can only be filled by drawing upon the ranks of the lower socioeconomic classes and minorities—groups whose members traditionally have performed the poorest in our schools. Anticipating this future, industrialists are pushing schools to change now.

It is interesting to note that local business people, those who still control schools, often find themselves opposed to the reforms espoused by powerful corporate leaders. This results because they are entangled in local political and personal considerations that give them a different view, even different problems and potential solutions.

A significant implication of industry's involvement in educational reform is that it may lead to a reallocation of resources for education. However, this will require new structures, especially for financing education. Undoubtedly there will be an increase in federal dollars. Moreover, property taxes cannot remain the base of educational funding, perhaps not even a significant element of that funding.

With changes in financial support will come changes in control. There will be a change in local control, since school boards will no longer pay for schools by controlling local property taxes.

What does this bode for high school sport? The case of no pass/no play in Texas shows what can happen when industrialists and politicians team up to reform a state's educational system.

If the purpose of schools is to prepare students to function effectively in society as adults, then the absolute minimum requirements today are the mastery of basic literacy and mathematical skills in order to prepare students for employment in tomorrow's work force. Athletic skills do not provide students with the means to function effectively as adults in contemporary society, nor do sports in anyway prepare young people for employment in the contemporary work force.

Summary

The economic needs of America, as perceived by the leaders of American business, have contributed strongly to the shaping of American education. Since sport has been such an integral part of American education for the past century, it is reasonable to assume that high school sport also has thrived with the approval of American business. Now some business leaders, especially those who represent large, national, high-tech industries, are working to reshape American education and the role of sport in our schools.

The role of American education changed during the second half of the twentieth century. Education is now more democratic, more accessible to young Americans, regardless of their racial or ethnic identity or their social class background. This has increased the heterogeneity of schools and changed the social function of American education.

At the same time, schools increasingly have been run by professionals, with a concomitant loss of influence by parents and local community members. In effect, in the first half of the twentieth century parents relinquished their educational role to professionally run schools. Sport has remained the primary medium for citizens to connect with their schools and gain a sense of ownership.

Now a new mythology is gaining acceptance. The new belief system holds that excellence in education is essential if American businesses are going to increase their productivity and competitiveness so that the United States can once again be number one.

The recent involvement of business leaders in education was illustrated by Texas industrialist H. Ross Perot's efforts to reform education in that state. The economic and political forces revealed in that effort, including the adoption of no pass/no play legislation, differ little from those in other states. That Texas may emphasize sport more than some states and spend less per student for education than most states only means that there are differences in degree, not kind, relative to the replacement of an old American myth by a new one.

For high school sport, the myths of yesterday are not supported by scientific data, making them tenuous as myths in an era grounded in science. This may make us uncomfortable, angry, or sad, but those emotions will not change the contemporary reality. In all likelihood, high school sports will change in the near future, as a result of educational reform. The nature of that change, how it is likely to come about, and how you can influence it locally in your community are the subjects of the next chapter.

Notes

1. Cited in Raymond E. Callahan, *Education and the Cult of Efficiency: A Study of the Social Forces that Have Shaped the Administration of the Public Schools* (Chicago: The University of Chicago Press, 1962), pp. 12–13.

2. David T. Kearns, "Why I Got Involved," *Fortune Special Education Issue: Saving Our Schools* (Spring 1990): 47.

3. Phil Gailey, "Texas Governor Speaks to Sweeten Adversity," *New York Times,* March 22, 1986: 10Y.

4. Lee Jones, "No Play Rule is Affirmed by High Court," *Fort Worth Star-Telegram,* Evening, July 10, 1985: 1A.

5. Roberta J. Park, "Sport, Gender, and Society in a Transatlantic Victorian Perspective," in *From "Fair Sex" to Feminism: Sport and the Socialization of Women in the Industrial and Post-Industrial Eras,* eds. James A. Mangan and Roberta J. Park (London: Frank Cass, 1987), p. 73.

6. Timothy O'Hanlon, "Interscholastic Athletics, 1900–1940: Shaping Citizens for Unequal Roles in the Modern Industrial State," *Educational Theory* 30, no. 2 (1980): 89–103; Joel Spring, "Mass Culture and School Sports," *History of Education Quarterly* 14 (1974): 483–99.

7. For an excellent review of the history of American education in the early decades of this century, see Callahan, *Education and the Cult of Efficiency.* For a brief review of the changes in school organization in this century, see Elizabeth M. Eddy, "The Reorganization of Schooling: An Anthropological Challenge," in *Applied Anthropology in America,* eds. Elizabeth M. Eddy and William L. Partridge (New York: Columbia University Press, 1978), pp. 326–49.

8. Andrew Carnegie, *The Empire of Business* (1902), pp. 79–81, cited in Callahan, *Education and the Cult of Efficiency*, p. 9.

9. *Springfield Republican*, cited in Callahan, *Education and the Cult of Efficiency*, p. 96.

10. For a case study of one of the few black head coaches who retained his job after desegregation, see Pat Jordan, *Black Coach* (New York: Dodd, Mead & Co., 1971).

11. Elizabeth M. Eddy, "Educational Innovation and Desegregation: A Case Study of Symbolic Realignment," *Human Organization* 34, no. 2 (1975): 163–73.

12. In 1912, the Texas Interscholastic Athletic Association (formed in 1905) and the Debating and Declamation League of Texas (founded in 1910) merged to become the University Interscholastic League (UIL) under the auspices of the University of Texas at Austin (Bill McMurray, *Texas High School Football* [South Bend, Ind.: Icarus Press, Inc., 1985], pp. 483–84). The Negro Interscholastic League (established in 1940 through the then all-black Prairie View A & M College) merged with the UIL in 1967. From around 200 scattered member schools in its early years, the UIL grew rapidly to a membership of 3,000 by 1920. It reached a peak membership in the early 1930s with about 6,000 before school consolidation became common in much of the rural state. Currently there are approximately 1,160 high school and 1,500 junior high and elementary school members in the UIL. Today the UIL is the largest interschool organization in the world. It conducts statewide competitions in twenty-two academic areas and twenty sports. It is estimated that each year one-half of all graduating seniors in Texas have participated in some type of UIL-sponsored event. In 1983, for example, 1,460,895 students participated in UIL-associated activities. This included over 560,000 (or 39 percent of the 1.46 million) in athletics; 392,000 (or 27 percent) in music events; 150,000 (or 10 percent) in speech; and about 15,000 (or 1 percent) each in drama and journalism.

13. Associated Press, "White Links Growth, Good Schools," *Forth Worth Star-Telegram,* November 21, 1984: 4D.

14. Karen Hastings, "White Calls Easing of School Test 'Fair,' " *Fort Worth Star-Telegram,* July 13, 1985: 31A.

15. Ibid.

16. Gailey, "Texas Governor Seeks to Sweeten Adversity."

17. Tim Madigan, "Poll Confirms School Officials' Views," *Fort Worth Star-Telegram*, Morning, November 28, 1985: 8B.

18. Gailey, "Texas Governor Seeks to Sweeten Adversity."

19. Jay B. Lewis, "Team Helps Town Face Tough Times," *Fort Worth Star-Telegram,* September 28, 1986: 18A.

20. Ibid.

21. Christopher J. Evans, "Yates," *Fort Worth Star-Telegram,* January 19, 1986: 11C.

22. Ibid., p. 1C.

23. Ibid., p. 11C.

24. Ibid.

25. Ibid.

26. T. R. Sullivan, "High School Football Coaches Feel Pressures," *Fort Worth Star-Telegram*, January 25, 1986: 7B.

27. Brock Mullins, "Coaches Say Pay Justified," *Fort Worth Star-Telegram*, February 9, 1992: B1.

28. Lee Jones and Karen Hastings, "Leave Pass-Play Rule Alone, House Urges Judges," *Fort Worth Star-Telegram*, Evening, May 22, 1985: 13A.

29. Lee Jones, "Playoffs, State Law Win Round: High Court to Settle No Pass-No Play Rule," *Fort Worth Star-Telegram*, May 25, 1985: 2A.

30. Ibid.

31. Associated Press, " 'No Pass, No Play' Remains Intact," *New York Times*, February 25, 1986: 28Y.

32. Ibid.

33. Callahan, *Education and the Cult of Efficiency*; Andrew W. Miracle, "Corporate Economy, Social Ritual and the Rise of High School Sports" (Paper presented at the Annual Meetings of the North American Society for the Sociology of Sport, Boston, November 1985).

34. In July 1985 a state official made the statement that "the business of Texas schools is education" in response to the state supreme court ruling upholding the constitutionality of no pass/no play.

35. U.S. Department of Labor, *Work Force 2000* (Washington, D.C.: Government Printing Office, 1987).

36. Harold L. Hodgkinson, *All One System: Demographics of Education—Kindergarten Through Graduate School* (Washington, D.C.: Institute for Educational Leadership, Inc., 1985).

9

The Future of School Sport

Athletics is where my character was built. It altered my life. I had the opportunity to go to school because of athletics and play professional football because of athletics.

> —High school football coach and former professional football player Willie Dearion[1]

Football games were not won with noble role models and the cotton candy that college presidents like to send out for the media. They were won by kids who had rockets for arms and hydraulic pistons for legs and biceps and triceps and quadriceps that could carry refrigerators home from Sears and cross-eyed looks suggesting that to maim someone was sublime.

> —Author H. G. Bissinger[2]

There is nothing about sports that makes them different from the rest of America, and therefore, they cannot serve as a special means for overcoming the problems of society.

> —Sociologist Murray Hausknecht[3]

The theme behind these three quotes is our theme: participating in or rather winning in sport builds character. Based on his own experiences as an athlete, Dearion believes in the myth. After a year in Odessa, Texas, following the fortunes of the Permian High School football team, author Buzz Bissinger does not. Sociologist Murray Hausknecht may not believe it either, but sport is perceived as a positive force by the majority of Americans, and has been for most if not all of the present century.

High school sport is immensely popular with students, many if not most educators, and some community members. While there is some variation in this commitment to high school sport by region, size, and type of city, and other local factors, there can be little doubt that high school athletics has been and still is a significant factor in American education.

We have described the ritual that is high school sport and analyzed the myths that give meaning to this ritual. This mythology stresses character-building and the educational value of sport. Analysis of the available data for each of the mythic elements has demonstrated little scientific support for any part of this belief system, even though for a few points the evidence is ambiguous or inconclusive.

Sport does not build character, at least not in the way many Americans assume that it does. Overall, sport does not promote substantial educational or socioeconomic attainment. High school sport does not reduce delinquency or racial prejudice. Moreover, during the course of an individual's life, high school sport does not promote social success or health. In short, there is no statistically measurable positive long-term benefit for those who played high school sports when compared with those who did not participate. On the other hand, there are no negative consequences for high school athletes.

The measurable benefits of high school sport are short-term social prestige for some high school athletes (i.e., mostly while they are still in high school), some institutional benefits for schools, and entertainment for the community.

In pointing out these facts, we are not anti-sport, although it may be perceived as such by those who have vested interests in maintaining the present system. The purpose of myths is to reinforce the belief that the present view of reality is "the truth," and that the situation always has been the way it is now. However, culture is never static but always changing. That the interest in high school sport in some areas of the country is less than it was, and that industrialists such as H. Ross Perot can question the character-building value of sport is testament to this change. It implies that high school sport is no longer universally accepted as the guardian of the moral development of our nation's youth. If we are not constrained by the belief that high school sport has these mythic properties, what changes, if any, do we make to increase sport's educative function? This is the subject of the present chapter.

Possibilities for Consideration

Schools without Sports

One reaction to debunking the myth of high school sport is to say that sports are educationally worthless and should be eradicated from high schools. Although we reject that line of action, it is not unprecedented. Obviously there can be education without sport. For example, some European countries such as Germany have no interscholastic athletics. In fact, there is some validity to the argument that schools without sports would help to focus the energies and commitment of students, educators, and community members on the primary reason for schools—academics. There is no doubt that some individuals from time to time forget that schools are really meant to be about reading, writing, mathematics, science, social studies, languages, literature, and the humanities. Today it is becoming difficult to see how sport fits into the curriculum. Moreover, without historical perspective it is difficult to understand why sport was ever introduced to American schools and rationalized on the basis of academic relevance.

Without sport, high schools would continue to operate much as they have for most students since desegregation in the 1960s.

Students would go to school each day, attend classes, grumble about homework, hang out with their friends, flirt with other students, and have fun. The difference would be that they would have to organize their social life around activities other than athletic contests.

There would be additional effects for schools without sport, but many of these would be subtle. Schools, as social institutions, might have less esprit, less cohesiveness, less commitment from students and the community. However, this might be offset by a redefinition of the purpose of schools and a resulting shift in the criteria used to judge them. For example, unable to rank schools on the basis of their football or basketball successes, we might rank schools on the basis of their social studies departments, their awards in mathematics, the percentage of students they send to college, or levels of improvement in standardized tests. In fact, such evaluation already is present and growing, especially the use of standardized tests to evaluate schools.

It might be expected that members of the community would feel more remote from schools after being disconnected from the last area of direct influence. However, we might suppose that new associations of support groups could form around academic areas of interest.

The change that might have the most impact would be the effect on those who are often labeled as "below-average" students. Students who barely scrape by in today's high schools might feel no compulsion to continue their education in a school where the primary, or perhaps even exclusive, focus was on academics. With no ball games or victory dances to entice them, such students might feel no compunction to attend high school. We think this argument overstates the case for sport since many marginal students (e.g., the burnouts described in chapter 3) who are in revolt against the school often reject sport as part of the total package of school values.

This argument deserves attention, however, because it has become part of the current mythology. As absenteeism reaches crisis proportions in urban high schools, the importance of the myth that sport keeps students in schools also increases. For example, in a January 1985 response to a report by his task force on public school athletics, then Chancellor of the Board of Education of the City of New York

Nathan Quinones[4] stated that, "A healthy school athletic program is vital to the physical, mental, and educational health of our students and to our concentrated efforts to reduce the number of students who drop out of schools before earning a high school diploma." It is presumed that without sport, and with a concomitant increase in the emphasis placed on academics, the percentage of the population under age eighteen who attend school would decrease. Similarly, the percentage of students expected to graduate from high school would drop. Such a possibility raises two concerns.

First, if students are only in school for sport, how much are they really learning? Can we reasonably expect that "students" who attend classes only to play sports or so that they can then participate in sports-related social events are likely to learn any significant amount of subject matter by osmosis? Even if they do learn a little on occasion, is it worth the costs of providing full-time instruction for students unable or unwilling to do more than part-time learning?

Second, what would happen as a result of academically disinterested students dropping out of the school system?[5] Some would argue that untrained they would be unable to secure employment and thus become a long-term economic burden for society. We would respond that for such students high schools today are actually involved in credentialing and not educating or training. The American economy of the twenty-first century might be viewed, only slightly simplistically, as one marked by a dichotomized work force—those prepared for high-tech jobs and those needed for menial service positions.

At stake is the baby-sitting function of American schools. Of all forms of institutionalized care in contemporary society, schools are the least expensive. It costs far less to keep a student in school during the day than to keep the same individual incarcerated around the clock. Reasonable individuals might question the legitimacy of viewing schools in this fashion, but it is not an inaccurate view for many students in many schools nationwide.

A further economic consequence of keeping older youth in school, even after the schools have given up on them academically and after they have given up on themselves, is that it keeps them from becoming full-time workers in the labor force. During periods of high unemployment, keeping large numbers of teenagers from being employed full-time means that older adults can compete more favorably for the limited number of available jobs. It is less costly for society, economically and socially, to keep unemployable teenagers in school than to cope with the displacement of their parents and grandparents as unemployed adults. However, the advantages of this mechanism disappear as society approaches full employment. Some economists are predicting full employment and a critical shortage of workers by the year 2000. Thus, this rationale is not likely to play a major role in the near future.

If the predictions of full employment before the end of the century are realized, there need be no masses of unemployable. Those who have benefitted from formal education might be expected to compete for jobs much as they do today. Those who have not will be able to find employment that does not require a degree, though admittedly it will be economically and socially less rewarding employment.

Generally Americans are committed to capitalism and a belief that economic rewards are strong motivators. When students realize that only those who learn subject matter content will earn credits, receive a degree, and have the possibility of finding high-paying employment, will not those students be motivated to stay in school and work at academic pursuits even though there is no football game on Friday night?

One negative result of the cessation of high school sports would be the loss of a cheap source of popular entertainment. This loss would be felt by many community members and students. However, today there are alternative sources of cheap entertainment. This has not always been the case, but with videocassettes and satellite dishes there is no lack of alternative entertainment, even for sports fanatics.

There would, however, be a real loss in terms of the shared experiences, the sense of community, that occur through high school sport. It is difficult to place a value on such experiences, but there is no doubt that they have helped and continue to help provide meaning to life. Observe any high school class reunion and it is striking the number of reminiscences that involve sport. Listen to Americans talk wherever they gather—at restaurants, bus stops, cocktail parties—

and not infrequently the conversations include references to what they assume to be shared, namely, high schools and high school sports. It helps to cement our society by providing a sense of commonality in a world of diversity. On the other hand, it could be argued that if this sense of community is gained at the expense of reinforcing artificial and inequitous differences between boys and girls, it is not worth the effort. Ultimately, however, the evaluation of this benefit of high school sport must remain subjective.

Sports without Schools

Now consider the reverse question of sports without schools. If there were no sports in high schools, what would happen to sports? It seems reasonable to assume that there would be virtually no significant long-term impact on sports participation by youth. Only the locus of sports involvement would shift.

Already there is a plethora of voluntary associations dedicated to sports in nearly every town, city, and suburb in the United States. The removal of sports from high schools would provide an impetus for growth by these associations. New ones would form in some areas to promote sports that now are organized solely by schools, although it is difficult to think of a school sport that does not already have a community-based counterpart in most cities. More commonly the cessation of high school sports would allow community-based associations to expand the age range of youth served and to extend the seasons of play. For example, local youth soccer leagues would experience an increase in the numbers of older youth participating in their programs and they could extend their seasons since they no longer would be limited by the conference play of high school soccer teams.

It is entirely possible that without high school teams, which now tend to dominate youth sports because they capture the attention of most youth, more, not fewer, teenagers would become involved in organized sports. High school teams are intended for and dominated by elite athletes, that is, the best athletes available in the local community. Students who have learned in elementary or middle school that they cannot make the team or will be bench warmers if they do, are discouraged from participating on high school teams. In most communities, the opportunity for high school-aged youth to participate in organized sports outside of school also is limited to elite teams. This is reinforced by the fact that usually the same athletes are playing on a school team and a nonschool team.

If there were no school sports, community-based organizations would be more likely to organize their leagues horizontally with a broad base instead of constructing them in a pyramid fashion. For young children in most American communities there exist opportunities to play sports regardless of skill or ability. It is only around the age of eleven or twelve that most associations begin to structure league play by ability level as well as age. As a result, by the time a player is fourteen or fifteen, there is seldom any place for the nonelite athlete. Without the reinforcing dominance of high school sports, it is possible that more communities would continue to provide league play for athletes with a wide range of skills and abilities regardless of age.

One can envision, for example, a local basketball or soccer organization to which an entire family might belong, with league play available for children of all ages and ability levels, as well as similar groupings for adults. High school sport, with its emphasis on spectatorship, is actually a deterrence to such systems now.

What is the proper balance between sports and academics in American high schools? We cannot provide an answer; rather, each community must examine the issues and reach that decision. We are not advocating the elimination of high school sports, we have intended only to show that even that radical scenario would not be devastating for schools or sports. This means that schools and communities can search for compromises or middle-ground positions that allow for a restructuring of high school athletics without having to base sport systems on century-old myths with little or no basis in fact.

A Reordering of Priorities

There are good reasons for high school sports, even though the existing myths are mostly hollow. Therefore, our proposals are intended to limit excesses and to assist in formulating educational policies that would benefit most constituents.

We have not addressed the questions of appropriateness; that is, under what conditions might the removal of sport from schools be warranted? Nor have we discussed how such policy decisions might be determined. These are complicated, situationally specific issues best left to individual communities.

Local options might take any of four courses. One option is to do away with interscholastic sports. While this might seem like an extreme or radical option, the discussion above has demonstrated that the likely effects would not court disaster. Schools would not die and probably would flourish academically. Organized youth sports would not disappear but would probably flourish in many communities.

A second local option that might be taken is to do nothing. Those communities that subscribe to the notion of "don't fix it if it's not broken" may be correct in taking no action. However, we suspect that there are few communities in the United States where at least a few citizens do not already believe the system needs repair. It is likely that in the course of the next decade virtually every American community will be forced to consider the education and school sport issues.

Another option would be to accept the entertainment function of high school athletics as an important part of the school's role as a quasicustodial institution. Forget the "sport-builds-character" myth and use athletics to keep the school and the community entertained. By charging fees for this function, the school might expand its educational and athletic facilities. The suggestion is to adopt the model of "big-time" college athletics and run high school sports as a business.

At the present time most high school athletic programs are not profit driven, but there are pressures which might induce some communities to adopt this model. As the money for extracurricular activities becomes tighter, less becomes available for athletics. The greater the doubt that sport builds character, the less likely that money will be available for athletics and the greater the need for athletic directors and coaches to find other sources of income to keep their programs alive.

Cable television companies and manufacturers of athletic shoes also may provide financial subsidies to high school basketball and football teams chosen for a local cable channel's "game of the week." The logical extreme of this option is that high school athletes might be paid for performing this entertainment function. Such a scenario might indeed spark a resurgence of interest among high school students who would be enticed back into athletics as a more lucrative part-time employment option than McDonalds or Burger King.

Before rejecting this option out of hand, consider that some high school athletic programs, particularly in football and basketball, already have many of the characteristics of Division I college sports. In communities that have a winning tradition in sports, coaches are expected to work as hard as their colleagues in the college ranks, players are expected to specialize in one sport and spend time in off-season conditioning and weight programs, and large crowds attend the games which are broadcast on television and written about in newspapers. Some high school football and basketball coaches get high salaries, and many of them suffer the same pressure and job insecurity experienced by college coaches.[6] Some high school coaches also recruit, although it is doubtful that this reaches the same degree as college sports. High schools receive money if their teams appear on "Sport Channel America"'s telecast of weekly football games. In 1989 Sports Channel reportedly paid $250,000 annually to the National Federation of State High School Associations for broadcast rights to selected games.[7]

All the elements that have caused corruption in college sport can be found in some high school sport programs, yet it is hard to imagine that we are witnessing the dawn of the era of the professional high school athlete. To some extent this is because we still believe in the "sport-builds-character" myth. Even at the college level most people tend to support the ideal that the athlete is an amateur, although it is getting harder to justify why a male basketball player at the University of Nevada, Las Vegas, or Georgetown, or a football player at the University of Miami or the University of Oklahoma should not share in the financial revenues that the universities receive from athletics. With some notable exceptions in football and basketball, most local communities probably would agree that high school students have enough to worry about without having to deal with the problems of quasiprofessional athletics.

The final option is for local communities to pursue the search for some middle ground, an appropriate balance, in an effort to curb the excesses of high school sport and to improve education simultaneously. If communities wish to adapt high school sport so as symbolically to meet the demands of a more technologically sophisticated society, we could expect some changes in the power structure of athletics.

No longer would the coach call all the plays and make all the decisions. A new emphasis would be placed on players making individual decisions and finding creative ways of solving problems in sport. Clearly the leadership role of coaches would change under such circumstances, since there would be no need for strident authoritarianism and autocratic control. At least coaches might not need to yell at players and officials as much under this scenario.

Furthermore, the specialization, so much a part of our sports, might be decreased. After all, we now need free-thinking adaptable workers who can slip easily into new roles that develop quickly in our rapidly changing economy. The days of the specialist are over; they become redundant too quickly.

Centralized authority and specialization have become typical of the structure of our sports through a process of evolution. Football, soccer, and rugby all developed from the same game form, but in the American version of football the coach has all the power, whereas soccer and rugby are still largely controlled by the players. Could soccer replace football as the most popular high school sport in the interests of technological creativity? Unthinkable, at least in the South.

However, since we have argued that sport developed to meet the perceived needs of the corporate economy in the first place, it is certainly possible that the structure of high school sport could be changed to increase the players' control. If this change occurred, the standard of play might be reduced since the players presumably would make more mistakes in strategy than the coaches do now. In an atmosphere that deemphasized school sport this might be an acceptable trade-off. Yet given the present importance of sport as a symbol of community success, it may be perceived as too high a price to pay in some communities.

There is some research that supports reducing the level of adult decision-making in sport. As part of a series of investigations into what makes people feel positive about their lives,[8] a sample of high school students were asked to complete self-report forms at random times during the waking day, including once during each class session at school; this form provided data on the individual's social situation, current activity, and subjective state.

The researchers report that for adolescents, sport is generally experienced more positively than other parts of their lives. Especially important is the finding that physical activity, such as that of sport participation, is associated with higher-than-average challenges. In the study, high challenges typically were found to be paired with high moods and high motivations. The researchers concluded that physical activity could provide a context in which the student may learn to experience challenges as potentially pleasurable. Thus sport might provide a context in which adolescents can safely explore their individual capabilities.

However, these researchers found that informal sports, as opposed to adult-controlled, highly organized formal sports, may provide the most attractive features for high school students. It seems that the highly positive association between challenges and skills exists in informal sport settings but not in adult-supervised ones. The researchers suggest that this is probably due to the fact that when they are in control, the adolescents can manipulate the balance between challenges and skills more easily. The implication is that sport should be thought of as a form of human endeavor that has its own reason for existence, not as some form of extended compensation or as a preparation for the future.

Emphasizing the process of sport as well as the outcome allows the athlete more opportunities for success. Instead of measuring success in terms of the outcome of the game or whether the team reaches the playoffs or wins the championship, it could be defined as how well the athletes perform relative to their own past performances. Another result might be a reduction in the pressure on athletes to sacrifice morality for victory. The research described in chapter 4 showed that athletes tend to adopt "game reasoning" to justify conduct in sport that involves cheating or injuring another player. When faced with the hypothetical decision of whether or not to injure an opponent intentionally, after having been instructed to do so by the coach, athletes justify their violent behavior by not thinking of the opponent as a person, or by accepting the authority of the coach without question, or just by doing whatever it takes to win.

This "end-justifies-the-means" philosophy is not what sport should be teaching if it is to have a positive effect on morality. Too often the pressure of victory gets in the way of making the right decision in the many moral dilemmas that athletes face in sport. Sport does provide situations in which athletes have the opportunity to show concern for opponents or act fairly, but often "sportsmanship" in these instances is the exception rather than the rule.

If school sport is to become a training ground for moral development, then coaches need to be trained in ethics and learn how to reward athletes for ethical behavior. At the present time, such training is rarely part of the preparation of school coaches. Based on the results of a 1986 survey,[9] only five states require coaching certification for some or all of their school coaches. None of these programs contain components on ethics or moral development, although New York State has a component entitled "Philosophy, Principles and Organization" in which such principles might be discussed. Twenty-five states require all coaches to hold a valid teaching certificate, but in twelve states neither a teaching certificate nor a coaching certificate is required of all coaches. The report noted that, while a teaching certificate was the most common requirement to coach, many states allowed exceptions.

Since many more coaching jobs than physical education teaching jobs need to be filled each year, educational administrators have left the decision of what standards should govern the hiring of coaches to the local school districts. There has been a great increase in "off-the-street" coaches without any form of certification, whose only attachment to the school is through the athletic teams they coach. This state of affairs is not conducive to sport being incorporated into the culture of the school, and questions have been raised about how a coach can communicate effectively with the school administrators, the teachers, or the parents under such conditions.[10]

If communities really are serious about using athletics as a means of developing character, they will have to put pressure on their local school board to provide qualified coaches who can develop programs that teach children about ethical dilemmas in sport and provide counselling on how to make moral decisions.[11] This image is a far cry from the model of the authoritarian win-at-all-costs coach usually associated with sport.

If the community entertainment function of high school sport were reduced, then other outcomes, specifically affecting the needs of the students, could be emphasized. Not least among these is physical fitness. Due to the time and effort needed to produce winning programs, coaches who also teach physical education are forced to make athletics their top priority. This is not necessarily their fault. Coaches know that their job security depends on a winning season, not a well-taught physical education class.

Lessening the status of school athletics would reduce this role conflict between the two activities of the teacher/coach, and allow such teachers more time to concentrate on educating the student body on the importance of physical activity. If the present status of fitness among school children is an indication, their education in this domain has been sorely neglected. While it would be wrong to blame high school sports for the low fitness levels of our nation's youth, the cult of sport has not promoted the idea that physical activity is healthy and enjoyable for everyone. This is hardly surprising since the elitism of interscholastic athletics has meant that the best perform while the rest watch. There is nothing in this model that encourages children to become physically fit themselves, or to learn about and enjoy the process of fitness.

In athletics, fitness is a means to an end (i.e., it helps achieve victory), rather than an end in itself (i.e., an enjoyable process), and many athletes will tell you that they hated fitness training. Who can blame them if the coach used fitness as negative reinforcement and made them run laps if they were late for practice or made mistakes. There is no evidence to support the contention that high school athletes are fitter than nonathletes in later life, or that involvement in high school athletics is an important prerequisite for a lifetime of fitness.[12] At the present time, many school systems exempt athletes from physical education classes, thus reinforcing the importance of athletics rather than physical education.

It is an anomaly that our society is in the middle of what can be described as a fitness boom and yet our youth have never been less fit. In fact, there is a crisis in fitness among America's children.[13] Forty percent of children aged five to eight already exhibit at least one heart-disease risk factor; 55 percent of girls aged six to seventeen and 25 percent of boys aged six to twelve cannot do one pull up. Data from the National Youth Fitness Study show that children of the 1980s have a higher percentage of body fat than children of the 1960s.

Clearly there is an important role for physical education to play in promoting a healthy and enjoyable life and reducing risk factors that can lead to heart disease, stroke, and lung cancer.[14] In addition, there is the potential societal benefit of lower healthcare costs. While some adolescents still will smoke cigarettes, get drunk, take drugs, overeat, and not exercise regularly in spite of (or because of) what adults tell them, some will use the knowledge to improve their health habits. Such an approach is especially important in light of evidence indicating that people are living longer, and that regular exercise plays a primary role in promoting longevity. Recently the American Heart Association has elevated physical inactivity to the dubious status of one of the four major risk factors contributing to heart attacks.

Increasing children's physical activity could substantially reduce the impending crisis to our nation that will occur as a result of spiraling healthcare costs.[15]

A modern equivalent to the PSAL programs described in chapter 2, involving large numbers of children, would have more chance of survival if it did not have to compete with the "real game in town," interscholastic athletics. In fact, the current trend in physical education is away from teaching sports skills designed to prepare elite athletes for high school and college sports and toward skills that prepare all children for life-long physical activity. Inclusion rather than exclusion is the goal.[16]

Coaches need training in how to teach fitness as an enjoyable activity. This would be a far cry from torture sessions that athletes endure as part of a weeding out ritual in which the social Darwinism idea of "survival of the fittest" is literally applied. That is, coaches may use training as a personal test of the athletes' willingness to endure pain, or as a form of punishment for athletes. This approach can make athletes hate fitness training and avoid physical fitness activities after their playing career is over.

Another result of reducing the entertainment function of school sport could be a more equitable distribution of resources between boys' and girls' sports. Increased participation by girls in school athletics has been one of the greatest changes of the 1980s, yet, because of its function as community entertainment, boys' athletics is often given more emphasis. Cheerleading, an activity that symbolizes the support role played by females in a "male" world, is still a high-status activity[17] in female high school clique systems, and the macho image still plays a part in male sports, particularly football.[18] If the entertainment value of high school sport was reduced, the common argument that sports are more important for boys than for girls because they attract more spectators also would diminish. This would decrease the effect of sport in reinforcing male superiority.

Finally, the use of high school sport as a symbol of community cooperation rather than conflict would increase if the "we're-number-one syndrome" could be reduced. Material in chapter 7 showed that tensions within and between communities brought into high school sport occasionally result in violence between competing athletes and fans. The current "win-at-all-costs" mentality fuels the flames of divisiveness, but it need not be this way. For example, the atmosphere preceding the football game between Permian High School and Odessa High School was unusually tense in the fall of 1990. Odessa had been the focus of negative publicity based on the best-selling book by Bissinger. To make matters worse, Permian High School had just been banned from the 1990 state football playoffs for violating summer workout rules. They had been "turned in" by the Odessa High School head coach. Aware of the tensions and the glare of publicity surrounding the game, the Odessa community made a special effort to promote unity between its two schools. There was a taped public-service announcement by fourteen students of both schools appealing for calm, and a joint performance by the marching bands of both schools before the game. The game occurred without incident.[19]

Actions that symbolize unity such as the marching band example are rare in sport, but should be encouraged when emotions run high. There is evidence that activities which require the cooperation of competing groups help to reduce tension.[20] School sports could be used to symbolize community unity much more than is presently the case. If less community pride was riding on the outcome of local school athletic competitions, these could be sources of positive interaction between opponents. Teams could visit with each other before the game and interact after the game if there was less pressure to win. Perhaps the left tackle from one team would be less likely to start a fight with his opposite number in the heat of competition if he had stayed as a guest in that player's house the night before. Where competing teams were racially or ethnically different, such interaction would provide an interesting learning experience that would help to break down stereotypes.[21]

The effect of the changes suggested above would be to make school sports more amenable to all students and to increase students' responsibility for organizing the events. If the elitism, sexism, specialization, and adult control that characterize the present situation in school athletics were reduced, then sport might really provide "character-building" opportunities for students.

Summary

This chapter has presented different options for the future development of high school sport. Of course, if the "sport-builds-character" myth remains in place, little will change. A function of myths is that they keep the believer stuck in time. Holding to the myth means it is a certainty that sport builds character, it always has and always will.

Our argument is that sport and culture are actually in a state of flux. Even though the institution of sport may seem like an island of stability in a sea of change, this perception is an illusion. Changes in sport in the past twenty years have included a great increase in minority involvement in many professional sports, a sixfold increase in women's involvement, and a fitness boom that has attuned millions of people to the joy of exercise. Commercials for everything from life insurance to life savers regularly include males and females running, swimming, pumping iron, and playing individual and team sports. Thousands of "ordinary" people, not just elite athletes, participate in marathons, mini-marathons, and ultra-marathons, or just walk for health and pleasure. A healthy lifestyle including sport and physical activity is now part of the American dream. The philosophical change that has accompanied this mass movement would make Vince Lombardi spin in his grave.

Of all the options we have presented, the attempts to bring school athletics more in line with the goals of education make the most sense to us. This is because we see value in sport, but do not accept the current mythology surrounding it. In our view, it is ironic that the "sport-builds-character" myth is actually impeding the opportunity for school sports to become a more integral part of the education of our nation's youth.

Notes

1. Marvin Wamble, "Football Builds Character: Fact or Fiction?" *Dallas Times Herald,* September 7, 1989: C8.

2. H. G. Bissinger, *Friday Night Lights: A Town, a Team, and a Dream* (Reading, Mass.: Addison-Wesley, 1990), p. 314.

3. Murray Hausknecht, "On the Burdens Sport Can Create," *New York Times,* November 25, 1984: Section 5, p. 2.

4. Memorandum from Nathan Quinones, Chancellor, Board of Education of the City of New York to Members of the Chancellor's Task Force on Public School Athletics, dated January 1985.

5. Realistically, if there were no sport in schools, would any more students leave school than the 25 percent who now drop out? Moreover, if sport does help to keep students enrolled, why is the dropout rate greater than the national average in states such as Texas (i.e., 40 percent) which now emphasize sport so highly?

6. Donald Lackey, "The High School Coach: A Pressure Position," *Journal of Physical Education, Recreation, and Dance* 57 (1986): 28–32.

7. Roger B. Brown, "Permian–Lee Game Will Air Nationally Over Sports Channel," *Fort Worth Star-Telegram,* October, 31, 1989: Section 3, p. 4; Michael Lev, "Advertizing: Gatorade Sponsoring High School Games," *New York Times,* October 9, 1990: C16.

8. Laurence Chalip, Mihaly Csikszentmihalyi, Douglas Kleiber, and Reed Larson, "Variations of Experience in Formal and Informal Sports," *Research Quarterly for Exercise and Sport* 55 (1984): 109–116; Mihaly Csikszentmihalyi, *Flow: The Psychology of Optimal Experience* (New York: Harper & Row, 1990).

9. Becky L. Sisley and Diane M. Weise, "Current Status: Requirements for Interscholastic Coaches," *Journal of Physical Education, Recreation, and Dance* 58 (1987): 73–85.

10. Robert Broderick, "Noncertified Coaches," *Journal of Physical Education, Recreation, and Dance* 55 (1985): 38–39, 55; Becky L. Sisley, "Off-the-Street Coaches: Methods for Improving Communication," *Journal of Physical Education, Recreation, and Dance* 53 (1984): 63–66.

11. For examples of such programs see: Donald R. Hellison, *Goals and Strategies for Teaching Physical Education* (Champaign, Ill.: Human Kinetics Publishers, 1985); Brenda Jo Bredemeier, Maureen R. Weiss, Donald L. Shields, and Richard M. Schewchuk, "Promoting Moral Growth in a Summer Camp: The Implementation of Theoretically Grounded Instructional Strategies," *Journal of Moral Education* 15 (1986): 212–20; Thomas Romance, Maureen R. Weiss, and Jerry Bockoven, "A Program to Promote Moral Development through Elementary School Physical Education," *Journal of Teaching in Physical Education* 5 (1986): 126–36.

12. See, for example, Patricia A. Brill, Harold E. Burkhalter, Harold W. Kohl, Steven N. Blair, and Nancy N. Goodyear, "The Impact of Previous Athleticism on Exercise Habits, Physical Fitness, and Coronary Heart Disease Risk Factors in Middle-Aged Men," *Research Quarterly for Exercise and Sport* 60, no. 3 (1989): 209–215; C. Roger Rees, Frederick F. Andres, and Frank Howell, "On the Trail of the 'Turkey Trotters': The Effect of Previous Sport Involvement and Attitudes

on Commitment to and Skill in Running," *Sociology of Sport Journal* 3, no. 3 (1986): 134–43.

13. James G. Ross and Russell R. Pate, "The National Children and Youth Fitness Study II: A Summary of Findings," *Journal of Physical Education, Recreation, and Dance* 58, no. 9 (1987): 51–56.

14. James F. Sallis and Thomas L. Mackenzie, "Physical Education's Role in Public Health," *Research Quarterly for Exercise and Sport* 62, no. 2 (1991): 124–37.

15. Healthcare cost the government 220 billion dollars in 1985, 660 billion dollars in 1990, and 880 billion dollars in 1992. At the current rate of growth these costs will be 1.6 trillion dollars by the year 2000, equal to the government's current total budget. See Ronald S. Feingold, "Health and Fitness in the Third Millennium," *International Journal of Physical Education* 30, no. 2 (1993): 10–17; Ralph S. Paffenbarger, Jr., Robert T. Hyde, Alvin L. Wing, and Chung-Cheng Hsieh, "Physical Activity, All-Cause Mortality, and Longevity for College Alumni," *New England Journal of Medicine* 314 (1986): 605–613.

16. Melinda Henneberger, "New Gym Class: No More Choosing Up Sides," *New York Times,* May 16, 1993: 11.

17. In Houston, Texas, a mother was convicted of plotting to commit murder in order to increase the chances that her daughter would become a cheerleader. This is a clear indication of the high status of this activity, at least in some parts of the country.

18. Bissinger, *Friday Night Lights*; Douglas E. Foley, "The Great American Football Ritual: Reproducing Race, Class, and Gender Inequality," *Sociology of Sport Journal* 7 (1990): 111–35.

19. Johnny Paul, "A Divided Odessa Huddles Up," *Fort Worth Star-Telegram,* September 29, 1990: Section 1, p. 1, 10.

20. Muzafer Sherif and Carolyn Sherif, *The Robbers' Cave Experiment: Intergroup Conflict and Cooperation* (Norman, Okla.: University of Oklahoma Press, 1961); Carolyn Sherif, "Intergroup Conflict and Competition," *Sportwissenschaft* 3, no. 2 (1973): 138–53.

21. C. Roger Rees, "The Olympic Dilemma: Applying the Contact Theory and Beyond," *Quest* 37 (1985): 50–59; C. Roger Rees, "Beyond Contact: Sport as a Site for Ethnic and Racial Cooperation," in *Sociological Perspectives of Movement Activity,* eds. Edith H. Katzenellenbogen and Justus R. Potgieter (Stellenbosch, South Africa: Institute for Sport and Movement Studies, University of Stellenbosch, 1991), pp. 24–33; C. Roger Rees and Andrew W. Miracle, "Conflict Resolution in Games and Sports," *International Review of Sport Sociology* 19, no. 2 (1984): 145–56.

10

The Evolution of a Myth

Most Americans believe that sport builds character. This idea originated in the athleticism of the British public schools in the mid-nineteenth century. It later appeared in the American playground movement and grew rapidly during the early decades of the twentieth century.

The athletic movement in Britain and the playground movement in America shared a concept of social development via experience in which many still believe. According to this position, moral development occurs through action, and nowhere is the action more vivid and involving than in athletics.[1] By the 1890s, this concept was linked with national development by Teddy Roosevelt and others. The same idea had been expressed in Britain almost a half-century earlier.

There is an overwhelming emphasis on winning in American sport. Moreover, it is believed by some that winning demonstrates moral superiority. This is one of the reasons Americans value high-level or elite sport performance. Apparently, we have not been concerned that all youths build their character through sport, just those with superior athletic talent. As a result, the majority of America's young people have been denied access to sport and its supposed character-building qualities.

We have symbolically equated being number one in sport with being number one in society. How does one become number one? Through hard work, dedication, following orders, and sacrificing self for the good of the team. To the extent that players and nonplayers alike accept the notion that these values result from sport participation and lead to individual success and moral perfection, they can be said to subscribe to the myth.

Americans' beliefs about sport seemingly require no proof. Certainly if we look for scientific evidence to support popular, cherished beliefs about sport, we shall be disappointed. Studies purporting to demonstrate proof for the sport myth either have examined small, special populations or they have used flawed methodologies. No studies capable of withstanding rigorous scientific scrutiny offer much support for any tenets of the myth. If the sport myth is to be supported with convincing scientific evidence, the research has yet to be done.

In addition to the belief that sport builds character, there are other associated beliefs about school sport. For example, it is because people believe so passionately in the intrinsic value of athletics as a character builder that the negative reaction to commercialism and drug scandals in modern sport is so intense. Some, such as Coach Joe Paterno of Penn State, have expressed the feeling that a traditional moral force in society is losing its impact.[2]

It is generally believed that sport decreases delinquency and drug use by increasing positive self-concept, enhancing skills, and demonstrating to the individual that success can be obtained by following the rules. However, examination of the evidence shows no clear support for the notion that sport participation deters delinquent behavior.

Some studies[3] have reported lower delinquency rates for athletes than nonathletes, especially among low achievers from blue collar backgrounds. Other researchers[4] who have examined the relationship of delinquency and extracurricular participation by type of activity (i.e., athletics only, service and leadership activities, service-leadership activities and athletics, or no form of extracurricular involvement) report that rates of delinquency were highest for those who engaged in no extracurriculars. Rates were lower and approximately the same for those in athletics or some other activity, while rates were lowest for students participating in both types of activities.

There are numerous problems associated with most research efforts studying the effects of sport participation on delinquency. For example, there are problems of defining and categorizing delinquent acts. Moreover, neither court records nor self-report accounts are likely to be accurate or comparable nationwide. In addition, there is the probable confounding fact that athletes may be conformists, and that athletic involvement is self-selecting in this regard. If athletes question the authority of the coach, or continually are caught breaking team rules, they can be thrown off the team. In addition, it is possible that authorities may treat athletes differently, more leniently, than nonathletes from similar social positions. For example, if the high school quarterback is stopped for speeding, he is likely to be known by the local cop. Perhaps he receives a warning rather than a ticket.

Nor is there convincing evidence that participation in athletics will prevent or reduce drug abuse among young people. In fact, sport has long been associated with alcohol use. Modern sports' extensive use of legal drugs to enhance performance, coupled with the widespread abuse of alcohol and the use of illegal recreational drugs by prominent athletes, cannot serve to deter drug use by school athletes.

There is also a suggestion that feelings of superiority, elitism, and the importance of general macho behavior are part of the modern self-image of male athletes. The recent spate of tragic incidents in which high school football players, copying a scene in the film *The Program,* endanger their lives by lying down in busy streets bears witness to this claim.[5] Clearly something more than the stupidity of drunken adolescents is at work here.

Perhaps feelings of male superiority over females are also part of this identity. There is certainly support for this assertion at both the high school and college level.[6] These feelings of superiority may lead athletes to engage in promiscuity or the abuse of women.

The report card is still out on other alleged effects of participation in school athletic programs. For example, some research has indicated that participation in school athletics has a positive effect on academic achievement and college aspirations. However, there is no consensus to explain why this should be the case. Some research reports that participation in nonathletic extracurricular activities has similar effects. Again the suggestion is that broad involvement in school life may influence students to engage in more normative behaviors.

A few studies have tested the hypothesis that participation in school athletics also might affect future occupational outcomes and future earnings, but the results are unclear. One reputable study[7] found that athletics had a positive effect on occupational prestige and income fifteen years after the first survey of seventeen-year-old males in one Michigan county. Another study[8] has presented evidence that athletics or social involvement in other extracurricular activities had positive effects on educational and job attainment among a sample of respondents in Ontario, Canada, six years after completing grade twelve. However, working with our colleague Frank Howell, we found no support for the hypothesis in a study[9] utilizing a national sample in which respondents were surveyed one year after graduation and again five years after graduation.

There are two effects of high school sport that have solid support from social science research: the impact of sport on school social life and on school/community relations.

Students generally find sport exciting and stimulating, which sets them apart from much of the rest of schools' offerings. Whether as athletes or as spectators, students' participation in sport allows them to rise above the humdrum monotony of school. Along with the other extracurricular programs, sport has been the primary arena for group effort, as opposed to the forced individualization of academic efforts. Sport also helps to define the school calendar, effectively marking the passing of the school year and symbolically reaffirming sport's significance.

The most important function of sport for American schools, however, is in determining the student social structure within the school. Groups are formed and prestige is bestowed largely on the basis of sport. Traditionally, athletes have occupied positions of higher status in American schools than those who excelled in academics, art, music, or any other skill area.

Similarly, the impact of sport on school/community relations can be enormous. Parents and the general citizenry in the community can participate in school athletics through booster clubs and other support groups. In the face of the increasing professionalization of American education in the twentieth century, athletics is now the only way in which parents and other taxpayers have any significant contact with most community schools.

Sport also serves to bind generations in a significant way. For example, boys, young men, and old men can "shoot hoops" together; individuals who would otherwise have little in common to talk about can trade stories, with athletes past and present "counting coup."

Traditionally, in some Native-American cultures such as the Cheyenne, successful warriors would describe their military exploits publicly—a process known as counting coup. Today, when former athletes gather, they too will tell stories about "big games" or "great plays." It is not clear whether the recent explosion in numbers of female athletes will have such effects on girls and women in the future.

In chapter 2 we presented Hobsbawm's theory that many modern traditions were invented in the late nineteenth century to meet the demands of life in newly industrialized society. We would extend that argument by adding that myths to support these invented traditions also were created. The significance of this is that if myths were invented at one time in the past, they can change at some point in the future, and that new myths can be created to achieve present needs.

However, this presents a paradox since the power of a myth lies in its capacity to convince those involved of its strength to withstand change. "This is the way it is, the way it has been and always will be. No question about it." A strongly held myth is not challenged. That individuals across America are beginning to question the myth of school sport indicates that this particular myth is weakening.

The message of this book is that myths change, that indeed they must change. As time passes and the circumstances that required a myth and promoted its invention change, original myths will have less and less fit with other components of the culture. This results in increasing tensions as individuals try to reconcile the widening discrepancy between traditional beliefs and current perceptions of reality. Eventually, the myth will be in crisis: either it will evolve, adapting to the new circumstances of social reality, or it will be discarded altogether.

For example, nineteenth-century industrialists did not propose a no pass/no play rule. Their need was for a docile, healthy, punctual, loyal work force; there was little perceived need for highly educated workers. Industrialists at the end of the twentieth century, however, perceive their needs quite differently. Thus most fully support legislation to strengthen the academic aspects of schooling—even at the cost of deemphasizing high school sport. It is within this context that we anticipate that the myth of high school sport will change.

We are a society which places tremendous faith in science. The traditional sport myth—the axiom that needs no proof—has been fractured by scientific data, by a public which now tends to think in terms of the application of scientific logic and reasoning. The idea that sport builds character can no longer be accepted fully and unequivocally by many Americans.

It might be argued that belief grounded in "facts" or "hard data" is no more real, no closer to truth than any myth. It is, however, useful, even essential in the modern world, that all elements of myth seem to conform to a scientific reality. This is the basis for our conclusion that the traditional myth of sport building character, which is not supported by scientific data, will change.

There is a growing movement to reassess the role of sport in American education. The movement will not be derailed by the anecdotes or personal testimony of a few true believers. It is inevitable that the search for new educational models will continue. It remains to be seen how most American communities will redesign the school/sport relationships. Nor is it clear what new myth about sport most Americans will come to believe.

It is because sport pervades so many layers of life and because no one in society can comfortably escape nominal participation in sport rituals that it has become so powerful, so sacred. Of course, not only has sport been ritualized, but there also has arisen an accompanying mythology to provide justification for sport rituals.

In our discussion about possible changes in the role of sport in the schools, we should keep in mind that the symbolic content of myth and the function of ritual can evolve. It is not always necessary to invent new myths and rituals. The communication of myth is inextricably bound up with ritual, i.e., with culturally prescribed behaviors that reinforce and often reenact the myths. When myth changes, however, it does not require a change in the ritual forms, only a reinterpretation. Thus school sport may continue to serve an important function as public ritual for communities, even if members of the community no longer subscribe to the myth that sport builds character. For example, a new myth that sport promotes health and fitness could be sufficient to maintain the ritual significance of sport in America's schools.[10]

As America's communities, large and small, face the issues related to school sport, society will benefit from open discussions and access to all existing information on the subject. Thus ours is a plea for local consideration of the issues by the individuals most directly affected by any decision regarding school sport.

We believe that there is an important role for youth sport in America, and that each community ought to determine the place of sport in its schools. There is no single option or plan that will work effectively everywhere. In examining the future of school sport, three alternatives have been discussed: (1) the separation of sport and school or schools without sport; (2) achieving a proper balance or the deemphasis of sport in schools; and (3) the introduction of new sport models for schools.

Any serious consideration of the role of sport in our schools demonstrates the unfortunate consequences of dichotomizing the issue into academics versus sport. If the primary goal of school is education, what would a cost-benefit analysis of school sport indicate?

The real dilemma, then, is how to balance the many competing demands of contemporary education. The needs of individual students (or even many students) should not be sacrificed for the benefit of the community, or for one or more segments of the community.

We expect mixed reactions to this book. Some readers, holding to the traditional myth, will accuse us of heresy. How dare we malign a sacred institution which keeps youth off the street, saves them from drugs, provides a way out of the ghetto, and brings school and community together? Others may find our message disturbing. Social ritual imparts a sense of security—all of us doing the same thing at the same time—while myth reassures us that what we are doing is good for us. Myth-busting causes uneasiness. If school sport does not, after all, build character, what can we believe? Is nothing sacred? Are the problems in sport symbolic of a wider crisis in society from which there is no escape?

It has not been our intention to spread anger and despair. We are all shaped by the rituals and myths of our culture, but through questioning myths that no longer seem true, we have the opportunity to adapt our beliefs to changing circumstances. By rejecting the "sport-builds-character" myth we can free ourselves from past constraints and move toward a more inclusive model of sport for American youth.

There is room for many more individuals to enjoy the process of participation in sport in a less stressful environment than presently exists. There is the opportunity for them to experience the joy of competition and cooperation within the boundaries of the athletic field or gymnasium without being sacrificed for the entertainment of the community. We, as adults, can support school athletics without getting caught up in the myth that we are number one through sport, that athletic competition is building character, raising grade point averages, or building the morality of the participants. To the extent that we can do this, we become the winners our cultural myths proclaim us to be.

Notes

1. Donald J. Mrozek, *Sport and American Mentality, 1880–1910* (Knoxville, Tenn.: The University of Tennessee Press, 1983), p. 40.

2. Rick Reilly, "Sportsman of the Year: Not an Ordinary Joe," *Sports Illustrated* 65, no. 27 (1986): 64–71.

3. Donald Landers and Donna Landers, "Socialization via Interscholastic Athletics: Its Effect on Delinquency," *Sociology of Education* 51 (1978): 299–303.

4. Walter E. Schafer, "Participation in Interscholastic Athletics and Delinquency: A Preliminary Study," *Social Problems* 17 (1969): 40–49.

5. J. K. Bernard, "Lethal Risk: Young Copy Cats," *Newsday,* October 23, 1993: 20, 23; Susan Forrest, "Costly Move: Car Hits Syosset Teen Who Was Imitating Film Scene," *Newsday,* October 19, 1993: 5, 29.

6. Timothy J. Curry, "Fraternal Bonding in the Locker Room: A Profeminist Analysis of Talk About Competition and Women," *Sociology of Sport Journal* 8, no. 2 (1991): 119–35; Douglas Foley, "The Great American Football Ritual: Reproducing Race, Class and Gender Inequality," *Sociology of Sport Journal* 7, no. 2 (1991): 111–35.

7. Luther B. Otto and Duane F. Alwin, "Athletics, Aspirations, and Attainments," *Sociology of Education* 42 (1977): 102–113.

8. Norman R. Okihiro, "Extracurricular Participation, Educational Destinies, and Early Job Outcomes," in *Sport and the Sociological Imagination*, eds. Nancy Theberge and Peter Donnelly (Fort Worth, Tex.: Texas Christian University Press, 1984): 334–49.

9. Frank M. Howell, Andrew W. Miracle, and C. Roger Rees, "Do High School Athletics Pay? The Effects of Varsity Participation on Socioeconomic Attainment," *Sociology of Sport Journal* 1, no. 1 (1984): 15–25.

10. Andrew W. Miracle and C. Roger Rees, "Sport as Myth for Modern Life" (Paper presented at the Annual Meeting of the Association for the Study of Play, 1989).

Index

231